LINCOLN CHRISTIAN COLLEGE AND SEMINARY

GOD ENCOUNTERED

OTHER WORKS BY FRANS JOZEF VAN BEECK:

Christ Proclaimed: Christology as Rhetoric
Grounded in Love: Sacramental Theology in an Ecumenical Perspective
Catholic Identity After Vatican II: Three Types of Faith in the One Church
Loving the Torah More than God? Toward a Catholic Appreciation of Judaism

GOD ENCOUNTERED

A Contemporary
Catholic Systematic Theology

Volume Two/3:
The Revelation of the Glory

Part III:
Finitude and Fall

FRANS JOZEF VAN BEECK, S. J.

A Michael Glazier Book
THE LITURGICAL PRESS
Collegeville, Minnesota

Grateful acknowledgment is made for the use of the following materials. Excerpts from "One Foot in Eden" by Edwin Muir (copyright © 1960 by Willa Muir) are reprinted by permission of Oxford University Press, the publisher (New York, 1965) of Edwin Muir, *Collected Poems*. Excerpts from the Introduction to *A Memoir of Mary Ann* by Flannery O'Connor (copyright © 1961 by Farrar, Straus & Cudahy, and renewed © 1989 by Regina O'Connor) are reprinted by permission of Farrar, Straus & Giroux, Inc. Excerpts from *The Waves* by Virginia Woolf (© 1931 by Harcourt Brace & Company and renewed © 1959 by Leonard Woolf) are reprinted by permission of the publisher. The illustration on the front cover, fol. 112r of *Codex Sanhippolytensis* N° 1 (15th cent.), is once again used by kind permission of the *Bischöfliche Alumnatsbibliothek*, Sankt Pölten, Austria.

Imprimi potest: Very Rev. Bradley M. Schaeffer, S.J., Provincial, Chicago Province. November 13, 1995.

Nihil Obstat: Rev. Charles R. Meyer, S.T.D., *Censor Deputatus*. October 23, 1995.

Imprimatur: Most Reverend Raymond E. Goedert, M.A., S.T.L, J.C.L., Vicar General, Archdiocese of Chicago. October 27, 1995.

The *Nihil Obstat* and *Imprimatur* are official declarations that a book is free of doctrinal or moral error. No implication is contained therein that those who have granted the *Nihil Obstat* and *Imprimatur* agree with the content, opinions, or statements expressed.

GOD ENCOUNTERED: *A Contemporary Catholic Systematic Theology. Volume 2/3. The Revelation of the Glory. Part III. Finitude and Fall.* Copyright © 1995 by De Nederlandse Provincie S.J. (F. J. van Beeck, S.J., agent). All rights reserved. No part of this book may be reproduced in any form or by any means without written permission except in the case of brief quotations embodied in critical articles and reviews. For information, address: The Liturgical Press, St. John's Abbey, Collegeville, Minnesota 56321.
Manufactured in the United States of America

FIRST EDITION

Cover design by Ann Blattner.

Library of Congress Cataloging-in-Publication Data

Beeck, Frans Jozef van.
    The Revelation of the Glory. Part III. Finitude and Fall.

    (God Encountered; v. 2/3)
    Bibliography: p.
    Includes index.
    1. Theology, Doctrinal. 2. Catholic Church—Doctrines.
    I. Title. II. Series: Beeck, Frans Jozef van.
    God Encountered; v. 2/3
    BX1747.5.B4 vol. 2/3
    ISBN 0-8146-5500-9

For Cardinal Joseph Bernardin
Archbishop of Chicago

Exercise oversight,
not as if you were being forced to do it,
but willingly, God's way,
and not out of a vulgar appetite for gain,
but eagerly,
and not as lords over your charges,
but as examples to the flock.

(1 PETER 5, 2–3)

98386

O admirabile commercium!
Creator generis humani,
animatum corpus sumens,
de Virgine nasci dignatus est:
et procedens homo sine semine,
largitus est nobis suam deitatem.

What admirable exchange!
Humankind's Creator,
taking on body and soul,
in his kindness, is born from the Virgin:
and, coming forth as man, yet not from man's seed,
he has lavished on us his divinity.

(Antiphon at vespers, January 1,
Feast of the Holy Mother of God)

Contents

Preface

This book is the *tertia secundæ* of *God Encountered.* Like its predecessor, it represents a change of plans. Subtitled *Finitude and Fall,* it is the first of a sequence of two in-between parts of Volume Two, numbered Two/3 and Two/4; the second and longer of the two will be subtitled *The Genealogy of Depravity.* Neither part constitutes the doctrinal heart of *God Encountered* conceived as a system of *Christian* theology. In the new arrangement, the treatment of the Christian understanding of God will be brought to completion only in Volume Two/5, to be subtitled *The Glory of God in the Face of Christ.*

Let us change the metaphor. The present book and its projected sequel describe and explore the landscape that takes its bearings from a horizon that is both protological and eschatological. Readers will recall that Volume Two/2 focused on the protology: the *exitus* of the One and Only Faithful God—the God revealed to Israel, not only as the Guiding Light of its own history, but also as the Creator and Establisher of All That Is. To match that theme, Volume Two/5 will focus on the culmination of God's *exitus* "in these last days." That is, it will elaborate the great Christian doctrines—those that account for the distinctive parts of the Christian creed: faith in Jesus of Nazareth, God's anointed servant, come to do God's will in the service of a humanity and a world as rich in potential as they are rife with mishap, mistake, and downright transgression; faith in Jesus rejected, put to death, buried, and raised from the dead to the glory of God; faith in Jesus expected to come in glory to do full and final justice; faith in Jesus worshiped and professed, in the power of the Holy Spirit, as God's Eternal and Living Word Incarnate and Only-Begotten Son, as the One who embodies and will fulfill the word of God's promise heard by the prophets of old and uttered by them in the power of the same Spirit.

The present book and its immediate sequel serve both to link Volumes Two/2 and Two/5 and to keep them separate. Still, no landscape can be neatly told apart from the horizon that bounds it. The link, therefore, is far from obvious, nor is the separation tidy. Nor does the landscape in which Christians (and, to a large extent, Jews and presumably Muslims as well) live and travel have configurations that are either definitive or clear. The Christian world is indeed all-inclusive; it stretches all the way from the promise-filled dawn of creation to the anticipation of final justice and peace in the blinding light of the eschaton; still, it is no less shifting and darkened for that. Every catholic theologian can say, with Edwin Muir:

> One foot in Eden still, I stand
> And look across the other land.

Little wonder that the theological insights and positions developed in this book and the following are a mixed lot indeed. But they are, in Edwin Muir's words, some of the "flowers in Eden never known":

> Blossoms of grief and charity
> Bloom in these darkened fields alone.
> What had Eden ever to say
> Of hope and faith and pity and love
> Until was buried all its day
> And memory found its treasure trove?
> Strange blessings never in Paradise
> Fall from these beclouded skies.

Let me change the metaphor again. The three chapters of this book and the four of its companion-to-be lie across the landscape of Volume Two of *God Encountered* like a dragon. Its giant, shimmering limbs sprawl across a territory not only fair but also very treacherous, and in any case only very partly inhabitable. The monster is sinuous, fascinating yet repugnant, gorgeous and hideous at the same time, and wrapped, after the fashion of dragons, in a haze of smoke—an effluence that often beclouds the contours of the landscape itself. Yet not all is negativity even here. For, despite their ominous subtitles, these two books, dedicated to the theology of finitude and outright sin, really want to convey in the *chiaroscuro* language of contemporary theology what the Nicene-Constantinopolitan Creed confidently expresses in the bright idiom of divine mercy, namely, that God's Word became Incarnate *"for us and for our salvation."* Catholic theology acknowledges finitude, failure, and sin, but, while shuddering at them, it is not fascinated by them. For in the tradition of catholic theology we can look finitude and sin straight in the face. Still, we can do so only because the eyesight by virtue of which we so look at them has been trained and indeed restored by the sight and the knowledge of Jesus the Christ. In fact (so the great Tradition has maintained), in focusing on Christ's person, history, and destiny, all of humanity has seen, in God's very mirror-image, not only the cosmos and its inherent uncertainties, but also its own self—precarious, wayward, and crooked, as well as permanently and unspeakably lovable and precious, made in the image and likeness of God. For it is in Christ that humanity recovers the memory which seemed by all accounts entirely lost: the indelible imprint left behind in the world and humanity by the invisible hands of a faithful God—a God who from the very beginning has deemed the world "good," and the world and humanity together "very good."

In this way, in the face of Christ, catholic theology sees the sight of sights and understands the truth of truths: Unconditional, Encompassing, Life-giving Love. For Jesus the Christ is, in a living person "like us in all things but sin," what the living Torah had long been, and still is, for God's Israel: the visibility and knowability of the invisible, unknowable God of Life and Love and Compassion (cf. Irenæus of Lyons, *Adversus Hæreses* IV, 6, 6).

Seen in this light, the chapters that follow are an exercise, not in theological misery, but in loving realism, conciliation, and reconciliation—in constructive cosmology, anthropology, and theology in their mutual interconnectedness. They reflect on the world and humanity, on their promise, their precariousness, and their potential for sinful degeneracy, and they do so, at least in the final analysis, theologically. For the horizon of the treatment of precariousness and fall to be offered in the present installment of *God Encountered* and the following is God's continuing self-revelation. After all, true theological understanding of a world and a humanity that are forever in process and development (as well as often in decline and fall) comes about in the kindly but revealing light that comes to them, on the one hand, from the living ever-faithful God who creates and, on the other hand, from God's Christ, in whose birth, ministry, execution, and resurrection all of creation is divinely assured of its return to God and its fulfillment in God.

This has turned out to be a very hard story to write. While the chapters offered here are complete, those of the next part, intractable as ever, are still unfinished. I am sure both of these two parts will show the marks of four to six years' worth of irresolution and struggle. In particular, I fear that readers will find a fair amount of prolixity and repetitiousness, for which I must apologize, not because it is the best

I have been able to do, but because I think I cannot continue revising and tightening up.

In kindly accepting the dedication of this installment of *God Encountered*, Cardinal Bernardin has given me an opportunity to do two things. The first is in order on account of the welcome I received from the Church of Chicago when I came to Loyola University over eleven years ago. Part of Paul's advice to the Church of Rome was that they should welcome those weak in faith, but not for the purpose of quarreling over opinions (Rom 14, 1). In recent decades, sound, serious Catholic theologians have been greeted with a lot of quarreling over opinions in more than one local church, obviously because they are systematically suspected of being weak in the faith, perhaps even intentionally. I wish to acknowledge gratefully as well as thankfully that none of this discouraging treatment has ever been meted out to me in the Church of Chicago, with its atmosphere of Christian hospitality—a mark of catholicity so gently and so effectively modeled by its present archbishop. Secondly, an important section in this book (§116) deals with a subject that Cardinal Bernardin has quietly, firmly, and for a very long time placed at the heart of his pastoral ministry: his championing of human life as a fundamental (and hence, indivisible) human (and hence, moral) issue. With this book, therefore, I wish to hail the Cardinal's efforts in this area as an exemplary exercise of the *magisterium ordinarium*, which in this case has been explicitly supported by Pope John Paul II in his 1995 encyclical *Evangelium Vitæ*.

Once again, I owe much to friends and critics. Among those who most helped shape sizable sections of this book, by encouragement, conversation, and criticism, I count James J. Walter first of all. Others who helped me by their interest in, comments on, and conversation about particular parts and specific issues are Guy Consolmagno, S.J.; Robert DiVito; Ronald Mercier, S.J.; Virginia M. Ryan; George Schner, S.J. (who also found numerous errors in the manuscript); Michael Schuck; Theodore J. Tracy, S.J.; Terry Walter; and Lawrence J. Welch and Shawn McCauley Welch, who read this book in manuscript and sent me their perceptive comments as well as a list of errors. Despite the fact that he is no longer my graduate assistant, Edward Peck offered to do the lion's share of the work on the indices. At The Liturgical Press, Father Michael Naughton, O.S.B., and Messrs. Mark Twomey and Peter Dwyer have continued to be a constant source of encouragement and sound advice, while Ms. Annette Kmitch's careful reading of the proofs was a real blessing—one all the more outstanding for being self-effacing: this book's readers will never get to see the errors she corrected. Finally, I would never have ventured out into the park of desktop typesetting had Caryn Bush and especially Michael Bradley not taught me, advised me, helped me, encouraged me, smiled at me.

Frans Jozef van Beeck, S.J.

Abbreviations

ABDict	*The Anchor Bible Dictionary.* Edited by David Noel Freedman. 6 vols. New York, London, Toronto, Sydney, and Auckland: Doubleday, 1992.
AristBWks	*The Basic Works of Aristotle.* Edited by Richard McKeon. New York: Random House, 1941.
CC	*Corpus Christianorum.* Turnhout: Brepols, 1953–.
CCC	*Catechism of the Catholic Church.* Washington, DC: United States Catholic Conference, 1994.
CF	*The Christian Faith in the Doctrinal Documents of the Catholic Church.* Edited by J. Neuner and J. Dupuis. New York: Alba House, 1982.
CSEL	*Corpus Scriptorum Ecclesiasticorum Latinorum.* Vienna: F. Tempsky, 1866–.
DH	*Enchiridion Symbolorum Definitionum Declarationum de Rebus Fidei et Morum. Kompendium der Glaubensbekenntnisse und kirchlichen Lehrentscheidungen.* Edited by Heinrich Denzinger; revised by Peter Hünermann and Helmut Hoping. 37th edition, in Latin and German. Freiburg: Herder, 1991.
DTC	*Dictionnaire de Théologie Catholique.* Edited by A. Vacant, E. Mangenot, and É. Amann. 15 vols. Paris: Librairie Letouzey et Ané, 1930–50.
EncPhil	*The Encyclopedia of Philosophy.* Edited by Paul Edwards. Reprinted edition. 4 vols. New York: Macmillan & The Free Press; London: Collier Macmillan, 1972.
FC	*The Fathers of the Church: A New Translation.* Washington, DC: The Catholic University of America Press, 1948–.
GCS	*Die griechischen christlichen Schriftsteller der ersten drei Jahrhunderte.* Leipzig and Berlin, 1897–.
GS	*Gaudium et Spes*: The Pastoral Constitution on the Church in the Modern World (Vatican II).
Hall	Stuart George Hall, *Melito of Sardis: On Pascha, and Fragments. Oxford Early Christian Texts.* Oxford: Clarendon, 1979.
LG	*Lumen Gentium*: The Dogmatic Constitution on the Church (Vatican II).

LXX	The Septuagint version of the Jewish Scriptures.
MT	The Masoretic text of the Hebrew Scriptures.
NPNCF	*A Select Library of Nicene and Post-Nicene Fathers of the Christian Church.* New York: Christian Literature Company, 1887–1992. (Reprint. Grand Rapids, MI: Wm. B. Eerdmans, 1979–83.)
PG	*Patrologia Græca.* Edited by J. P. Migne. 162 vols. Paris: 1857–1866.
Philok	*The Philokalia.* Edited by G.E.H. Palmer, Philip Sherrard, and Kallistos Ware. 3 vols. London and Boston: Faber and Faber, 1979–86.
PL	*Patrologia Latina.* Edited by J. P. Migne. 221 vols. Paris: 1844–1864.
PlatoCDia	*The Collected Dialogues of Plato.* Edited by Edith Hamilton and Huntington Cairns. *Bollingen Series,* LXXI. Princeton: Princeton University Press, 1961.
RW	Jan van Ruusbroec. *Werken.* 4 vols. Edited by J. van Mierlo, J.B. Poukens, L. Reypens, M. Schurmans, and D. A. Stracke. Mechelen: Het Kompas; Amsterdam: De Spiegel, 1932–34.
SacMundi	*Sacramentum Mundi: An Encyclopedia of Theology.* New York: Herder and Herder; London: Burns and Oates, 1968.
SC	*Sources chrétiennes.* Paris: Cerf, 1940–.
SchrzTh	Karl Rahner. *Schriften zur Theologie.* 16 vols. Einsiedeln, Zürich, and Köln: Benziger Verlag, 1954–84.
TDNT	*Theological Dictionary of the New Testament.* Edited by Gerhard Kittel and Gerhard Friedrich, translated by Geoffrey W. Bromiley. 10 vols. Grand Rapids, MI: Wm. B. Eerdmans, 1964–1976.
TDOT	*Theological Dictionary of the Old Testament.* Edited by G. Johannes Botterweck and Helmer Ringgren, translated by David E. Green. Grand Rapids, MI: Wm. B. Eerdmans, 1977–.
TheoInv	Karl Rahner. *Theological Investigations.* 21 vols. Baltimore: Helicon/New York: Herder and Herder/Seabury; London: Darton, Longman & Todd, 1966–88.
Vg	The (Latin) Vulgate text of the Scriptures.

Part III

FINITUDE AND FALL

CHAPTER 12

Introduction:
"That Mysterious Limp"

FUNDAMENTALS: ANTHROPOLOGY AND THEOLOGY

[§112] SELF-ACCEPTANCE, IDENTITY, AND ESTRANGEMENT

[1] Finite we may be; we are not the prisoners of finitude. It is true, every time we adopt a position, especially if we go about it carefully, we deal with a thoroughly particular reality. That is, we involve ourselves in a limited, finite act of affirmativeness, and in doing so we lay claim to *some* understanding of truth and *some* judgment of value. But we also sense that in every particular position we take we are taking a stand on what is only

a small island in a measureless ocean of elements not traversed; it is a floating island, and much as we are more familiar with it than with this ocean, in the last resort it is carried; and only because it is carried can it carry at all.[1]

This means: our every *particular, thematic* affirmation is undergirded by a deep, broad affirmativeness that remains unthematized; that is, our native *capacity* for understanding and commitment (or so we realize upon reflection) has roots far deeper in us and a compass far wider in us than the limited understanding and commitment required by all the particular positions we adopt is liable to suggest. Our every act of understanding and commitment draws upon a native, implicit, intuitive sense of identity that involves a fundamental affinity with the widest conceivable reality. For this reason, every single instance of affirmativeness on our part implies a basic claim—a claim about our authentic selves and about the wider reality around us, and even (in and beyond all reality, real and imaginable) a claim about ourselves and the mystery of mysteries: God.

Let us once again explicitly formulate this implicit claim: *in* all our particular positions, and as the condition for their very possibility, we rely on our fundamental, mainly formless, and thus largely inexpressible, yet darkly intuitive and deeply reliable intellectual and affective attunement to all that is real, and ultimately, to the living God (cf. §108, 3, a; §109, 8, [*v*]).

[2] This authentic attunement to all reality in us is not something thought up, something willed, or something intended, let alone something achieved by conscious effort (cf. again §109, 8, [*v*]); it is simply there—*an a priori, transcendental given* [*a*].

This given, while simply given, is not an inert fixture. Rather, it comes with an inherent appeal to our deeper, reflective selves: it presents itself to us for our *acceptance.* Acceptance, in fact, is what anything given invites. Humanly speaking, whatever is given remains incomplete—an offer and nothing more—until it is acknowledged and appreciated precisely *as* given. Acceptance is what turns a mere given into a gift.

Now our given attunement to God and to all reality (which is also the source of our innate desire for growth toward human maturity: §87, 1–2, a) involves both self-awareness and freedom; thus it is in the nature of the given itself that it should somehow become a matter of conscious and deliberate acknowledgment. But how could something so integral to our personhood and so pervasively present in every position we adopt be a matter of indifference? And since our orientation to other persons, as persons, is an original fact, how could we overlook these persons' attunement to ourselves, and treat their existence as a bare, neutral fact (cf. §64, 2, [*l*]; §95, 4)? And even more, how could the given orientation to God, both in ourselves and in others, fail to invite our conscious notice, reflective appreciation, and endorsement —that is, our *free* endorsement?

[a] The fact that the transcendental attunement is something to be accepted has consequences. Among other things, it has consequences for the credibility of any explicit, thematic claims to as well as about it. Consequently, it has consequences for the ability—our

---

[*a*] This "given," it will be recalled, is termed *immanence* by Maurice Blondel. It is the mainspring of all human beings' native quest for action, of their growth by self-actualization, and, in the final analysis, of their movement toward transcendence. Cf. §87, esp. 2, a.

own and others'—to endorse the attunement itself in explicit intellectual terms and to live by it in a fully deliberate fashion. For in and of itself, the attunement is and remains a transcendental, deeply enabling *a priori* condition that underlies and undergirds all our positions; to the extent that we are aware of it at all, we are aware of it by participative knowledge (cf. §63). That is, we will never be able to get it wholly into focus or to grasp it adequately; it will never swim into our ken as a clear *object* of knowledge detached from ourselves and our self-consciousness. Reflection may indeed bring it to the surface; but any explicit claims about our transcendental attunement (and hence, any express endorsements of it) must remain *interpretative*, and hence, delicate and somewhat precarious. Therefore, to get others to understand and accept such claims and endorsements, we will have to appeal to their self-experience, or at least to their willingness to enter into that self-experience and to come to trust it as a matter of habit. All of this only serves to further drive home the fact that any positive endorsement, on our part, of our transcendental attunement as a reliable guide to life is a matter of free choice.

[3] In stating this, we have touched upon yet another mysterious paradox inherent in humanity. We deeply realize that, in the words of the thirteenth-century Flemish Beguine Hadewijch,

we have not yet become what we are, and we have not yet grasped what we have, and the things that are our own are still so far removed from us.[2]

Put differently, what is deepest as well as most distinctively human and personal in us is our attunement to all of reality and to God. Yet this attunement, which is also the germ of our authentic identity, is *both* something simply given *and* still a matter of free choice. What is given is this: if in actual fact we exist as human beings (and we do), we do so in sheer, inalienable, immediate dependence on the transcendent God who creates us by both constituting us as other and dwelling in us, antecedently to any distinction between holiness and sin or good and evil, as Ruusbroec rightly emphasizes (cf. §90, 4). The sheer *givenness* of this dependence calls for a *free* response of unconditional gratitude and abandon; yet, from the nature of the case, the given could not possibly *compel* such a free response. Here, therefore, at the point where we are most deeply touched by the creative presence of God (cf. §82, 3, b), we have ourselves but for the taking (even if, it is true, only ourselves). Still, if we are to become our true selves (which is, really, the only thing we *can* become, since it is the only thing we are originally made to be), we have no choice but to accept positively who and what we are (even if, paradoxically, we will never succeed in adequately *grasping* either this "who" or this "what," since it would take all of our "who" and all of our "what" to do any such grasping). So, elusive as our deeper, God-given selves may be, it is up to us to discover, nourish, and even cherish them. We can attain growth in authenticity and maturity only by fundamentally accepting ourselves, freely, and in the last resort, thankfully.

This is obviously an unusual option, yet it is also the most fundamental of all options. For it is the choice, not *between* ourselves and something other than ourselves, but *of* ourselves as we are meant to be. Put differently, it is the option between our true, accepted, even appreciated selves and our mistaken, misprized, resented, even rejected selves. That is, it is the kind of choice that is capable of determining a person's basic stance in life. It is, therefore, the most decisive, and for that reason, the freest imaginable option as well, since it initiates and empowers our given freedom to make other choices—the ones that do involve real alternatives [*b*].

[4] Thus we have once again arrived at the point where anthropology turns out to hinge upon theology. Our true, accepted, appreciated selves will emerge and grow only to the extent that we have opted for a life of authenticity—that is, for a life that positively corresponds to the wellspring at the core of our being: our fundamental attunement

---

[*b*] Here we have struck upon two fundamental theological concepts. The first is self-acceptance: we ourselves are the first gift God offers us, as Romano Guardini (who knew about self-acceptance from a lifelong battle with depression) explains in a touching little book, *Die Annahme seiner selbst*. The second is the concept, well-known in twentieth-century Catholic theology, of the fundamental option (*optio fundamentalis*). The term designates the transcendental attunement to God *inasmuch as it is positively endorsed by a free (if largely implicit) commitment to the good life* on the part of individual persons. The fundamental option is a bridge concept: it connects our *basic* ("transcendental") *freedom* (by which we have the *capacity* for *total* commitment) with *freedom of choice* (which we exercise by making choices involving *contingent*, finite realities). The fundamental option, in other words, creates the *historic* precondition for all our subsequent choices, which (unlike itself) *are* between real alternatives. Fleshed out, tested, matured by these particular choices, the fundamental option will develop. As we grow in both authentic identity and openness to God, our endorsement of our native attunement to transcendence will become habitual; it will become the fundamental disposition that more and more permeates, quietly but noticeably, whatever positions we will choose to adopt. It will also deepen our sorrow whenever we have, in particular instances, acted in ways contrary to this disposition. This will result in various virtues, especially *wisdom*. For a reliable survey of the basic literature on the fundamental option, cf. Bernard J. Rabik, *Freedom in Fundamental Option*, esp. pp. 23–67; for Karl Rahner's thoughts on the subject, cf. *Grundkurs des Glaubens*, pp. 101–06 (ET pp. 93–99).

to God [c], on the strength of which we also enjoy an affinity with all that is.

Our fundamental option for authenticity is both vigorous and delicate. It can persist despite failures and even sins (even though, obviously, it is weakened by them). In fact, it is precisely *because* of this option that we can come to a keen awareness of our failures and sins, bear the awareness, have the heart to repent, and even draw wisdom from failure and sin, and, tested by our sobering encounter with reality, fundamentally come to live a life of virtue, of faith in God, and of carefree abandon to God. By contrast, to the extent that we get mired in self-concern (in Luther's idiom, to the extent that we get engrossed in ourselves, taken over by the *cor curvum in se* ("the heart bent over on itself"), our self will get encrusted. Often, too, it will get lost in a crowd of uncoordinated social roles, masks, and *personae* that we feel impelled to adopt (cf. §201, 3, a). When (and to the extent that) this happens, no amount of self-seeking, self-maintenance, self-assertion, and even self-absorption will add up to a deep sense of self-identity; instead, one or more mis-taken, misprized, resented, even rejected quasi-selves will gradually stifle our true identity (cf. §125, 7, a–k); we will be habitually governed by worry, regret, discontent, temptation, desolation, *ennui*, or *accidie;* ultimately, a recurrent, vague sense of the pointlessness of life in general will wear us down, leading to an incapacity for genuine abandon. We will be only half capable of enjoying life's comforts and meeting life's challenges; we will find ourselves cut off from the source of repentance for our failures; both integrity and conversion will progressively elude us. Such loss of contact with our own reality is likely to make us feel that life has somehow dealt us a bad hand; this in turn will stunt our capacity for faith and trust in God, not to mention our ability to communicate ourselves to others in a constructive fashion (cf. §95, 1–2) [d].

---

[c] Such a life unfolds, of course, under the influence of *grace* in all its forms. Again, it is the undying merit of Henri de Lubac to have rejected the notion, current in sixteenth-century Thomism, that purely natural beatitude, with all reference to grace removed, is a possible and acceptable fulfillment for human beings. For de Lubac as for the great Tradition, "the paradox of a natural desire for the supernatural [is] built into the very concept of the human" (Avery Dulles, "Henri de Lubac: In Appreciation," p. 182). On this issue, cf. §82, 3, [g]; §91, 2 and [b]; §95, 5, [pp]; §109, 9, a and c–d.

[d] In the biblical idiom, the authentic self open to the living and life-giving God is designated by the word *spirit* (Heb. *rûaḥ*, Gk. *pneuma*), while the self-enclosed self, estranged from God and hence, distorted in itself and marked by mortality, is called *flesh* (Heb. *bāśār*, Gk. *sarx*). Both metaphors have been the subject of capable studies; an example is John A. T. Robinson's very accessible *The Body* (esp. pp. 11–33). For

[5] In this way, paradoxically, finitude accepted grows upon us: it becomes a cherished home, opening out onto the Infinite and its freedom as well as onto the whole world around us. By contrast, finitude rejected turns into a place of exile that imprisons us.

In observing this, what have we encountered once again but the mystery of human identity and transcendence? This time, however, our reflections have led us to a realization, not so much of its promise as of its inherent *precariousness*. Little wonder that Henri de Lubac, toward the end of an impressive series of testimonies to humanity's capacity for God, can characterize humanity as follows:

Hence, in this creature different from all other creatures, that 'unstable ontological constitution,' which makes it at once greater and smaller than itself. Hence that waddling quality, that mysterious limp, which is typical, not just of sin, but primarily and more radically of a creature that is made out of nothing, yet which, oddly, approximates God. *Deo mente consimilis.* At the same time, and inseparably, 'nothing' and 'image'; radically nothing, and substantially image nonetheless.[3]

But this implies that humanity's mystery *can* become opaque and turn into a practically impenetrable riddle; created with a native openness to transcendent perfection, we are inherently capable of self-impoundment, by dint of estrangement, degeneracy, and decay.

Very importantly, therefore, our potential for authenticity and freedom is to be understood *dialectically*. We exist, and continue to exist, in essential dependence on God's creative presence in us. On the one hand, this is a realization that is deeply cheering and reassuring: not even the worst kind of estrangement from ourselves, from others, and even from God can eradicate the divine resemblance at the core of our created being—the presence that calls us home to ourselves because it relates us to God (cf. §90, 3; §98, 4, b, [bb]). Yet on the other hand, this realization is something profoundly troubling. In the actuality of our conscious and deliberate lives, we do have the ability to let God's indefeasible fidelity to our being become a source of complacency and false assurance; that is, instead of accepting ourselves, we *can* merely

---

full and generally reliable treatments, cf. the articles *pneuma* and *sarx* in *TDNT*, and *bāśār* in *TDOT*. (As of this writing, the volume containing *rûᵃh* has not appeared; cf. the German original.) Note, too, that both metaphors have fields of reference that exceed individual persons by far; they often function as metonyms that boldly typify whole situations. A telling sample of this is YHWH's warning, issued to Israel, not to rely on Egypt for protection: "The Egyptians are human [*ādām*] and not God, and their horses are flesh and not spirit" (Is 31, 3).

take ourselves for granted. If (and to the extent that) we should do so, our capacity for genuine abandon will give way to carelessness, our potential for self-appreciation and enjoyment to a mere craving for gratification, our growing sense of identity to inauthentic self-satisfaction and self-absorption, and our aspiration to thankfulness to the kind of banal happiness that leads to forgetfulness of the blessing of being. And as in this fashion we drift away from the consciousness of our origin, the lives we lead will fail to express our native originality and dignity, and we will end up habitually (and, perhaps, increasingly) belying the ineradicable divine fidelity that keeps us in existence.

This has an ominous consequence. Our original blessing, which is God's creative indwelling in us (cf. §82, 3, b; §90, 4), will turn into a tacit indictment of ourselves—of the inauthentic persons we are becoming. Miserably, whether implicitly or by overt design, we will be turning the One who keeps sustaining us as our Creator into our Accuser and Judge. And on top of that, according as our original, authentic, open self gets encrusted with self-concern, we will become divided selves.[4] The congruence we so badly need—the congruence between the ego and the self, or between the *personae* we adopt and the identity we are inwardly prompted to actualize—is hard enough to attain even if we are fortunate enough to succeed relatively well in our struggle for authenticity. But if, and to the extent that, we should lapse into real inauthenticity, congruence stops being merely difficult. Instead, it gets habitually impaired. Our appearances get dissociated from our reality; less and less will we be what we appear to be, and *vice versa.*

[a] Against the background of this ominous possibility, Gregory Nazianzen's beautiful characterization of the authentic Christian life, dedicated to the pursuit of true wisdom, stands out in bold contrast: "To be, rather than to seem to be, a friend of God."[5]

[6] Needless to say, therefore, the awareness of our essential dependence on, attunement to, and desire for God that is at the core of our sense of identity and self-worth calls us to responsiveness and responsibility (cf. §98, 5); we cannot simply take it for granted; while ineradicable, it is not meant to lull us to sleep. Both the dependence of the immature and the complacency of the inauthentic are pathways to decay. Realism, therefore, demands of us that we temper our delight in the privilege of existence and of our developing sense of who we are by a sobering awareness of our inherent penchant for estrangement, degeneracy, and decay. Acknowledging the deep trepidation

we find within ourselves at the precariousness of our being is a deeply human (and Christian) thing to do. Familiarizing ourselves with this inconvenient but ultimately trustworthy companion is even more human and Christian.

[§113] THE DIALECTICS OF INNER CONFLICT AND CONVERSION

[1] The fundamental-theological reflections offered in the previous section have consequences of much importance, both anthropologically and theologically. Hence, they merit careful elaboration.

First of all, while the deep trepidation we discern in ourselves may be a potent *indicator* to our capacity for estrangement, degeneracy, and decay, it is not its true *measure*. For cut off from our inner sense of the God in whom we are rooted, we neither have a reliable sense of ourselves, nor can we know and appreciate the truth about ourselves; for, ultimately, it is only by being de-centered that we discover the central truth about ourselves (cf. §109, 8). The true measure of our inclination toward human estrangement, degeneracy, and decay, therefore, is not our trepidation. It is the deeper reality which the trepidation only bespeaks and conveys: the God-relatedness at the core of our being. It is this relatedness that is meant to awaken in us *both* thankfulness at the original blessing of our conscious and free affinity with created being *and* trepidation at our ontological potential for deterioration [*e*].

[2] Secondly, all of this is not changed (or at least not fundamentally changed) if and when our inherent potential for estrangement, degen-

---

[*e*] This combination of trepidation and thankfulness in the human self-awareness matches the combination of penitence and praise in the *tôdāh*-tradition (cf. §45); in both cases, the former is less fundamental than the latter. It also calls to mind Martin Heidegger's explanation of the affinity between authentic thought and the sense of thankfulness that springs up from the realization that the fact that there is being at all is an ineffable favor, right in the face of existential anxiety (cf., e.g., *Was ist Metaphysik?* p. 9). Students of Paul Tillich will have noticed that the "trepidation" referred to here resembles Tillich's notion of "anxiety," which he defines as "finitude in awareness" (*Systematic Theology*, I, p. 191). But the present treatment also differs from Tillich's, especially in one respect. Unlike Tillich (cf. *Systematic Theology*, II, p. 45), our treatment contends that even in our present situation of estrangement we have access to our essential being, not just logically or purely notionally, but really and experientially. In other words, our essential being and its dynamics can be (substantially if incompletely) brought to explicit awareness by transcendental reflection. From this it follows that existential self-awareness bears witness not only to existential anxiety or trepidation, but also (and more fundamentally) to the deep thankfulness which flows from our attunement to the Infinite—the core of our integrity as human persons.

eracy, and decay takes the fateful step into *actual* failure, sin, and depravity. In that case, an ineradicable, residual awareness of our essential relatedness to God will continue to goad our conscience, at least for some time. Only it will now move us, no longer just to trepidation at a possibility and a propensity, but to disgust at a reality. This disgust vis-à-vis evil and sin—known as a "guilty conscience" or *remorse*—is consonant with our innermost nature; for what we hear in the call of conscience is, ultimately, the voice of the indwelling God. More proximately, however (and here the theological plot really thickens), the disgust we may sense is derivative; it is (again) an *indicator* to our sinfulness, not its true *measure*. Consequently, while the divine indwelling that grounds our conscience is ineradicable (cf., again, Ruusbroec's explanation in §90, 3), not each and every troubled or remorseful response on the part of our conscience to particular unfortunate choices we have made is a reliable guide [*f*].

That is to say, not each and every instance of moral abhorrence is of God or unites with God. We have an inherent penchant for inauthenticity and self-absorption, by which we may lose touch with God, our true selves, and reality at large. One prominent form of this self-absorption is self-righteousness; consequently, not even righteous indignation at human sinfulness—our own and others'—is in every instance rooted in our deepest affinity with God; hence, it is not in every instance a reliable guide to God. Human beings will denounce the sins of the world they live in; they will even zealously confess their own part in them; known sinners are very capable of ardent self-reproach, and even more capable of it when found out. Yet no matter how sincere and conscientious such sentiments may be, and no matter how justified they may appear, they just may be, in cases, forms of the very inauthenticity and depravity they profess to detest—forms all the harder to detect for the robe of righteousness they wear.

In the unreliability of individual and communal conscientious experience something else becomes clear as well: perversely, evil is something we are capable of *sanctioning*, as a group of experts in the human sciences explained, a quarter century ago, in a disturbing collection of

---

[*f*] This is true even though, existentially and sometimes even in the last resort, an erroneous conscience may be the only guide to moral action people have. All of this is consistent with Newman's observation that, while our sense of duty remains unalterably oriented to the transcendence in which it is rooted, our moral sense, being less stable, may be mistaken in what it understands to be good or evil (§105, 3). So, while our felt experience of the former is always trustworthy, our felt experience of the latter may be misleading.

essays entitled *Sanctions for Evil.* Let us put this in the Jewish-Christian idiom. We are the *prisoners* of sin. No wonder the great Tradition, taking its cue from Saint Paul, speaks (among other things) of "slavery."

[a] Newman's distinction between the sense of duty and the moral sense (cf. §105) provides illuminating parallels to Paul's distinction, elaborated in the third chapter of the Letter to the Galatians, between the Promise made to Abraham and the Law handed down from Sinai. The Promise and Newman's "sense of duty" have this in common, that they are genuine *measures*; by contrast, the Law and Newman's "moral sense" are no more than (more or less reliable) *indicators.* The Promise to Abraham is unmediated; by virtue of God's creative faithfulness, it cannot to be nullified; it is the ground upon which both Jews and Gentiles can be justified in God's sight. Analogously, the sense of duty is unmediated; it is the direct echo, in the moral conscience, of our ineradicable attunement to God; it can ultimately draw human persons into a justice measured by God's holiness alone, and thus prevent them from resting in their own justice. The Law, on the other hand, is mediated by cosmic and cultural elements and powers (*i.e.,* "given by angels": cf. Acts 7, 38. 53; Gal 3, 19; Heb 2, 2; cf. Deut 33, 2 LXX). That is, it is (at least in Paul's argument in Galatians) only an instrument of the divine pedagogy as it applies to Israel's phase of immaturity; and while it fosters justice by the sanctions it sets (even though it also manifests the sinfulness of those who live under it), by the same token it encourages self-righteousness and a spirit of bondage, and thus it inhibits freedom in the Spirit. Analogously, the moral sense reflects the authoritative moral understandings current in the community to which we belong; it mediates between our sense of duty and the ways in which we act. Thus, while it may help enhance our authenticity (and our capacity for penance) and our relatedness to God, it may also help foster tendencies toward moral self-absorption, slavery to questionable cultural prejudices and habits, and an attitude of self-righteousness.

[3] The points just made indicate that the actualization of the human inclination toward failure, sin, and evil, brings about (and is experienced as bringing about) a fundamental inner conflict—that is, an *ontological self-contradiction.* This contradiction demands that it be understood dialectically: not only sinners themselves, but even their sinful tendencies and actions, remain anchored in God; consequently, in the very act of aiming at evil and performing it, they continue to

operate on the basis of their native tendency toward the good; if we do evil, we do so because we are seeking to do something at least in some way good.

The great Tradition has given evidence of its appreciation of this tangle. It has done so by developing a number of difficult, yet, on closer inspection, coherent fundamental-theological positions and doctrines on human failure, sin, and evil [g].

Some of the more important of these deserve some brief but careful discussion.

[a] First of all, the Jewish-Christian tradition appreciates the fact that the dialectics of failure and sin often give rise to perplexities that are downright labyrinthine. This especially applies to the *inner experience* of sin and righteousness, which can take both individual and communal forms. Not surprisingly, therefore, the Tradition has generally repudiated as both untheological and inhumane any positions on the human struggle with evil that are the equivalent of the merciless cutting of the Gordian Knot.

There is a parallel here. The great Tradition has consistently appreciated every form of righteousness as a gracious gift from God, rather than as straightforward moral option, obviously achievable by anyone or any community of sound intent. By the same token, it has resisted the temptation to make short shrift of sin, by treating it as something simply to be stamped out, since it has always held that virtue and vice are inextricably interwoven, like the wheat and the tares of Jesus' parable. Accordingly, it has interpreted the history and vicissitudes of humanity and the world, laced with evil and sin as they are, in terms of *drama*, in the form of both tragedy and comedy. No wonder the stubborn inconsistencies and self-contradictions

---

[g] In rational theodicies, often at a loss as to how to reconcile a God who is both omnipotent and good with a universe and a humanity that are plainly imperfect, the problem under discussion raises the haunting question of divine participation in, and responsibility for, evil and sin. The Jewish-Christian tradition has squarely faced this issue. It is theologically committed to merciful love, not absolute omnipotence, as the prime divine attribute; it is also committed to the essential goodness of the world and hence, to the interpretation of evil and sin as a negative, "privative" feature of the good (it inheres in something good while "depriving" it of some of its expected goodness: cf. §13, 3, e, [*j*]), and hence, as not formally willed by God (cf. *S. Th.* I, 19, 9, *in c.* and *ad 3*; cf. §115, 4, a). Thus the great Tradition will deny that evil and sin demonstrate that God is either impotent or indifferent in regard to evil and sin in the world. It will also refuse to interpret God's apparent unwillingness to come to the help of the ignorant and the wayward as cold, merciless divine pedagogy; rather, it will appeal to human responsibility, and in the final resort, to God's Providence (cf. §118).

and the unresolved tensions generated by failure, sin, and evil are favorite themes in Western literature; random examples come to mind, like the first three acts of Shakespeare's *Measure for Measure*, dominated by the figure of self-righteous Angelo; Molière's *Tartuffe*, Robert Burns' satire *Holy Willie's Prayer*, and numerous characters in the novels of Graham Greene, like the whiskey priest in *The Power and the Glory* (whose first title was *The Labyrinthine Ways*) and the self-righteous Rycker in *A Burnt-out Case*.

[b] Taught by the New Testament, the great Tradition, especially in the West, has reflected on some of these fundamental complexities under the rubric of *concupiscence* [h]. Understanding this difficult theological concept takes two steps.

First of all, concupiscence must be understood as a *natural* condition. All human beings must actualize their fundamental freedom and identity and work out their salvation by way of particular choices, both of the body and of the mind. This feature of human existence has its match in the natural structures of the cosmos in which we are situated. The only choices the world offers us are particular ones, even if it remains true that everything is connected with everything, so that particular choices usually involve wider commitments (cf. §108, 1–2, b)—a theme that will have to concern us later on (cf. §216). In any case, in no particular choice, no matter how moral and constructive, can we ever hope to invest our integral (that is, in the final analysis, spiritual) selves. Not surprisingly, therefore, both our natural desires and the exercise of our natural freedom of choice are beset by ambiguity. We can never be absolutely sure how much we really want what we desire or decide, or seem to desire or decide, or even whether we really want something at all, simply because no particular option available to us is ever entirely convincing spiritually (which is another matter that will require our attention further on: cf. §123). Thus there is a natural lack of congruence between our overt natural desires and our deep, spiritual desire and sense of moral responsibility. As a result, sometimes we will find ourselves giving in to our desires in a way that embarrasses us, some-

---

[h] "Concupiscence" equals Gk. *epithymia*—a word that occurs in almost every New Testament writing. Only twice (Lk 22, 15; 1 Thess 2, 17) does it simply mean "desire"; in the remaining 35 New Testament instances (among which the five instances of "the desires of the flesh" are notable), it has negative connotations of one kind or another: self-seeking, lack of self-control, lack of harmony, blindness, ignorance, licentiousness, corruption. In the patristic literature, the idea is often conveyed by the term *pathē* ("passions"); cf. §11, 1–2; 5.

times we will find ourselves inhibited by them, also to our embarrassment; few things are as elusive as the attainment of harmony between the cosmic self that lives by impulse and partiality and the spirit that seeks wholeness and yearns for abandon. Concupiscence, understood as the *natural maladjustment* between the human spirit's native desire for transcendent goodness and its experience of being strongly attracted or repelled by contingent, morally ambiguous options, keeps us *naturally* at odds with our true selves and hence, with God. For we can attain wisdom only if we allow our natural desires to move us, yet it takes that very wisdom to direct those same desires critically and constructively. Put differently, while our natural desires drive home to us our native zest for growth toward full identity, they also arouse our native trepidation at the possibility of forfeiting it. Thus natural desires keep us inwardly off-balance; we experience in our minds and souls events that the Greek fathers know as instances of *propatheia*—well described by Adolphe Gesché as "those transient, furtive, non-deliberate turbulences that are neither sinful nor acts of passion, and which affect [the soul] without overcoming it," and as "that critical state, morally undifferentiated because unavoidable, yet which *in and of itself* can lead the way to moral failure."[6] Small wonder we falter, but (so the Catholic tradition has affirmed, especially against the Reformers and the sixteenth-century Louvain theologian Michael Baius) this kind of *natural* faltering in and of itself involves no sin (cf. DH 1925, 1927, 1930, 1935, 1938, 1940, 1946–47, 1950–51, 1967; CF 1986–88).

But this is not all. For, if turbulence and faltering are the themes of (to borrow from William Blake) our Songs of *Innocence*, positive disharmony and failure set the tone of our Songs of actual *Experience*. In the *fallen* world in which we live, we are positively affected by the actual occurrence of imperfections and sins—those of others first, but then our own as well. Consequently, *propatheia* is now often almost undistinguishable from the sins to which it so regularly gives rise, and concupiscence is now a major force for evil. Our desires, those of the mind as much as those of the body, are badly scrambled. Natural desire still looks "only natural," and so does *propatheia*, but both now often positively misdirect our native ability to make responsible choices, both as individuals and as social groups. Paul's occasional references to concupiscence as being tantamount to actual sin (Rom 6, 12ff.; 7, 7. 14–20) may have to be treated as hyperboles (as the Catholic tradition has wisely insisted); still, *propatheia* and concupiscence *as we actually experience them* most certainly

drive home the reality of our sinfulness (as the Reformation has proclaimed with special vigor, and as the fathers of the Council of Trent
acknowledged as a matter of both faith and experience: DH 1515).[7]
For the universe to which our natural desire is attuned has become
beclouded by human sin. Therefore, natural desire must now operate under the raw conditions of hard labor, in moral impotence, and
shackled by concupiscence as we know it all too well: desire darkened[8] and turned disordered because it is rooted in sin schooled by
it. Consequently, natural desire is now as prone to sin as kindling
(*fomes*) is to catching fire (DH 1515–16; CF 512–13) [*i*].

[c] This has further theological repercussions. The Jewish-Christian
tradition acknowledges and even treasures agonies of such *inner*
depth and persistence that only paradoxes will do justice to the
dreadful tension between good and evil that brings on the agoniz-
ing. Examples are the contest between the attractiveness of a robust
life without God and the deep privilege of a laborious life with
God—a contest that is the motor force of Psalm 73. Then there is
the torment of Job, caught between outrage at undeserved suffering
and determination not to blaspheme God. There is Paul's dramatic
account, in the first eight chapters of the Letter to the Romans, of
the struggle between concupiscence and righteousness, between
flesh and spirit, and between the Mosaic Law and the Spirit of
God—a struggle echoed in the eighth book of Augustine's *Confessions*.

Thus the Tradition recognizes that human evil and sin are (and
are experienced as being) a matter of fundamental, ontological conflict. This makes paradoxes unavoidable. For, firstly, *although* the
self-contradiction of sin and sinful desire is of human making, and
hence, a human responsibility alone, its resolution cannot be
brought about by any brave moral resolve on the part of human
persons themselves; this is so because the self-contradiction has
marred our essential relatedness to the transcendent God, and

---

[*i*] The explanation of concupiscence just given is deeply indebted to Karl Rahner,
who, more than any other Catholic theologian in this century, deserves the credit for
having developed an understanding of concupiscence that is coherent both anthropologically and theologically. Incidentally, his conception is deeply catholic in that
it emphasizes that desire and the tensions and quandaries connected with it are
natural and thus not sinful in themselves; yet it rightly satisfies the Reformation's
demand that justice be done to the virtuous Christian's continuing experience of sinfulness—a theme frequently neglected in Catholic theology before the era of ecume-
nism. Cf. especially his seminal essay "Zum theologischen Begriff der Konkupiszenz"
(ET "The Theological Concept of Concupiscentia").

hence, the root of our very capacity for morally responsible choices. But, secondly, *because* the self-contradiction is of human making, and hence, a human responsibility, its resolution must not be brought about by supra-human powers alone; divine omnipotence must not be expected to remedy humanity's predicament by eminent domain. In sum, neither brave autonomous effort at moral self-management will do, nor will passive reliance on commanding divine power allegedly capable of bringing relief from outside (let us say, in the form of a *deus ex machina*, or, for that matter, by God's omnipotence or indulgence powerfully overriding human willfulness). For on the one hand, any simple removal of sin effected by God acting in solitary sovereignty would not do justice to the moral integrity and responsibility of human persons; but on the other hand, if sin had to be overcome by human effort alone, this would not do justice to the total dependence on Transcendence that is at the core of all human integrity and responsibility (cf. §98, 5).

Thus the resolution of the impasse of evil and sin and the healing of concupiscence can come about only if *both* divine transcendence is acknowledged afresh *and* human responsibility is restored; and this restoration must include the retrieval of their mutual (that is, asymmetrical) relatedness. Any resolution of the impasse, that is, must engage both the transcendent God and responsible humanity—again, in their mutual, asymmetrical relatedness. Ultimately, therefore, the resolution can be expected only from an endlessly compassionate God—that is, a God so utterly transcendent as to be able to touch the conflicted and misguided human heart by the gracious divine presence, at a depth inaccessible to the conscious, deliberate self (cf. §89, 2, [*jj*]). Only this God can provide the deep enlightenment that enables human beings to acknowledge the truth, and thus stir them to authentic repentance. Only this God, too, can awaken and capacitate the deep inner delight in responsible self-discipline required to meet the humanly speaking) impossible divine demands. This is precisely the paradoxical resolution that Augustine conveys in the prayer he reiterates, like a refrain, in the tenth book of the *Confessions*: *da quod iubes et iube quod vis* ("if you grant what you command, you can command what you will").[9]

[d] This also helps account for the great Tradition's appreciation of *spiritual direction* and *discernment of spirits*. The drama of conversion from sin and the bouts of self-absorption that are part of sinful living often produce opaque and intricate plots; not every good

intention in them is reliable, nor every desolation a sign of evil, nor every consolation a sign of God's presence. For that reason, we need the guidance of the Christian community and of proven guides to Christian living, as we pick our way around our inner selves and the powers at work in ourselves and in the world we live in by spiritual discernment, in search of the deep harmony that is the sign of true human authenticity as well as the creative, healing presence of God (cf. §79, 2, a; §125, 5, g).

[e] Here also lies the root of the Christian understanding of the resolution of the paralyzing deadlock brought about by sin and evil. The great Tradition places this resolution, not in the stamping out of sin or its destruction, but in the sinner's *conversion* and *reconciliation* with God. Far from being obliterated, expunged from the record, canceled from the memory, or ignored, *sin and its effects are remembered and acknowledged*; mature forgiveness is based not on forgetting, but on remembering. Thus sin and its effects become the very stuff of conversion and reconciliation, and hence, of the praise of God: the willing acknowledgment of sin matches the acceptance of God's forgiveness and the willing abandon to it, as well as the celebration of God's mercy (cf. §45, 2–7).

Forgiveness, therefore, comes in the form of the victory of mercy over judgment (Jas 2, 13). This assurance of mercy in turn involves the abandonment of all forms of fear of divine judgment—a fear that so often engulfs the sinner, in the form of the rush into self-judgment, whether of the self-justifying or the self-condemning kind (cf. §401, 2, b). Under the influence of divine grace, then, the sinner's debilitating concern with self must give way to an inner posture of *participation*—that is, of the ability to stop being self-rejecting and self-defeating, and to live with oneself in self-acceptance, reconciled with one's real sinful self, as well as with one's past errors and misdeeds, which the grace of forgiveness turns into potential sources of wisdom. In the words of Julian of Norwich: "sin will be no shame, but honor to us" [j].[10]

---

[j] At its best, the great Tradition supports self-acceptance (cf. §136, 5–6), and treats self-abasement, self-rejection, and self-defeat as forms of self-absorption, evil, and sin; Hopkins' "My own heart let me have more pity on; let/Me live to my sad self hereafter kind/Charitable" is a deeply Christian prayer. In this rejection of negative self-assessment, we are justified in recognizing echoes of the Jewish-Christian tradition's opposition to all forms of dualism (cf. §98, 3–4; §115, 3, [b]; §125, 5, b, [vv]). The all-creating, all-merciful God has no opponents (cf. §79, 4), not even those who very much act as if they were. Degeneracy, sin, and evil are parasitical on the fundamental, ontological integrity and goodness that betray creation's divine origin: "Evil

In the last resort, therefore, as Augustine came to see with such great inner clarity, the sinner's recovery of identity is *both* authentic *and* a free gift from God; it consists in a personal catharsis brought about by divine grace. In this catharsis, the human heart, forever restless, usually struggling, frequently wayward, sometimes hardened, finds itself at long last released from the grip of its moral impotence (cf. Rom 7, 15–25). The forces of estrangement and sin are disabled, disarmed, and defeated, and the inner victory is won only when the misguided heart's native attunement to God is restored; and this comes about when the liberating impulse of divine graciousness works on the soul it has first patiently worn down by means of the vicissitudes of life, sometimes jolting, sometimes cajoling: God makes mercy in human beings by "melting and mastering" them "whether at once, as once at a crash Paul, or as Austin, a lingering-out sweet skill."[11]

True conversion thus becomes a delightful, liberating, inner sense of victory rooted in the deep experience of transcendence. At last, we find ourselves free enough to admit defeat; and as we find ourselves becoming increasingly capable of mature abandon to God, we recover our long-lost selves. We acknowledge how badly we have failed, and the regret at our past follies is likely to continue forever. Still, our self-centered distress at past failure has been turned into "compunction"—the kind of regret that purifies life and turns our awareness of our loss of innocence into a humble, quiet hunger and thirst for salvation.[12] Our exile may still be upon us, but we are no longer at a complete loss. Concupiscence may still be with us, but, having been healed at the root, its power is no longer unchecked. As a result, the authority of God's law no longer evokes in us a sense of moral impotence and discouragement. The riddle that had us immobilized has been cracked; the sense of the mystery at the core of our being is accessible once again. Finally, we can at least *begin* to choose freely, and virtue can once again become what it was always meant to be: intrinsically more delightful than vice [k].

---

cannot exist except in the good" (*malum non potest esse nisi in bono*: Aquinas, *Q. D. de Malo*, 1, 2, *in c.*); consequently, God can call forth good from evil. In the New Testament, this conviction takes the form of radical calls for non-violence and long-suffering. Jesus bids his disciples not to punish evil, nor to oppose the evil that threatens them, and to match the Father's encompassing mercy for good and evil alike by loving their enemies (Mt 5, 38–39. 44–45; Lk 6, 27–36); Paul exhorts the Roman community not to seek vengeance, but to defeat evil by doing good (Rom 12, 19–21).

[k] Readers of Augustine will have discerned in this paragraph allusions to two classical passages. One is Augustine's exegesis of Jn 6, 44: "No one can come to me

[f] Earlier, in the treatment of the dynamics of Revelation, it was explained how the experienced presence of mature others (and, through and in and beyond them, of the transcendent God) will evoke in us the sense of responsive identity (cf. §122, 1, f). We can now add that the analyses just conducted suggest parallels between the anthropological-theological dynamics of revelation and those of conversion and reconciliation: it is *in encounter* that we come, first to an initial acknowledgment of failure and sin, and from there on, to mature repentance and forgiveness. These parallels support the fact that the great Tradition has firmly maintained that any fully *theological* understanding of sin is a matter of *divine revelation*.

Not that the Tradition has overlooked the fact that there is such a thing as a natural sense of evil, which can be developed into a fundamental theology of sin; in fact, it has positively warranted its development. It has fostered the assumption that the Christian doctrine of sin is very much supported by ordinary life experience [*l*]. In other words, John Henry Newman was but restating in personal terms an age-old consensus, shared by pagans, Jews, and Christians alike,[13] when he pointed out that human life experience very much suggests that there must be something sinfully wrong with humanity and the world (cf. §114, 1). Irresistibly aware of its radical attunement to the light of stable truth and to the life of dedicated goodness, humanity is forced, again and again, and by the vicissitudes of its own history, to face its intellectual and moral impotence—its inability to attain either truth or goodness in fullness or with any permanence or assurance. Immanently called to growth and development by means of action (cf. §87, 1), humanity has also been

---

unless drawn by the Father who sent me" (*Tract. in Joh.* XXVI, 4; *PL* 35, 1608), which appeals to Virgil's line *trahit sua quemque uoluptas* ("all are attracted by what specifically delights them": *Ecl.* II, 65); here Augustine argues that the activity of our *will* does not fully account for our faith; the fact that we are *attracted* by God-given interior delight does. The second is the passage, in the seventh book of the *Confessions* (X, 16; *CSEL* 33, p. 157), where Augustine professes that he owes his inner enlightenment to the divine light, which is known by "love alone." In writing this, Augustine implies that his conversion to, and reconciliation with, God have also reconciled him with the world; he now realizes that, as long as he was estranged from God, he was living in the world as in a place of exile, in a land that does not fit the soul attuned to God: "far from You, in the region of dissimilarity" [*in regione dissimilitudinis*]. Augustine is borrowing the latter phrase from Plotinus (*Enneads*, I, 8, 13), who in turn echoes Plato ("the bottomless abyss of unlikeness": *Statesman* 273^d6–7; *PlatoCDia*, p. 1039).

[*l*] Note that this corresponds with a contention made long ago, namely that the Creed warrants and authorizes natural theology with a universalist appeal (cf. §59, 4). For analogous points, cf. §62, 1, a; §64, 1–2; §91, 1; §93, 9.

forced, by dint of disappointment, to recognize the tragic character of effort—especially of noble effort: every so often the more earnestly we try, the deeper the hole we dig for ourselves and each other. Thus the experience of our common existential predicament—of humanity's wearisome inability to free itself from the circle of frustration it seems to have drawn around itself—readies us for both the regret and the relief which the revealed doctrine of sin, together with its correlate, the doctrine of salvation by grace, bids us profess and accept [m].

That relief has two correlated ingredients.

The first is the grace of willing penitence: our own salutary recognition, in the light of the revealed Word of God, of our sin: of the injury that we, along with all of humanity, have presumed to offer, and continue to offer, to a boundlessly good and gracious God, who in being both creative and gracious reveals and communicates the divine Self in the gift of the Holy Spirit.

The other is the grace of justification: in the penitential acceptance of God's revealed judgment that we are sinners, we are freed to accept as a blessing the divine mercy that envelops and carries and embeds the judgment. In this way, we are remade by the mercy that restores us both to our original kinship with God and to our own authentic identity and ability to act freely, as the Decree on Justification of the Council of Trent explains ever so carefully (cf. DH 1525– 26; CF 1929–30) [n].

---

[m] Few modern theologians have more keenly analyzed the human existential predicament in its various aspects as an urgent, if ineffectual, quest for the revelation of the "New Being" than Paul Tillich. Cf. esp. his *Systematic Theology*, pp. 81–159. This remains true, even if, in the last resort, one would have to conclude that Tillich's account of the correlation between human predicament and divine self-revelation restricts the latter to the narrow scope of the former; cf. F. J. van Beeck, *Christ Proclaimed*, pp. 202–17.

[n] This may be an appropriate place to point out that the catholic tradition's understanding of original justice is analogous to its understanding of the dialectics of justification; in fact, the analogy suggests that the concept of original justice has been tacitly extrapolated from the experience of justification. In the actuality of human life, there is no neutral stance in regard to God; either we move away from God, rejecting grace and implicitly disfiguring our authentic selves, or we move toward God, coming to repentance by grace, being enabled to love God, and thus also growing into our true, responsive identity. Analogously, in treating original justice, the Tradition has (with very few exceptions) succeeded in resisting the idea that Adam and Eve (here imagined as historical individuals) lived in a state of pure nature. Rather, they were portrayed as endowed with the supernatural gifts of holiness, justice, and the freedom from every form of concupiscence—gifts that filled them to overflowing, in the form of the praeternatural gift of immortality (cf. DH 239; 1511; CF 503; 507; cf. also §125, 2, a, [m]).

[g] The original shape of any divine revelation—of the living, self-revealing Word-Presence of God—is not so much the rise of doctrines as the interpretation of historic events. These events involve encounters with witnesses to God and godliness; of such encounters, doctrines are the authoritative, tradition-shaping expression and interpretation (cf. §95, 7–8). Things are no different in the case of sin: its revelation occurs primarily in revelatory *events*. Such events, we must anticipate, will be experiences in *contrast*: it is in the encounter with witnesses to God's holiness that human sin will appear in fierce relief—all the fiercer for the fact that sin is self-contradictory. This calls for elaboration.

[h] At an initial, primal, "pistic" level of divine pedagogy, the experience of the human condition's contrast with God's holiness is liable to take a strongly cosmological shape. Humanity cannot but be awed at the vastness of God's power manifested in the cosmos. But that transcendent power turns out to awaken in the believer not only awe and faith and trust, but also dread in the face of majesty, and hence, guilt and fear in the face of holiness, along with the salutary awareness of the urgent need for conversion. Consistent with this, in the pistic imagination, worldly power and prosperity are blessings by means of which Almighty God both shows the divine favor and demands obedience to the divine command; conversely, weakness and impoverishment tend to be interpreted as a natural, divinely-imposed punishment for sin. Thus, early Israel's success on the battlefield is interpreted as a reward for its faith and obedience, just as its national prosperity betokens the blessing of Almighty God. Conversely, things like the superiority of Israel's enemies resulting in military defeat, disease resulting in death, awe-inspiring or astonishing natural events, and even prophetic threats drive home the divine displeasure. (Incidentally, the Jewish Scriptures abound in examples of this type of contrast, but Peter's profession of sinfulness upon seeing the great catch of fish [Lk 5, 8] shows that it is by no means absent from the New Testament.) Thus, in the pistic world, sin is revealed as an offense against Almighty God, and the very temerity involved in sin is rightly expected to draw down upon sinners the just rigors of divine punishment. In fact, faith in this connection between sin and punishment is so strong that when a deserved punishment fails to materialize, the (all too human) reaction is that God must have had a change of heart moved to pity at the sight of the people's conversion. This primal type of penitence, while not de-

void of genuine awe, is strongly inspired by fear. To that extent it is imperfect; if it is deepened (as is appropriate), it will advance to the "charismatic" level.

[i] In the charismatic imagination, the revelation of sin is characterized by *inwardness*. It arises from the embarrassing contrast between the clear demands for justice, goodness, or truth implicit in the whole world-order and in the testimony of God's privileged witnesses on the one hand, and human irresponsibility on the other—the ·deep crookedness, corruption, and deceit that typify much human activity, even of the well-motivated. Typically, at this level, prophetic witnesses touched by the holiness of God will call for conversion of heart and drive home, on behalf of the God they witness to, the need for justice, goodness, and truth as inherent human duties, regardless of circumstances. This strongly anthropological type of penitence, inspired by personal and communal awareness of moral responsibility, can in turn be deepened again, so to reach the properly theological, "mystical" level.

[j] Here, where union with God is immediate, the revelation of sin arises in all its theological starkness, from the contrast between the transcendent God's faithful love and the human insistence on self-assertion, self-maintenance, and self-justification turned wayward and even violent. At this level, any prophetic witnesses must be prepared to be so devoted to God as to be ready for martyrdom, for the contrast between divine love and human sin becomes so embarrassing to the sinner as to be intolerable; accordingly, sinners, desperately and blindly attempting to justify themselves, will attempt to remove the very witnesses that embody God's demanding and forgiving love. In this way, sin is revealed in its full, brutal ugliness. Just people, powerless but patient,and marked by their silent abandon to God, accept martyrdom at the hands of those they seek to touch with the love of God. Thus the voluntary poor and the true believers and the willing prophets of all times and places—the "cloud of witnesses" (Heb 12, 1)—become the mirrors held up by God to reveal to humanity what it has done to itself by dint of human sin.

In the Christian imagination, this revelation culminates in the treatment meted out to the person of Jesus, "the greatest moral evil ever committed."[14] Trotted out by Pilate in full view of the mob (Jn 19, 5), Jesus reflects, in the most human, innocent, accepting, and compassionate of faces—the *Ecce Homo* face so often and so unforgettably painted by Georges Rouault—the inhumanity inflicted on him, and in him, on the whole human family. Here the sin of the world has found itself revealed in the humanity of God, who, paradoxically, in the very act of exposing the full ugliness of sin also absorbs and outsuffers it, thus taking it away. And in the process, something even deeper and more paradoxical is revealed: God's omnipotence, which the Jewish-Christian understands as manifested to best advantage in the divine lenience and mercy [o], capable of drawing "the greatest of goods"[15] out of the greatest evil—that is, drawing everlasting life out of death dealt by overpowering sin.

[4] Let us conclude. These elaborate fundamental theological anthropological reflections, offered by way of introduction to six long chapters on evil and sin, amount to a firm caution to theologians. The affirmation of humanity's moral responsibility (and of the culpability connected with it) is part and parcel of the Jewish-Christian tradition (§98, 5); but then again, so is a healthy distrust of the deadly human eagerness to comprehend, evaluate, and (especially) pronounce upon evil and sit in judgment on it [p]. Where sin and evil are concerned, therefore, much as theologians, like the proverbial preacher, may be "agin' it," they will do well to curb their zeal for categorical positions on the subject [q].

Happily, therefore, the Jewish-Christian Tradition positively cautions us against projecting even our most deeply felt responses to the onslaught of evil all too hastily on to God. For our vision of God is skewed by our skewed selves. The defensive, self-conscious, self-justifying embarrassment of Adam and Eve hiding from God in the garden after eating from the forbidden fruit (Gen 3, 7–11) is part of their estrangement from their true selves—the estrangement that has skewed their vision of God. What should give the theologian further

---

[o] In the words of the Roman Missal: *Deus qui omnipotentiam tuam parcendo maxime et miserando manifestas* (Opening Prayer, 26th Sunday in Ordinary Time).

[p] In fact, the failure of Adam and Eve to obey God's command not to eat of the tree of the knowledge of good and evil (Gen 1, 17) reflects Israel's belief that sin is precisely rooted in humanity's presumptuous claim to autonomous judgment in matters of good and evil. The claim implies that humanity can sit in sovereign judgment on itself and its actions—a claim that (so the Jewish and Christian traditions hold) imprisons us (cf. § 126).

[q] In the catholic tradition, this has taken the form of the rejection of two extreme positions adopted here and there in the wake of the Reformation. The first is the characterization of fallen humanity as totally depraved, and hence, the proposition that those not justified by grace commit sin in everything they do, since there no longer exists such a thing as a naturally good action (cf. DH 1557, 1575; CF 1957, 1975). The other extreme is the proposition that the justified enjoy an absolute assurance of salvation (DH 1540–41, 1566; CF 1941–42, 1966).

pause are other biblical commonplaces. Thus there is the consistent prophetic assurance that God seeks, not the death of sinners, but their conversion (Ez 33, 11). There is also the prophetic habit of consistently placing Israel's unfaithfulness in the context of, not only divine wrath and punishment, but also, and more decisively, of God's love and mercy; furthermore, there is the consistent prophetic witness to YHWH's persistent commitment to the Covenant and even to the deep renewal of the Covenant manifested in Israel's return from Exile (cf., for example, It is 55, 6–9; Jer 3–31; Ez 36).[16] Finally, Jesus' parable of the tares and the wheat (Mt 13, 24–30. 36–43) should certainly come to mind, as should Jesus' injunction not to judge (Mt 7, 1 par. Lk 6, 37; cf. Rom 2, 1; 14, 4. 13; 1 Cor 4, 5; 5, 12; Jas 4, 11ff.), and his reminder that God causes the sun to rise on the good as well as the evil, and the rain to fall on the just and the unjust alike (Mt 5, 45).

It is a matter of fundamental theological integrity, therefore, to hold that there is nothing simple or straightforward about evil. Consequently, evil and sin are nowhere easy to unmask or identify; not surprisingly, there is no divine authorization for their quick, forceful defeat. Consequently, too, it is *simpliste* to disparage and condemn evil as a matter of course, or to present sin as open rebellion, of the kind that obviously calls for divine wrath and punishment, or to treat sin as error to be uncompromisingly denounced, or as depravity firmly to be rooted out, by clear divine warrant [r]. All evil is dark indeed, like a riddle, but to the eye of faith its darkness never succeeds in wholly extinguishing the original light; the riddle puts wraps around the hidden light of truth and goodness immanent in all that is, but it does not overpower it or crowd it out (cf. Jn 1, 5); the mysterious presence of God in every creature remains ineradicable; it demands that it be respected. That is, all evil remains parasitical on the good; no wonder it carries *within itself* the invitation to conversion; if this were not the case, not even God would be able to draw good out of evil.

These realizations may be disconcerting, especially to the zealots among us. Still, they at least drive home the theological conviction that the human penchant for depravity, depravity itself, and even the human abhorrence at depravity demand a *theological* interpretation—one that does justice as much to God's unflagging immanence in creation as to God's transcendent holiness that is offended. At the core of

---

[r] In other words, the fact that expressions like these occur in the Bible with great frequency is a wholly insufficient warrant for a theologically undiscerning use of them.

that interpretation is the realization that (in Ruusbroec's words) "the nobility which we have, by nature, in the essential unity of our spirit" is inalienable, "for all persons, good and evil, have this within themselves" (§90, 3). God does not cease to love the sinner, who continues to bear an essential likeness to Christ (§90, 5).

[a] This christological interpretation of God's abiding presence to humanity is elaborated, with true originality of vision as well as great tenderness, in the theology of God's loving response to the sinner developed by a younger contemporary of Ruusbroec, the English mystic Julian of Norwich. In her skillful and elegant monograph on Julian, *Wisdom's Daughter*, Joan M. Nuth explains how "the parable of the lord and the servant," which was part of Julian's original visions, contains a very puzzling element. Eagerly on his way to doing his lord's work lovingly, the servant had fallen into a ditch and gotten himself so severely injured as to be unable to serve the lord; he merely lay there, feeble and feeling foolish, blinded in reason and perplexed in mind, and almost forgetful of the love that had first moved him to set out on his tasks; *yet the lord kept looking upon him only with love.* Julian finds herself unable to reconcile this mild response on the part of the lord with the Church's teaching on the damnation of sinners, until she realizes, after a long period of perplexity, that the servant in the ditch represents, not only fallen Adam, but also (and more importantly) divine Wisdom freely and humbly incarnate. Thus, in the end, she comes to the realization that "God sees sin and salvation from the perspective of eternal wisdom and love": "because of the true union which was made in heaven, God's Son could not be separated from Adam."[17]

[5] A final caution. Divine reassurances extended to sinners like those found in Julian's writings are, of course, no invitation to excuse sin or to take it easy on morality. In the Jewish-Christian tradition, the proverb *tout comprendre, c'est tout pardonner*[18] is simply a blasphemy. So is Heinrich Heine's death-bed quip *Bien sûr qu'il me pardonnera; c'est son métier.*[19] Similarly, any "liberal" account of human evil, designed to bring it within a purely anthropological compass and thus to reduce it to the status of understandable (that is, readily excusable) snags in cultural or moral development, whether personal or communal—let us say, an account that would understand sin merely as the natural, par-for-the-course consequence of finitude—is theologically unacceptable.

[a] Let us quickly add, however, that such purely anthropological accounts of human evil are phenomenologically and experientially unsatisfactory as well. For, first of all, they make *all* human failure essentially harmless, which is patently false. Furthermore, by robbing, as a matter of principle, every human person of moral responsibility, they reduce humanity to a worldwide nursery. Finally and ultimately, they turn the awesome mystery of God's anguish on behalf of the sinners—an anguish that translates into infinite mercy and compassion—into a tale of toothless, careless, loveless leniency that holds the human recipients of divine mercy cheap by making no moral demands on them. In the seventh chapter of his classic monograph *God Was in Christ,* Donald M. Baillie has given us a profound treatment of this crucial difference between costly mercy and mere indulgence.

[b] Still, the mere temptation to anthropologize is no excuse for crude theologizing. Theology must insist that evil and sin are not readily understandable; that they can be appreciated and understood only in relation to mystery; that ultimately, what will renew our sense of religious awe is the recognition that an imperfect world and sinful human persons and communities remain rooted in the creative and self-revealing presence of an utterly Sovereign, Holy God, who is and remains involved in, and committed to, the work of the divine hands. Obviously, therefore, any genuine theology of evil and sin is liable to put our experience and understanding of human life to a substantial test [s].

[§114] HISTORIC SIN

[1] The analyses just conducted have already alluded to a proposition that will now require our thematic attention, namely that human sin is a fact of life. This proposition consists of two elements.

Firstly, as a matter of record, the Jewish-Christian tradition has not stopped at regarding the human hold on authenticity, goodness, and truth as merely precarious. If it has emphatically recognized that humanity is characterized by a penchant for estrangement, degeneracy,

---

[s] The positions adopted in this and the following sections are meant to fulfill the promise first made in §12, 1, b, and subsequently reaffirmed in §79, 4, c and [dd]. Cf. also §84, 4; §125, 7–8; §140, 1–2.

and decay, it has professed even more forcefully that the latter are a matter of *historical actuality*.

Secondly, as pointed out already, the Jewish-Christian Tradition has not thought of this in merely *anthropological* or even purely *ethical* terms. Sin, that is, is not just a regrettable, tragic failure, on the part of a humanity otherwise replete with promise, to reach the fullness of its immanent potential to its own satisfaction, legitimate enjoyment, and mature sense of moral responsibility. At root and above anything else, the Tradition has taken a *theological* view of human deficiency: it has maintained that humanity's degeneracy is properly moral and religious—it involves humanity's relatedness to God [*t*]. In other words, humanity has in the last resort failed and even deliberately refused to accept itself at the hand of God, and hence also, to turn itself into the stuff of thankful praise, awe, service offered to God, and of intimacy enjoyed with God. In fact, so the Tradition has gone on to insist, in the last analysis the failure has taken anthropological and even cosmological shape only because it is, at bottom, so overwhelmingly religious and theological. In other words, it is sin against the living God that has prompted humanity to jeopardize and even revoke its commitment to responsible stewardship, on God's behalf, in regard to both itself and the cosmos.

John Henry Newman is a most eloquent and careful witness to this truth. When he was recounting, in the *Apologia pro Vita Sua*, the "history of his religious opinions," he explained that, precisely as a believer in God as the world's Creator, he could only be deeply disappointed by "the general facts of human society and the course of history." Thus he could write:

> And so I argue about the world;—*if* there be a God, *since* there is a God, the human race is implicated in some terrible aboriginal calamity. It is out of joint with the purpose of its Creator. This is a fact, a fact as true as the fact of its existence; and thus the doctrine of what is theologically called original sin becomes to me almost as certain as that the world exists, and as the existence of God.[20]

[2] In observing the painful contrast between the intimations of humanity's original promise and the experience of its actual condition, Newman is a witness to the great Tradition, starting with Israel's *tôdāh*-tradition all the way down to the experience of faithful Jews and faith-

---

[*t*] This proposition is the exact match of Newman's contention that an analysis of the moral conscience must ultimately arrive at God (§105, 3–6)

ful Christians today. The profession of sinfulness is simply a constituent element of the all-encompassing sacrifice of praise and thanksgiving offered to God (cf. §45, 2–6; §113, 1, [e]). A good example of this
is a temple psalm whose central section professes the awesome power
of God and whose conclusion is a vision of the eschatological restoration of the whole world, by the effective presence of God, to harmony,
beauty, and fertility; yet the psalm starts with a profession of sinfulness:

> Yours is fittingly a song of praise,
> O God, dwelling in Zion;
> Yours is the pledging of vows,
> You, hearer of prayer.
> To You all flesh draws near,
> Burdened with deeds of iniquity.
> Too much for us, our transgressions;
> You take them away.

(Ps 65, 2–4)

At one level, of course, Israel's rehearsal of its history is thoroughly
anthropological and ethical: it marches to the beat of human—say,
socio-political or moral—triumph and defeat. But far more properly,
Israel's account of its history is religious and theological: it marches to
the beat of what all its secular triumphs and defeats point to, symbol-
ize, and, indeed, embody: God's faithfulness and mercy, and Israel's
own penchant for disloyalty and hardness of heart. Thus the central
theme of Israel's history as a nation is the thesis that the merciful God
encounters and saves and disarms and wins over (at least regularly) an
Israel that insists on being misguided.

[a] In the case of Christianity, the interpretation of human waywardness takes a similar tack. Let us demonstrate this by means of
a very different, rather more modern example, taken from the world
of doctrine. The theological themes of justification, sanctification,
and salvation, while clearly rooted in the Bible, vigorously appeal to
human experience—a fact that helps explain why they have moved
so close to the center of the Christian consciousness since the Reformation (cf. §20, 1–2). Still, their full meaning becomes clear only
if it is acknowledged that they imply not only that there is something
radically wrong with *humanity*, but also that this wrong has ramifica-
tions that are beyond humanity's compass. For even at their most
experiential, justification, sanctification, and salvation concern humanity's relationship with God. The "radical wrong" they imply,

therefore, must be that humanity as we know it suffers, not merely from injuries to its own moral and religious being, but also from actual, habitual, and indeed immemorial injuries to its relatedness to the living God, which constitutes the core of its moral and religious being. Justification, sanctification, and salvation, in other words, are implicit professions of humanity's inability to do justice, consciously and freely, to God.

[3] In Aquinas' five ways, humanity's native relatedness to God is explored under three hierarchically ordered rubrics: *dependence, resemblance,* and *dynamic attunement* (cf. §102, 10). Accordingly, any injury to this relatedness can be expected to involve an estrangement from God in respect of any or all of these fundamental forms of relatedness. That is, both individually and socially, humanity finds itself in a self-imposed, ill-fitting, unnatural predicament of *autonomy, dissimilitude,* and *aversion.* No wonder these inauthentic postures never become quite satisfactory. Though bent on independence, we find ourselves anxious and irresolute about ways to affirm it; though intent on establishing an identity, both personally and socially, we find ourselves at a loss for satisfactory patterns and archetypes by which to model, test, and measure it; though determined to move beyond present, unsatisfactory conditions of existence by means of action, so as to seek fulfillment, we find ourselves misguided about which way genuine growth and development lie. We are torn.

[4] Most humiliatingly, however, if hardly surprisingly, humanity finds itself, in all of these impasses as well as beyond them, turning its native desire for the living God into an uneasy pursuit of a variety of counterfeits of God. *Sin is idolatrous,* and it is in the nature of idolatry to wear a religious mask. Humanity's quest for total autonomy, after all, is and remains rooted in its original desire for God; no wonder it remains residually religious; a modern commentator, writing in a different context, has rather perceptively characterized the result as follows: "God is out though godly attitudes may be in."[21] What, therefore, originally was the unquenchable desire for the wholly transcendent One will take the shape of a deep human need for spiritual contentment. Consequently, in due course, religion is liable to become little more than a respectable form of self-absorption; in the end, people will look for a god to believe in largely in the interest of self-maintenance and self-regard. Thus the worship of God, whose original purpose is to set humanity free, will turn into a source of enslavement—a crutch for the needy, the unhappy, the irresolute, and the unfulfilled, as the great

nineteenth-century humanistic atheists and their disciples have not tired of pointing out (cf. §70, 4, a–b; §99, 2).

Not surprisingly, movements and establishments of one kind or another (and, indeed, whole cultures) will seek to meet a hungry humanity's religiously inspired thirst for, and fascination with, *miracle, mystery,* and *authority*. Material, palpable *idols* (cf. §310, 10) and their purveyors will have us marveling at the easy gratification available to us; but they will also lead to humanity's degradation, and thus dull our awareness of our deeper, less immediate desires. Misguided and misleading *ideals* (cf. §318, 4) and their prophets will capture the consciences of many of us, inducing them to sell our souls and enslave them to causes and prejudices that excite (but often secretly stunt and alienate) those who support them. Most insidiously of all, *ideologies* (cf. §142, 14, a) authoritatively taught by self-styled martyrs, sages, highpriests, pundits, and gurus of every kind will claim to give humanity a definitive, all-encompassing, and indeed self-deifying account of itself and of the world. Such ideologies will seduce us with the prospect of universal justice, harmony, or happiness; but in reality they seek to have us agree to a humanism whose core is humanity's self-deification. This can only result in a quasi-religious conformity from which there is virtually no exit, and which would prohibit us retracing our steps to the freedom of the children of God (cf. §215, 5, e) [*u*].

[5] The Jewish-Christian tradition has called all of this *sin*. Sin is *the deep injury both to humanity's relatedness to God and to its own native integrity, historically enacted*—that is, brought about in the actuality of human life in all its historic forms by human agents acting with an appreciable measure of understanding and freedom of choice. And, inasmuch as humanity is made in God's image—that is, ineradicably dependent on God, attuned to God, and aspiring to God—sin is historic insult of-

---

[*u*] Attentive readers will have noticed in this paragraph a progression with which they are by now familiar: cosmology → anthropology → theology (cf., for example, §102, 10). Besides, readers of Dostoevsky will have recognized the source of some of the phrases used in this paragraph: *viz.,* chapter 5 of Book Five of *The Brothers Karamazov,* entitled "The Grand Inquisitor." It is to be noted that in the context of the novel, the legend is the literary creation of an atheist, Ivan Karamazov. In Ivan's cynical view of humanity and the world, the liberating religion of mercy, freedom, and love initiated by Jesus Christ is no more than an illusion; Christianity's only realistic opportunity to benefit humanity lies in the Roman Catholic, papal, and Jesuit attempts (so Ivan claims) to establish the religion that can meet the true predicament of humanity and the world: not the freedom and love offered by the Savior, but the Grand Inquisitor's "corrected" version of it. That version is an ultimately idolatrous system of enslavement that seals the fate of wounded humanity by eradicating both its awareness of its native dignity and its last memory of Jesus Christ.

fered to the living God by a humanity estranged from its deepest authenticity.

[a]   The concept of sin properly understood, in other words, involves both anthropology and theology, in their mutual (if always asymmetrical) relationship.   But it also involves another pair of elements: the historical and the radical (or "transcendental").

The essence of sin is best approached by starting with the latter pair.   Sin, in all its forms, is *historical* injury offered to God, at any level of consciousness and deliberation, on the part of human persons or communities; however, since historicity is not incidental to humanity but integral to it, this historical occurrence strikes at humanity's *roots*, even if it does not extirpate them.

Thus we encounter the former pair: theology and anthropology. In injuring (even if not annihilating) their essential rootedness in and relatedness to God, human persons and communities injure themselves, not only in regard to their own identity, but also in regard to their historic responsibility to do justice to all of humanity.

[6]   However, since humanity is inseparable from the cosmos, the injury involves cosmology as well: sin affects humanity's ability to take responsibility, in a constructive fashion, for the cosmos *as well as for itself as a cosmic phenomenon.*   To this fundamental philosophical and theological theme we must now turn, in a demanding chapter.

CHAPTER 13

"Creation Made Subject to Frustration" (Rom 8, 20)

FUNDAMENTALS: COSMOLOGY AND ANTHROPOLOGY

[§115] NATURAL EVIL

[1] Sin, so it was stated at the end of the previous chapter, affects humanity's ability to take responsibility, in a constructive fashion, both for the cosmos and for itself as a cosmic phenomenon.

This implies an important proposition. If humanity must take responsibility for the cosmos "in a constructive fashion," this suggests that at the very least the cosmos is perfectible. But this implies the conviction that there exist deficiencies in the cosmos—deficiencies that can neither be properly called sin nor regarded as the effect of sin. That is, there are imperfections in the cosmos that are not the result of humanity historically and answerably acting, at least in some degree, in ways that are at odds with God, itself, and the world. Such imperfections are called "natural" imperfections. Now since humanity is radically part of the cosmos, it stands to reason that such natural imperfections should occur in humanity as well; humanity suffers from flaws that are neither sinful nor the consequence of sin.

Speaking anthropologically, this conviction is a matter of universal human awareness. Human beings of all times and all places seem to understand, whether thematically or unthematically, that both humanity itself and the cosmos "need work." The civilizing imperative is a distinctively human attribute. We naturally experience ourselves and the world around us as perfectible; we act on the assumption that there exists, as an integral ingredient of ourselves and of the cosmos we participate in and inhabit, such a thing as "natural evil" or "physical evil."

Bene intelligit qui bene distinguit.[1] To understand is (at least in part) to make distinctions, and the task of understanding natural failure, natural deficiency, and natural evil is no exception to this rule. Accordingly, if we are to develop a sound understanding of *sin* in its anthropological-theological distinctiveness (which is the task of this volume), we are likely to be helped by a precise understanding of *natural evil* in its cosmological and anthropological distinctiveness (which is the primary task of the present chapter).

To distinguish is not the same as to *separate*. In fact, we may anticipate that reflection on natural evil will lay bare fundamental connections between it and human sin—between a fallen world and a fallen humanity. This anticipation is rooted in the radical continuity that prevails between humanity and the cosmos—a continuity that *God Encountered* is committed to respecting (§9, 1, [*I*]; cf. §115, 7, [*g*]).

[a] This continuity immediately comes home to us when we travel from the abstract, relatively harmless expression "natural evil" to the realm of concrete instances. The latter are apt to drive home just how troubling the notion of natural evil is from an anthropological point of view (as against a purely cosmological one). Such instances also face us with the fact that "natural evil" raises a host of theological issues, all of them connected with *humanity's position in the cosmos*—the age-old philosophical and subject treated, in this century of science and technology, with so much clarity, passion, and sense of proportion by Max Scheler in *Die Stellung des Menschen im Kosmos* (ET *Man's Place in Nature*). The Second Vatican Council gave a courageous (if in places somewhat guarded) treatment to the issue in its Pastoral Constitution on the Church in the Modern World (GS 33–39; DH 4333–39). In any case, humanity and the cosmos are inseparable; yet the decisive difference that humanity makes in the cosmos gives rise to relationships of great complexity. This suggests that natural evil is a demanding and irritating theme; that is to say, it will resist attempts at theological interpretation as long as we fail to confront and properly clarify *the relationship between cosmology and anthropology*—a theme touched on more than once already (cf. §87, 2, esp. [*gg*]). The elaborate analyses in the present section will have occasion to show this.

[2] Let us start our inquiry on a strictly anthropological note. Faced with questions about natural evil, most of us feel at once that it is both heartless and unwise to be wholly imperturbable and "philosophical" about the issue. It is inhumane to acknowledge the seriousness of harmful and hurtful natural occurrences and at the same time to smooth them over as "only natural": devastating earthquakes, fires,

and floods; the native cruelty of many animals; the destructive effects of countless micro-organisms on the health of plants, animals, and human persons and communities; the frequent incidence of congenital human deformities (which the successes of modern medicine tend as much to bring out into the open as to alleviate); the noiseless disappearance (or so it would appear) of millions of faceless, unremembered human beings into the dark folds of the past, irrelevant (or so it seems) to the course of human history; the large numbers of human beings caught in conditions so primitive that even basic human civilization and morality are impractical; and even more, that nightmarish test of our faith in a just and good world: the painful deaths of innocent children, sometimes even at the hands of their own abused, deranged, or irreversibly criminal parents. Dr. Rieux's statement, in Albert Camus' novel *The Plague*, may be theologically questionable, but it is not far-fetched: "I will refuse to the death to cherish this sort of creation where children are put to torture."[2]

But, disasters aside, there is the frequent occurrence of small mishaps with tragic consequences; the debilitating hitches in physical, intellectual, and emotional development on the part of human individuals and communities; harmless yet potentially dangerous mental conditions like insensitivity or absentmindedness; and a whole variety of minor but practically uncontrollable human inadequacies that are not a matter of morality, at least not fully [*a*].

[*a*] Some of these examples imply that natural evils also occur in human contexts—understandablly so, for by virtue of being part of the cosmos humanity suffers the natural consequences of finitude and materiality. In other words, human beings cannot help affecting the world of otherness and being affected by it. In the tradition of moral theology, this realization has given rise to a crucial proposition: "Acts of a human individual" *(actus hominis)* are not necessarily "human acts" *(actus humani)*. "Acts of human individuals" are understood to be simply (or at least mainly) cosmic: people drop from heights, digest food, instinctively respond to stimuli, panic, "lose it," and so on. The fact that these activities occur in human agents or are performed by human agents is not by itself sufficient reason to regard them as *specifically* human acts. For by "human acts" we mean *acts that typify humanity as such.* Thus Thomas Aquinas can explain that acts are human insofar as they proceed from persons *acting deliberately and freely* (cf. *S. Th.* I–II, 1, 1, *in c.*). After all, he explains, all human beings are natively oriented to an ultimate end, *viz.*, fulfillment in God; this orientation is the very definition of morality. It follows that *acts are moral inasmuch as they are human* , and *vice versa*: "human acts and moral acts are the same thing" (*S. Th.* I–II, 1, 3, *in c.*). It is consistent with these traditional conceptions that natural evil as it occurs in "acts of human individuals" is nowadays often termed "pre-moral evil" or "ontic evil." And it is only fair to add to this that the term "pre-moral evil" is also widely considered applicable to *morally doubtful effects and side-effects unintentionally or even reluctantly caused* in the course of human acts that are substantially deliberate.

Looming largest of all among natural evils, however, there is the phenomenon of *death*. What is meant here is death in its everyday, "natural" form: neither purposely inflicted nor freely embraced in an act of self-abandon. To call death "only natural" amounts to ignoring not only humanity's almost universal fear of death, but also the fact that the death of human beings has been regarded, from time immemorial and across the whole planet, whether in protest or in resignation, as humanity's defeat *par excellence*:

> O pity and indig ˈ nation! Manshape, that shone
> Sheer off, disseveral, a star, ˈ death blots black out; nor mark
> Is any of him at all so stark
> But vastness blurs and time ˈ beats level.[3]

Yes, death is the enemy that respects no living soul, obliterates all that is distinctively human, and even makes the pursuit of divine wisdom look pointless (cf. Eccles 2, 13–16).

Let us sum up. Ever so many natural occurrences, no matter how understandable they may be philosophically, hurt and damage the world and, directly or indirectly, humanity as well. In the face of so much human suffering, no wonder we find ourselves reluctant to be impartial in the face of "purely natural evil."

[3] The notion of "purely natural evil" has a second, even deeper anthropological obstacle to contend with. In the actual, existential condition of humanity, many "natural" flaws and deficiencies are interconnected with, and indeed, almost inseparable from, undeniably willful, fully human failure, evil, and even sin. We can think of very harmful "natural" evils that are substantially (if perhaps only indirectly) caused by human activity: large-scale deforestation and the depletion of the ozone layer, with their (humanly speaking) damaging effects of soil-erosion, droughts, famine, disease, and loss of needed biodiversity. As a matter of fact, our inclination to protest against occurrences which, while produced by mere cosmic process, cause human and non-human suffering is largely rooted in our recognition that there exist basic interconnections between human agency and cosmic accident and disaster. Much as we may realize that the latter are "only natural," they nevertheless strike us as positively misplaced—that is, as *wrong*. No wonder we call them evil too.

How do we come to feel this way? Not in the last place because we know from experience that perfectly understandable natural evils jeopardize humanity's physical safety and well-being: human beings de-

serve better treatment at Nature's hands, we say. But more importantly, we know that natural evils inhibit the full deployment of humanity's
distinctively spiritual potential—intelligence and freedom. In particular, human communities quite often live in dread of the forces of
nature and of invisible powers associated with them; this prevents the
unfolding of their ability to worship, give thanks to, and believe in a
good and merciful God, and to draw inspiration and guidance for a
fully human life from that faith [b]. Most importantly, however (as
from horrifying experience we are only too well aware), natural evils
and the pain they cause will ever so often provoke human persons and
communities to the most appallingly *immoral* responses: wicked outbursts of fierce, irrational, and even deliberately violent self-defense or
(what amounts to the same) self-assertion at the expense of others.
Humanity's ability to cope with natural evil in a morally satisfactory
fashion is obviously very, very limited; no wonder we find ourselves
resisting the idea that there is such a thing as simply natural evil.

[4] Still, despite all this resistance, the notion of natural evil remains
understandable. The ontological condition of a finite, material cosmos that is to an appreciable extent in a state of flux, and of a finite
humanity that participates in the material conditions of this cosmos,
warrants the expectation of a certain amount of *natural* imperfection
and deficiency.

[a] Saint Thomas Aquinas implicitly agrees with this whenever he
observes (as he frequently does) that "natural evil" really exists.
However, he invariably adds that it is not essential but merely incidental. Essentially, the infra-human world, while finite, is good,
stable, and reliable; no wonder (so Aquinas maintains) it typically
holds its own. This applies not only to the material universe as a
whole, but also to each species of beings within the universe. Natural evil does occur, of course; its essence lies in the fact that it de-
prives particular goods of the goodness naturally befitting them (or
"owed to them"). Still, it occurs only *ut in paucioribus*—as a minority
phenomenon [c]. This only stands to reason; the natural order is

---

[b] The interpretation of natural failure as "evil" opens the door to fundamental issues regarding God's power and goodness (cf. §113, 3, [g]). This becomes con-
spicuous in dualistic cosmogonies, in which evil ("what should not be") is seen as the
product of an evil *power* at opposite poles from God—as something deeply chaotic
that God must contend with, and which at least partly eludes the scope of the divine
sovereignty (cf. §98, 3–4; §113, 3, e, [j]).

[c] S. Th. I, 63, 9, *in c.* Cf. *ibid.*, I, 49, 3, *ad 5*, where, significantly, Aquinas adds that
humanity is the exception: human beings, being rational, are rightly (because nat-

willed by God; no wonder it prevails; in the normal course of events in the infra-human universe, stability and goodness carry the day. Consequently, natural evil is no conclusive argument against either God's existence or God's transcendent attributes.

Neo-scholasticism followed Aquinas in maintaining that finitude is the ontological condition of creation; accordingly, it viewed "physical evil" simply as part of the real world, regardless of the occurrence of sin. Accordingly, twentieth-century neo-scholasticism has produced important, thoroughly modern studies of the problem of evil in the tradition of Aquinas. Thus there is the treatment, both historical and systematic, by the great French Dominican A.G. Sertillanges (d. 1948), in his posthumous two-volume work *Le problème du mal*. More recently, the Swiss theologian (and later Cardinal) Charles Journet (d. 1975) gave us the more modest, but wide-ranging and penetrating monograph *Le mal* (ET *The Meaning of Evil*).

[b] Philosophical treatises on the problem of evil are more typical of the modern era; still, most of them bear out their indebtedness to scholastic thought. The classic treatment of evil in the *Theodicy* of Gottfried Wilhelm Leibniz (1646–1716) is a good example of this. Very much like Aquinas, Leibniz observes that "moral evil" (or human sin) is to be distinguished from "metaphysical evil" (or the imperfections that result from plain finitude). Still, this is where the similarity ends. For, first of all, Leibniz adds a third (and typically modern) category of evil, namely "physical evil," by which he means human pain and suffering. Secondly, after making his distinctions, Leibniz proceeds, by the consistent application of rational, geometrical method (cf. §7, 1, a), to capture all the phenomena once again under one and the same rubric: evil. He goes on to explain that *all forms of evil* (including, he adds, with the liberal-intellectual optimism characteristic of the early Enlightenment, moral evil) are no more than a "concomitant" phenomenon—a phenomenon merely incidental to the totality of goodness that objectively typifies the cosmos; hence, they do not amount to a decisive argument against God's transcendence, omnipotence, and goodness (cf. §119, 2, c).[4]

---

urally) expected to live by reason, yet they are outnumbered by people who live by mere sense experience. Note that in this latter passage, Aquinas, along with the entire Tradition, does not attribute humanity's failure to live by reason to humanity's *physical* makeup. Humanity's distinctive moral problem is not the body, but concupiscence (cf. §113, 3, b–c). By concupiscence human beings do not succeed in availing themselves of their *spiritual* faculties is such a way as to govern the dynamics inherent in their cosmic functions.

[c] This is, perhaps, an opportune moment to mention two notable contemporary treatments of the problem of evil which, while not in the catholic or scholastic tradition, continue the tradition of theological and philosophical reflection on the subject. Quite recently, Edward Farley has offered us, in his book *Good and Evil*, an impressive fundamental theological account of the Christian understanding of human evil, which succeeds in combining the best of classical Protestantism with a lively dialogue, both with the great Tradition and with modern philosophy and phenomenology, including the most prominent contemporary authors. Even more recently, in a book titled *God and Evil*, David Birnbaum has given us a coherent and interesting philosophical and fundamental theological Jewish perspective on the issue.

[5] Let us return for a moment to the classical interpretations of natural evil proposed by Aquinas and Leibniz. For all their differences, they raise one and the same problem. It is not anthropological, but distinctly cosmological. It is this: *from a modern scientific point of view* it is not at all clear that the notion of "natural evil" is a meaningful concept.

The single most influential factor behind these objections is the rise of the idea that the cosmos is not stable. The world is *in process*, and it is so essentially, and not just incidentally. The universe as a whole is evolutionary.[5] In the contemporary scientific world picture, therefore, the failures that both Aquinas and Leibniz could think of as only incidental and episodic bulk as a mass phenomenon. The so-called natural order, including humanity as a biophysical phenomenon, is increasingly turning out to be not just *occasionally affected* by off-course, chance occurrences, but permanently; in fact, the cosmos and humanity are, to a significant extent, the *product* of occurrences. In other words, the basic patterns of the natural order are now understood (at least to a significant extent) not as stable entities governed by inherently reliable natural laws, but *statistically*, which implies that they involve *large numbers*. This has far-reaching consequences. If natural goodness and natural evil are both the outcome of processes of configuration and deconfiguration that are to an appreciable extent indeterminate, then the line between the two is much harder to draw than either Aquinas or Leibniz could imagine. Consequently, too, we have reason to be much less confident than either of them could ever have been when they implied that instances of natural, metaphysical evil and instability could easily be identified in the context of the general, prevailing natural goodness and stability.

Let us elaborate. Given the complex dynamics that produce the basic structures of the cosmos, the latter's coherence is a matter not of the assured stability (let alone immutability) of its configurations, but of the occurrence of configurations and combinations and structures of precarious balance—the result of intricate, only very partly predictable, evolutionary cosmic processes. These processes eventuate in ways that are by no means wholly predictable or predetermined by stable (let alone simple) "laws of nature"; no wonder they have been characterized, with some justification, as "chaotic."[6]

Small wonder that modern philosophic thought on natural goodness and natural evil is significantly influenced by modern science. Thus Hans-Georg Gadamer, who has struggled with the truth-claims typical of scientific civilization like few other humanistic philosophers in this century, can sum up the human experience of the cosmos as "the experience of being as existing in equilibrium, determined by a balance of existing forces."[7] Things are not substantially different in regard to humanity's position in the cosmos as a whole; an early scientific genius like Pascal intuited this precarious balance when he wrote that "one vapor, one drop of water are enough to kill" humanity. He was on target: in physical and biophysical respects, humanity is "but a reed, the weakest part of nature."

Pascal added, of course, that we are to draw, for our sense of what we really are, upon the privilege of consciousness: for all its weakness, the human person is "a reed that thinks" (§96, 3). The problem with this is that history has shown that this turn to anthropology brings no assured relief to the human understanding, since the consciousness of our spiritual advantage *over* the cosmos will exacerbate as much as alleviate our trepidation about humanity's destiny *in* the cosmos. There is horror in the realization that the human race, this sole repository of thought and self-consciousness in the known universe, is just about as vulnerable to destabilizing natural occurrences as any comparable infra-human biophysical configurations. Just how blessed is a humanity that must exercise its transcendence—its openness to the whole world—in the teeth of the certainty of individual death, time after miserable time? A humanity, that is, that is fated to *know* that it has no guarantee of security in the world, let alone of perpetuity? A humanity, therefore, whose indomitable capacity for culture in all its forms is at least partly inspired by the determination to ignore the prospect of extinction and the anxiety generated by it? That is to say, a humanity that can live and find fulfillment only by insisting that the retreat from skillful engagement with the world of objectivity into the safety of human consciousness has anxieties in store for the human mind that are even worse than the threat of cosmic imbalance?[8]

In this impasse, what is required of the theologian is a measure of intellectual resolve. History and nature, anthropology and cosmology must embrace, or at least face, each other again (cf., once more, §87, 2, d, [gg]). Facing up to the cosmos as modern science has come to understand it may just hold out to the human mind a fresh understanding of humanity's unique position in the cosmos as well as the promise of a new freedom.

[a] In appreciating the pervasiveness of the statistical element in Nature, modern cosmology is putting the axe to the root of classicist positions on the constant, determined nature of things and, indeed, on "Nature" itself understood as wholly stable and in that sense perpetually normative. Natural order and natural harmony, we now realize better than ever before, are a matter of *configurative balance.* For all its striking coherence, the wild profusion of physical, biophysical, and psychophysical structures in the cosmos is incessantly subject to the pressures of chance; below the surface, the existing structures, dynamic as they are, are potentially as fertile (or at least almost as fertile) in producing a whole range of failures, random events, and, indeed, chaotic occurrences as in ensuring the stability and the regularity that give the appearance of assured natural goodness and success. Of random occurrences, the vast majority are individual and incidental, and hence, short-lived. In Nature viewed as the all-encompassing web of dynamic relationships that make up Planet Earth, developments that are off-course and combinations that are dispensable are usually maladapted; they are overpowered by the larger, dominant combinations and structures on which they have to depend for survival; consequently, they are not so much evil as *unsuccessful*—often to the point of being irrelevant by comparison with the prevailing structures and the dynamics wielded by them. Thus even the effects of major natural disasters are usually absorbed and neutralized with relative ease by the wider environment; not infrequently, contagious diseases induce, in the populations they attack, the immunological resistance that will sufficiently attenuate their virulence; in most cases, biological oddities like genetic mutants turn out to be so dysfunctional as to be easily defeated by the milieu in which they would have to survive.

But this is precisely where the question arises if the lack of success of such anomalous, quirky, or thwarted products of evolution justifies the judgment that they are "naturally evil." If this were the case, might we not be forced to call the many extinct products of past evolutionary processes naturally evil? The large reptiles of past eras were obviously unsuccessful; but were they evil?

Occasionally, however, physical or biological processes do spawn new situations and combinations and organisms that *are* successful. They begin to participate in "Nature" as viable entities. Frequently they do so as destabilizing features that bring on conflicts, crises, and (occasionally) the failure of pre-existing combinations and systems and organisms, which in turn may cause or occasion the fall of other systems and organisms, or the rise of new ones. (Now which are desirable or undesirable, good or evil, the sassy new or the toppled old?) Such incidents are relatively rare, of course, but they do remind us that the dynamics of unpredictability are very much at work in and underneath the "natural order," with its appearance of stability and regularity.

[b] All of this becomes especially urgent once we realize that humanity shares in the predicament of all cosmic existents: "human nature" *as a biophysical and psychophysical phenomenon* enjoys no timeless stability; rather, it is the evolutionary outcome of cosmic processes in which the odds remain hard to tell; it continues to depend on them, it remains exposed to them, and it must maintain itself in the teeth of them. In other words, humanity is and continues to be, to a significant extent, dependent on what we can responsibly call chance [*d*].

[*d*] This leads to two conclusions. Firstly, we now understand that cosmic change is not merely *incidental* to the allegedly "stable nature" of cosmic configurations; rather, it *intrinsically* affects their apparent stability. In the classical world picture cultivated by both scholasticism and the early Enlightenment, this observed stability gave rise to the notion of "nature." As late as 1735, the great botanist Carl Linnaeus (1707–1778) could still argue, in the first four *Observationes in Regna III. Naturæ* that open his *Systema Naturæ*, that the present state of the vegetable and animal realms is the direct reflection of God's creative activity in the beginning. Linnaeus' reasoning is that all individuals now alive in whatever species can be traced back only to the first parents in that species. By contrast, in the world picture accepted in modern science, process has won out over "Nature." This makes it *simpliste* to associate, in any *immediate* fashion, God the Creator with the "nature" of every particular cosmic entity as we know it or with the "natural stability" of the cosmos as a whole. Secondly, scientific and philosophical considerations like these are apt, in the long run, to affect our judgments on the way in which the Roman Catholic tradition has upheld moral norms by appealing to the natural law, if, that is, the latter is taken to be predicated on physical and biophysical realities viewed as natural invariables (cf. §50, 1, b).

These realizations demand, or at least invite, a rereading of Aquinas' *quinque viæ* (cf. §102), perhaps along the following tentative lines.

[c] First of all, from a contemporary point of view, the interpretation of the cosmic phenomena on which Aquinas' first three *viæ* are based—namely, *change* and *contingency*—has changed. Natural entities are no longer understood as clearly identifiable, wholly stable beings which accidentally affect each other in significant ways, and which substantially come into being and vanish again. They are now understood as relatively stable temporary and local configurations produced by *process*, and never entirely without an element of chance. To the modern scientific view, in other words, the cosmos presents itself no longer in the guise of an ascending scale of discontinuous, essentially static entities, but as a welter of dynamic processes of physical and biophysical evolution occurring among entities that are composite and hence, only relatively stable in themselves and only imperfectly discontinuous with each other [*e*]. These processes have fashioned, and continue to fashion, the form of Planet Earth and everything in it and on it as we know it, as is borne out by the paleontological vestiges of the existence of configurations and organisms and human persons and communities that once were. And on an incomparably larger scale and within the framework of incomparably greater units of time and space, human thought has even begun to discern and understand, as a precondition of the present "state" of the universe, the elemental processes that fashioned it at the outset and continue to do so.[9]

As a result, if we should want to follow in Aquinas' footsteps, we may now want to argue somewhat as follows. We do have a thoroughly dynamic, evolutionary cosmos—but one that is all the more strikingly coherent for having eventuated, statistically speaking, within an astonishingly narrow range of possibilities. In this cosmos, one

---

[*e*] Readers familiar with scholastic philosophy will have recognized, in what has just been explained, an allusion to Aquinas' classical definition of *unity* as a transcendental property of Being. Something is one inasmuch as it is *in se indivisum et ab aliis distinctum* ("undivided in itself and distinct from all else": cf., *e.g.*, *S.c.G.* II, 40, *Item*; *Q. D. de Ver.* 2, 15, *in c.*; cf. *S. Th.* I, 11, 4, *in c.*). Our point, therefore, can also be formulated as follows. Finite reality enjoys imperfect unity; things finite, and things material in particular, are both intrinsically composite and extrinsically not altogether distinct from each other. The latter part of this thesis can also be expressed by stating that all things finite are to a degree "alienated" from themselves (cf. §122, 1, a–f). Put differently, for us cosmic beings, to exist as what we are is to (co-)exist with what we are not.

tenuous (but increasingly coherent) chain of configurations has, in the teeth of overwhelming statistical odds, caused intelligent humanity to emerge from and in this cosmos. It has not only survived in it, and even (as the anthropic principle[10] proposes; cf. §80, 3, [c]) developed a reliable (if very provisional) understanding of its coherence and its functioning. This has enabled it, especially in recent centuries, to develop technologies that have significantly affected the shape of its cosmic environment.

Interestingly, now that we are beginning to be able to give an intellectually acceptable account of this evolutionary development, we find ourselves even less willing than Aquinas to settle for indefinite regress as an explanation. It is intellectually pointless to attribute the emergence of humanity and the cosmic matrices from which it has arisen to *pure chance*—utterly indefinite, wholly shapeless, unintelligible process (§102, 8). Instead, the evolutionary dynamics of the cosmos as we now understand it become both more mysterious and more understandable if we have recourse to a transcendent, supra-cosmic source of dynamic coordination and coherence, which all call God.

[d] Secondly, in thus reinterpreting Aquinas' first three *viæ* in an evolutionary perspective, the fourth way gains an even more crucial significance than it already had in its original context. For, in all likelihood, we are more thematically conscious than Aquinas ever was that it takes a radically anthropological point of view to read the cosmos and interpret it reliably and realistically (cf. §102, 6). That is, for the cosmos to fall into a coherent and intelligible pattern what is required is the precarious step into *reflection*. That evolutionary step into reflection is, of course, exactly what typifies hominization:[11] emergent human *consciousness* (Pascal's "*pensée*": cf. §96, 3 and note 4) is the most recent, maturest fruit of the cosmic knack for evolution, carried forward on the strength of recombination and reconfiguration [f]. Consequently, humanity finds itself placed, by an initiative or initiatives which it cannot attribute to itself, in a position of strategic responsibility in the cosmos. That is, humanity finds that

---

[f] Teilhard de Chardin insists on the cosmic nature of thought. One way in which he conveys this is that he interprets the emergence of thought *both* as the world's own latest evolutionary step in interiority as well as expansiveness *and* as the supervention of a true novelty in the cosmos. The advent of consciousness, therefore, is a development truly analogous to the evolutionary novelty that preceded it: the emergence of life. At the terminological level, Teilhard conveys this analogy by the analogy between the terms "biosphere" and "noosphere."

it is the most decisively advanced, privileged constituent of the cosmos known to itself, since it alone enjoys both the inner stability and the openness to take the measure of the very cosmos in which it also continues to participate. By virtue of consciousness, therefore, humanity finds it incumbent on itself to discern authoritatively—if always provisionally, and, so to speak, while holding its breath—what is good and evil (that is, constructive and destructive) in the cosmos.

[e] Obviously, what is left undecided in this quick rereading of the first four *viæ* is the very difficult question of *natural finality*—the heart of Aquinas' fifth way. For, more than ever before, Aquinas' interpretation of the stable nature of things as the dynamic source of reliable tendencies toward transcendence is on shaky ground. No wonder modern science has been reluctant to apply the concept of "natural finality" (with its connotations of essential stability) to infrahuman cosmic existents. But this is not necessarily the end of the argument. For the tradition has always viewed the natural finality of things in the perspective of divine Providence as the coordinating and directing principle of all worldly vicissitudes; the final court of appeal in the matter of cosmic finality is trans-cosmic. Cosmic matter, however erratic, obviously lends itself to chains of combinations and arrangements of increasing inner complexity and wider outside influence. The world, in other words, appears to be "going somewhere." On these grounds, could we successfully transpose Aquinas' vision into a modern key by suggesting that cosmic process bespeaks (or at least suggests) a transcendent principle of attraction by which all cosmic configurations, mutually attractive as they so often are, are guided toward a unified end, surpassing all particular ends yet also encompassing them?

In many of his writings, but especially in his visionary essay *The Phenomenon of Man,* a modern scientist as well as a creative theologian like Pierre Teilhard de Chardin has done just that. He depicts the dynamics at work in the configuration of lifeless matter and, further up the evolutionary scale, of living and sentient organisms, as analogous to the specifically human tendencies toward interiority and transcendence.[12]

[f] The present treatment has implied that the modern cosmological world picture has theological consequences. The recent *Catechism of the Catholic Church* bears witness to this (though, perhaps, in tones a little too cool to convey fully the sense of pained wonder appropriate to the statement). We read: "Why did God not create

a world so perfect that no evil could exist in it? With infinite power God could always create something better. But with infinite wisdom and goodness God freely willed to create a world 'in a state of journeying' toward its ultimate perfection. In God's plan this process of becoming involves the appearance of certain beings and the disappearance of others, the existence of the more perfect alongside the less perfect, [and] both constructive and destructive forces of nature. With physical good there exists also *physical evil* as long as creation has not reached perfection."[13]

[6] The rhetorical questions parenthetically asked a few paragraphs ago (§115, 5, a) intended to suggest that our analyses, sketchy as they are, have consequences for the concept of natural evil. Even more importantly, they are bound to affect our judgments about particular phenomena that are claimed to be actual instances of natural evil. But even if we should insist on continuing the classical habit of simply equating the incidence of irregular, destabilizing occurrences in Nature with "natural evil," the same question arises. Should we not acknowledge at least an essential element of relativity in our definition of natural evil? *Relative to what* are natural evils evil?

Let us capture this issue in a somewhat more formal argument—one that will lead to important conclusions about humanity's position in the cosmos.

To form categorical judgments about anything, we need sufficient definiteness on the part of the object. Failing that, we must resort to discretionary, interpretative judgments, for which we need, on our part, a sufficient degree of both participation and transcendence: participation to ensure familiarity with the object (cf. §63), and transcendence to ensure the critical distance needed to judge. In the case of the determination of natural evil, the ontological structures of the cosmos are in and of themselves insufficiently unified, distinct, and stable to warrant entirely definitive value judgments regarding *particular systems and occurrences* (cf., again, §115, 5, b, [d]). This precludes any easy differentiation between concrete instances of natural good and natural evil.

Consequently, we must look elsewhere for a point of vantage to judge from. That point of vantage must be *humanity* itself. Humanity is the tribunal that combines genuine participation in the cosmological order with decisive transcendence over it, at least in principle, by virtue of its participation in the noosphere. In other words, it is by recourse to *anthropology* that the dynamic, ever-evolving structures of the cosmos are to be interpreted as well as evaluated. Accordingly, questions about natural goodness and evil as they occur in the cosmos are to be responsibly resolved, at least in the first resort, by anthropological criteria.

This implies that the concepts of natural goodness and natural evil are not a matter of cosmology alone. The fundamental reason for this lies in hominization as an integral element in cosmic evolution: as a result of the emergence of humanity, *the cosmos as we know it is itself no longer reducible to bare cosmology.* Put differently, we can legitimately appeal to the anthropic principle to lay claim, on behalf of both humanity *and the cosmos,* to a responsible understanding of the cosmos and its dynamics as a whole (cf. §80, 3, [c]).

[7] This insight becomes crucial when it comes to determining concrete cases of natural evil. To be adequate, the *method* of determination must obviously match the actual state of the cosmos ("Nature"); and the cosmos as we now know it includes humanity as its crowning attainment—that is, as its intrinsically *normative* attainment [g]. The determination of particular instances of natural evil, therefore, is a matter of both cosmology and anthropology taken in their ontological interrelatedness—a proposition to which we will have occasion to come back (§115, 10, b).

This conclusion calls for yet another step in our reflection, for the ontological interrelatedness that prevails between the infra-human cosmos and humanity involves two integral components: mutuality and asymmetry. Let us start with the former.

[8] The cosmos and its processes obviously continue to embed and encompass humanity. That is, they engage humanity in processes of *mutuality,* or *interdependence.* These processes are mediated by human *bodiliness,* which can be defined as the actualization, in individuals, of all of humanity's involvement in physical and biophysical cosmic process (cf. §122, 1, [a]) [h].

---

[g] Again, note the underlying premise here—one that permeates this theological system: for all humanity's preeminence, there is continuity, not discontinuity, between humanity and the cosmos: cf. §9, 1, [*l*]; §59, 6, [g]; §78, 3, [r]; §80, 3, [c]; §87, 2, a, [x], and d, [gg]; §94, 6, a; §99, 3; §102, 4, a, [*l*]; §104, 1.

[h] This implies a conception of the human body that runs counter to classicist, Cartesian philosophical anthropology. What is here proposed is this: the body must be regarded as not altogether discrete, and hence, as not totally individuated. This idea is wholly compatible with the patristic conception of human nature as the physical "lump" (Gk. *phyrama,* Lat. *massa*) taken on *in its entirety* by the Word (cf. Gregory of Nyssa, *Catech. Or.* 32 [ed. Srawley, p. 116]; Anastasius of Antioch, *Or.* III, *De Incarn.,* X–XI [*PG* 89, 1340–41]). The notion is already found (albeit with a negative

This involvement in turn is a matter of mutual exchange—that is, of a blend of passivity and activity. Both individually and communally, humanity as a biophysical and psychophysical phenomenon is involved in a lifelong process of borrowing from, and lending to, the material cosmos—of being affected by its structures, and of affecting them in turn. To start with, humanity remains part of the cosmic metabolism; likewise, it continues to *need* the cosmos as a physical and biophysical matrix. Obviously, as a phenomenon both living and sentient, humanity enjoys an intrinsic ability to respond actively to the structures of the cosmos and to take them on in a constructive fashion; as a self-conscious, spiritual phenomenon with a transcendent goal, it even has the ability to enjoy, understand, and engineer cosmic structures—that is, to make something of them in truly deliberate and purposeful fashion.

To say, therefore, that mutuality prevails in humanity's relationship with the cosmos does not involve the proposition that humanity is simply engulfed in an undifferentiated cosmic jumble. Neither humanity nor, for that matter, the countless creatures that make up the world of things are wholly submerged in randomness—even though randomness does become more prominent according as we descend further into the more fundamental structures of the cosmos. Thus,

---

bias) in Melito of Sardis' *Peri Pascha*, 103, where the risen Christ calls upon all human beings, regardless of lineage, "lumped together in sins" [*hai en hamartiais pephyramenai*] as they are, to come and receive forgiveness of sins (Hall, pp. 58–59). Cf. also F. J. van Beeck, *Christ Proclaimed*, p. 158, n. 44. Modern conceptions about matter also make it scientifically sound to view human bodiliness, not as radically individuated, but as the *common matrix* in and through which individual human persons are related to humanity and the physical and biophysical world *as a whole*. Thus Teilhard de Chardin can write: "*My* Matter is not *one part* of the Universe that I could be said to possess *totaliter*; it is the *totality* of the Universe possessed by me *partialiter*" (*Science et Christ*, p. 34; ET *Science and Christ*, p. 13; cf. Gustave Martelet's illuminating discussion in *The Risen Christ and the Eucharistic World*, pp. 39–47). This notion also allows us to retrieve the classical notion of the human individual as a *microcosm*, reflecting, in its own unique way, the *macrocosm*. – However, the notion also raises a theological problem. The understanding of the body as wholly discrete and individual seems to enjoy the favor of the magisterium: the Fourth Lateran Council teaches that the dead will arise *cum suis propriis ... corporibus, quae nunc gestant* ("with their own bodies, which they now bear": DH 801; cf. CF 200). On closer inspection, however, the phrase turns out to be an isolated idiom and no more. This allows us to interpret it as the equivalent of a far more traditional phrase: *in hac carne, qua nunc vivimus* ("in this *flesh* in which we are now alive": DH 72; CF 15; cf. DH 85, 684, 797, 854; CF 25). The latter expression affirms the reality of the resurrection of the dead by means of an idiom ("the flesh") that is biblical in origin and connotes humanity's present estrangement from God (cf. §112, 4, [*d*]). But it also conveys that our corporeity, like our estrangement, is the organ of our participation in a *generic* reality: through our bodies we are part of human*kind* viewed as a distinctive biophysical component of the cosmos—a cosmos (so the Jewish and Christian traditions hold) that is to be renewed *as a whole* in the resurrection.

even within the limits of the material cosmos, humanity shares with other meaningful combinations and systems in the cosmos, especially with organisms that are alive and sentient, a measure of real transcendence over near-undifferentiated process. Most prominently of all, like all living beings, humanity dynamically interacts with the material cosmos by turning part of it into an area of effective *influence*, both actively and passively: we avail ourselves of combinations of lifeless elements, not only consciously, by using them as tools, but also biophysically, by actively supporting a vegetative *environment* that surrounds us with life, and in doing so, supports us. As sentient beings, we take a further step: we exhibit a radical affinity with our closest cosmic neighbors, the animals, and especially with our next of kin, the more developed vertebrates. Like them, we both adapt to and create an Umwelt—a *habitat*, an area or sphere of effective, *experienced presence*, and we do so instinctively, and not just rationally. In fact, in relation to some (plants and) animals humanity's *Umwelt* involves an area of useful, and even enjoyable symbiosis; ever so many animals and plants share our bodies and our habitats and provide us with the ability to digest our food, and with clothing and food (though some, it must be granted, merely take advantage of us); other animals animate our habitats by dint of sight and sound, and help shape them as well as us by the constancy of their habits; with many animals we even go so far as to engage in habits of affective companionship—of instinctive care and mutual affective significance.

Let us sum up. Humanity's relationship of mutuality or interdependence with the cosmos includes some forms of the *limited asymmetry* that is characteristic of all living beings. For it is characteristic of living beings to transcend their environments on the strength of *vital initiative*, which enables them to be dependent on the environment in such a way as to turn it to their own advantage. In the case of animals, and especially of the higher arthropods and vertebrates, this limited asymmetry is even more apparent; vital initiative here takes the shape of instinctive, passionate drives and ambitions; animal superiority over the lifeless and vegetable realms involves the ability to turn environments into genuine habitats.[14]

[9] Still, in and through and especially beyond these inchoatively asymmetrical forms of interdependence and mutuality at the biophysical and psychophysical levels, humanity exercises a truly distinctive, inalienable integrity, which is also the basis of its relationship of *authentic asymmetry* with the physical, biophysical, and psychophysical cos-

mos. In fact, upon reflection, the simple fact that we are *conscious* of having relationships of mutuality and interdependence with the cosmos, our environments, and our habitats implies that we are not bounded by them and limited to them. Unlike plants and animals, in other words, *we cannot help transcending cosmic situations as such, somehow*. Humanity, while genuinely cosmic, is also natively spiritual, and hence, not reducible to the physical, biophysical, and sentient cosmos and its structures. As Hans-Georg Gadamer puts it:

No living organism so labors to transform its own environment into a world of culture as humanity.[15]

That "world of culture" is marked by the imprint which meaningful human communication leaves, and continues to leave, on the world of natural objects. Consequently, as a matter of principle, cultures invite meaningful communication, across times and places, with other cultures; this is how they intimate humanity's openness to the whole world and, indeed, to a beyond.

But neither cultures nor the human transcendence that expresses itself in them make us citizens of a realm of reality separate from the body and the world we live in; transcend the cosmos as we may, we remain continuous with it as well (cf. once again, §9, 1, [*I*]; §115, 7, [*g*]); one very obvious indication of this is that it is and remains appropriate (if not wholly adequate) to classify humanity among the vertebrates and treat it as one species of primates. The philosophical and theological traditions of Western and Christian civilization have expressed this by stating that the human being is a unity of body and soul, and even if the latter element is of an essentially higher order of ontological intensity than the former, since it involves every human being in an immediate and inalienable relatedness to God (cf. §109, 9, c, [*z*]), both are integral to the constitution of humanity.

The great Tradition, never loath to take its cues from the natural order, has always thought that this higher ontological intensity is even ascertainable phenomenologically. Thus Gregory of Nyssa, in *The Constitution of Humanity*, can rely on Stoic anthropology and indulge in an elaborate phenomenological analysis of humanity's appearance and habits. This enables him to lay bare both humanity's dependence on the cosmos and its ceaseless aspiration to higher things. And in the end, it leads him to the conclusion that the human spirit, amazingly, gains knowledge, by way of the senses, of everything that exists in the world, *yet it cannot, in the last resort, fathom itself*. This remarkable fact,

Gregory goes on to explain, makes sense only if we infer that the human spirit mirrors and reveals, right here in the cosmos, the incomprehensible nature of the transcendent God.[16]

Aquinas, more interested in cosmology than Gregory but equally observant, takes his cue from Aristotle and compares the human body with the animal body. The similarities are obvious, but so are the differences; the human capacity for transcendence, the fruit of the spirit, has plainly left its mark on humanity's physical appearance. The human body is relatively indeterminate; it is far less specialized and far less aggressive or defensive even than that of its closest relatives, the higher mammals; that is, it shows that it is attuned to a life not restricted to specific environments, habitats, and functions (cf. §130, 7; cf. §130, 1); it is open to all elements and ready to meet the challenge to deal with them all. Centuries later, Friedrich Nietzsche was to notice the same phenomenon; it led him to characterize humanity as "the not yet immobilized animal."[17] And in our own day, we have witnessed humanity succeeding not just in settling in almost every environment on earth but even in reaching for space by adapting itself to it and it to itself, by means of a variety of technologically very resourceful tools. It is precisely this combination of lack of physical differentiatedness (*æqualitas corporis*) and the agility and subtlety of the human hand that both bespeaks and befits the spirit:

The intelligent soul grasps universal concepts, and hence, has a capacity for innumerable things. For this reason, nature could not possibly have confined it, either to limited natural ways of assessing things, or even to limited defensive or protective auxiliary functions, as is the case in other animals, whose souls enjoy powers of perception and management to deal with a fixed number of limited circumstances. . . . Horns and claws serve some animals by way of weapons; a thick leathery skin, and quantities of hair and feathers are their protection. These bear witness to their being replete with the terrestrial element, wholly unlike the balance and delicacy of humanity's physical makeup; thus they would be inappropriate in humanity. Instead of them, human beings possess reason and hands. With the help of the latter, they can equip themselves with weapons and covering and the other necessities of life, in an infinity of ways—which is also why the hand is called "the instrument of instruments" [*i*]. This is also more in keeping with rational

---

[*i*] Thomas Aquinas borrows this characterization of the human hand from Aristotle, who writes: "the soul is like the hand; for just as the hand is the tool of tools, so the mind is the form of forms" (*De anima* III, 8, 432^{a}1; cf. *AristBWks*, p. 595); he quotes the same passage more fully in *Q. D. de anima*, 8, ad 20. There is an interesting parallel to this entire discussion in one of Aquinas' minor writings (*Opusc. contra impugn.* V, *ad 1*; ed. Mandonnet, IV, p. 68). Here Aquinas quotes Aristotle's discussion of the relationship between human reason and human hands found in *Parts of*

beings, since they are characterized by an infinity of ideas; it allows them to equip themselves with an infinite variety of instruments.[18]

In Aquinas's vision of humanity's position in the cosmos, therefore, human bodiliness is not only a match for the spirit; it is also put to the test and challenged and stretched by the spirit, which guides the body (especially the hands and the organs of speech) in devising tools and social institutions to compensate for humanity's biophysical defectiveness [j]. And conversely, the human spirit must allow itself not only to be tempered by the body's exigencies, but also excited by its potential.

Only in this way will human beings succeed in exercising their distinctive identity, which consists in being (to borrow the title of one of Karl Rahner's seminal works) *Geist in Welt*: "Spirit in World." Let us put the same conception in the idiom of Maurice Blondel: humanity, while firmly embodied, enjoys (at least as a matter of principle) that hallmark of spirit which is *immanence* (§87, 1); immanence involves that dynamic capacity for inalienable inner resourcefulness and deliberate self-extension in active engagement, by virtue of which humanity is capable of establishing both deep self-identity and real presence to the other.

Animals IV, 10; 687^a2-687^b25 (ed. Peck-Forster, pp. 370–375).

[j] Aristotle tends to view the human body in rather narrowly technical and rational terms. But he does note the delicacy of the human lips and tongue, to which (in combination with the teeth) he attributes the capacity for articulate speech (*Parts of Animals* II, 16–17; $659^b29-660^a28$; 661^b12-16). Curiously, though, he does not explicitly relate this capacity to human intelligence or to the mind. (But cf. *Generation of Animals* 786^b20-22 for a slightly different conception.) Aquinas, on the other hand, very much sees a direct link between articulate speech and human reason; he also interprets the refinement that typifies the human body as a whole as an expression of spirit (e.g., *S. Th.* I, 91, 3, *ad 3*). These are sound insights, both phenomenologically and anthropologically. The hand, after all, is obviously not a tool geared only to technical ends, but also a prime organ of interpersonal communication, both of the intelligent and the affective kind. We gesticulate to convey understanding, we use our hands to write, we join hands (in a variety of ways) to convey personal commitment, attachment, and tenderness. Analogously, the organs of articulate speech (lips, teeth, tongue, larynx, and vocal chords) enable us to engage in distinctively human forms of intelligent and affective expression and communication, like explanations and smiles and intelligent laughter and studied song, not to mention kisses. Aquinas' emphasis on the human body's spiritual features places his treatment closer to Gregory of Nyssa's *The Constitution of Humanity*, with its striking demonstration of the body's spiritual character based on an analysis of the connections between humanity's erect posture, the shape of the human mouth, the capacities of the human hand, articulate speech, and the ability to communicate in writing (cf. esp. chaps. VIII–IX; *PG* 44, 148C–152A; ET *The Making of Man, NPNCF*, Second series, vol. 5, pp. 394–95).

[a] In one of Aquinas' most celebrated passages, the emergent self-consciousness that is the privilege of humanity as it deals with the world of otherness is described as capacity for *reditio completa*—the complete closing of the circle initiated by self-transcendence. The distinctive feature of beings endowed with intellect, so Aquinas explains, is their ability to engage cosmic realities in such a manner as to transcend them by virtue of the self-awareness actualized and attained in the very act of engagement. Thus he writes: "the most perfect among the things that are (say, intellectual substances) completely return to what they are [*redeunt ad essentiam suam reditione completa*]. For to the extent that they know something outside themselves, they in a way go outside themselves; but inasmuch as they know that what they are doing is knowing, they already begin to return to themselves. . . . But this return is completed inasmuch as they know what they themselves are [*reditus iste completur secundum quod cognoscunt essentias proprias*]."[19]

[b] This is, perhaps, a good moment to point out an immediate as well as hugely important implication of what has been explained so far in this section and what is still to follow. *Since there prevails an essential asymmetry between humanity and the cosmos, efficient causality does not adequately account for human activity in the cosmos; and consequently, since humanity is an integral part of the cosmos, appeals to efficient causality alone cannot adequately account for, or do justice to, the cosmos as a whole.*

This theme has already come up in a previous discussion. In the wake of epistemological positions developed by the nominalists, a fundamental mechanization of the world picture began to occur in the West toward the end of the fourteenth century.[20] This led the New Learning to attenuate the age-old sense that there prevails a basic affinity between the cosmos and humanity; eventually that sense was lost altogether. Concurrently, efficient causality came to be thought of as the chief form of activity, and hence also, of God's activity in regard to the cosmos (§103, 1–2). Needless to say, this tendency favored scientific and technological development; but it fixed a chasm between the human mind and "objectivity," between science and humanity, nature and freedom, and consequently, between cosmic effectiveness and moral responsibility. The latter is, of course, precisely what is at issue in the present discussion.

[10] Humanity's distinctive immanence manifests and actualizes itself in *action* (cf. §87, 2, a–b). If humanity is to find its integrity and become what it truly is, it must engage and take on the cosmos—both its

random dynamics and what has resulted from them: the physical and biophysical configurations in the cosmos, including the human phenomenon itself. And what is more, it must do so in a specifically human way—that is, *intelligently and deliberately*. By virtue of both its evolutionary position and its spiritual transcendence, therefore, humanity is called to enjoy, understand, integrate, ennoble, and even transform and turn to spiritual purposes itself and the cosmos in which it continues to participate. For, though humanity's integral reality qualitatively transcends cosmology, cosmic realities never cease to be integral to humanity. In its quest to establish its own integrity, therefore, humanity must find ways to order, humanize, and in that sense "spiritualize" both itself and the cosmos—to help the emancipation of humanity and the world from decombination, disintegration, randomness, and the sheer play of large numbers. It must do so by taking advantage of the fact that the physical and biophysical cosmos, including humanity as one ingredient of it, already displays its potential for meaningful configuration and harmony. Humanity, therefore, is to discover, understand, cultivate, and enhance such patterns of stability and harmony as are already there, waiting to be more fully actualized.

This is a momentous realization. Since the advent of humanity's spiritual presence in the cosmos, *the emergence of meaningful configurations and their maintenance is no longer wholly at the mercy of the odds of physical and biophysical and psychophysical process and its knack for coordination*; it has become a human capacity, and a human (that is *moral*) responsibility as well. This capacity and the responsibility inherent in it are infinitesimally small-scale when viewed in the context of the cosmos as a whole; still, within the compass of Planet Earth, they are appreciable, as humanity's stupendous impact on the global environment bears out. And, given the fact that civilization is a matter of tradition (that is, of cumulative, self-reinforcing, self-enhancing, and often self-correcting historic process) the emergence and maintenance of meaningful configurations in the cosmos and especially on Planet Earth must *increasingly* become a matter of human ingenuity, intelligence, and freedom. Put in the biblical idiom, humanity is, by creative divine appointment, creation's steward, charged with its cultivation, starting with the earth (cf. Gen 1, 28–29; 2, 15. 23); we could even go one step further and call humanity, made in the image and likeness of God, co-creator with God. This remains true, even if there is no denying that raw, undeliberate cosmic process remains an overwhelming influence in the cosmos, even within the relatively narrow compass of Earth, where the influence of humanity can no longer be overlooked.

In the preceding account of humanity's place in the cosmos, we have adopted a consistently evolutionary perspective. This compels us to accept integral humanity as the tribunal inherently equipped, by its own immanent aspiration to identity through self-actualization, to make *judgments* about the macrocosm and to act on them deliberately. Indeed, in the Jewish-Christian tradition, humanity is what it is by virtue of the divine image and likeness; accordingly, it is creative. Naturally, human creativity remains rooted in God; hence, it relies on a core of co-creativity. That is, humanity is essentially equipped, because inalienably charged, to take moral responsibility for itself and the cosmos. This takes the form of the never-ending task of bringing humanity as well as the whole world home, proximately to humanity itself and its purposes, and ultimately to God (cf. §98, 5).

[a] At the risk of running ahead of our argument, let us forge, from this last proposition, a basic, coherent theological principle regarding the human responsibility for the cosmos. Fundamental human self-acceptance, it was argued before, involves the acceptance, as the precondition for all authentic spiritual growth and development, of humanity's attunement to all reality and, ultimately, to the living God; the awareness of this implies a call to responsiveness and responsibility (cf. §112, 5). In light of what has just been argued, however, human self-acceptance equally involves the recognition of itself—humanity—as the privileged outcome of cosmic process. In consequence of the latter, human self-acceptance must encompass a fundamental acceptance of moral responsibility for the well-being and development of the evolving cosmos whose outcome it is. This includes a basic responsibility for humanity itself, insofar as it is a cosmic phenomenon capable of being cultivated and civilized [k].

One way—albeit a negative one—to take the measure of both the nobility and the delicacy of this vocation to cultivate humanity and the world is to realize its enormous potential for failure and downright destructiveness. Humanity has plainly proved itself capable of turning cosmic and human potential to admirable purposes; it has also proved, in varying degrees of deliberateness, and often with the best of intentions, its ability (and even its tendency) to cause natural evil. It has brought on deficiencies and disasters not of the wholly accidental kind in the global environment, in the vegetable and ani-

---

[k] Note the word "basic." *Actual* responsibilities are always to be conscientiously discerned and adjudicated by reference to moral capacity and concrete circumstances.

mal realms as well as in human habitats; it has treated human individuals and especially human communities themselves, not only as usable commodities, but also as obstacles to be got rid of; it has attacked and destroyed notable forms of human civilization; it has gone so far as to procure the plotted death of human beings and even of entire communities. Thus humanity has a proven and (unfortunately) characteristic ability to act in such a way as to subordinate productive (if always precarious) patterns of balance—both of the cosmic and the human kind—to the pursuit of dubious purposes. From time immemorial, humanity has upset and laid waste cosmic and human configurations which, despite their obvious imperfection, were essentially good and worthy of notice [*l*].

[b] This realization enables us to add a needed refinement to our understanding of the relationships between natural evil and sin. There is obviously nothing sinful in the pristine cosmic processes that disturb and jeopardize the patterns of cosmic balance favorable to the emergence and development of humanity; but there *is* sin in all more or less deliberate *human* efforts at influencing or changing these balances *in ways that are misguided because undiscerning.*

[c] But now we need a norm to discern just what is misguided and what is not. This norm must plainly be derived from humanity's position in the cosmos. The human responsibility for the cultivation of the cosmos from a position of *authentic* transcendence entails an obligation to remain faithful to humanity's integral, evolved self— that is, *to itself along with the cosmic precedents that have favored its emergence.* Let us phrase this differently. If we adopt a consistently evolutionary perspective, we have sound *anthropological* reasons to respect many *cosmological* (*i.e.*, physical, biophysical, and psychophysical) structures in the cosmos, and to see to it that the power we have at

---

[*l*] Note an important qualification. Humanity must indeed bear much blame for the many ways in which it has *de facto* abused both itself and the cosmic systems that have favored its emergence and survival. Still, it is repugnant to conclude, from this observation alone, that humanity *as such* is a negative ecological factor or a cosmic pollutant. The reasons for this are obvious. Logically, the position is self-contradictory: human beings cannot in one and the same act define themselves as bad for the cosmos and claim to have valid judgments to make about it. Philosophically, the position amounts to subordinating humanity to the cosmos—which militates against cogent evidence to the contrary implicit in the evolutionary process as we know it. Psychologically and morally, the position is a gesture of despair; it implies a wholesale denial of humanity's proven (if always precarious) capacity for responsible action in regard to both itself and the cosmos. Finally, theologically speaking, if humanity itself is a natural evil, this would amount to interpreting its emergence as a case of the cosmic penchant for self-destruction—an implicit profession of scientific atheism.

our disposal to cultivate the cosmos be carefully schooled by the cosmos' own proven (if always precarious) potential for meaningful combination and arrangement.

This schooling must include two primary elements. Firstly, we have discovered that we have scarcely begun to appreciate the biophysical and psychophysical complexity of the cosmos. Secondly, we have come to realize that *natural good and natural evil are notoriously hard to tell apart* (§115, 5). These two realizations imply that, from an anthropological point of view, all quick judgments about the cosmos (including all quick identifications of natural evil in it) are suspect. Humanity must learn how not to undercut itself. It must learn how not to add to the blind violence already rife in the cosmos, by impatient exploitation, indiscriminate use, undiscerning "development," quick fixing, furious experimentation, and inconsiderate attempts at damage control. It is only human to grasp that the precariously balanced environments and cultures that have been, and continue to be, the matrixes of humanity's own growth and development be unnecessarily, let alone wantonly, jeopardized or upset.

Neither Nature nor human customs that have become second nature must be canonized, of course. Still, it is also true that *natura artis magistra*: for all our scientific and technological sophistication, Nature and its ally, immemorial non-scientific human practice, remain fairly dependable tutors in the search for productive ways to go about art and artifice. Unfortunately, both Nature and traditional human wisdom are still very inadequately understood and all too frequently downright despised, in the name of scientific expertise that arrogates to itself the right to define the "state of the art." *Natura parendo vincitur*.[21] Only to the extent that this is realized is humanity's position of transcendence in the cosmos likely to remain a reliable civilizing force (cf. §120, 5) [*m*].

[d] In an elegant and learned monograph, entitled *The Cosmic Covenant: Biblical Themes of Justice, Peace, and the Integrity of Creation*, the

---

[*m*] This reflection provides a theoretical basis for the traditional catholic respect for the natural law, reverently read off from the physical and especially the biophysical structures of "Nature." But it also suggests that respect for the natural law can be reconciled with a decisively expanded recognition of the use of *recta ratio* in the responsible manipulation of Nature. After all, Nature's potential (which is integral to Nature) is at least partly hidden and undeveloped, and it is distinctively human to discover and develop it. It follows that much of the natural law, too, remains to be discovered and developed. This suggestion implies, of course, that science and technology, as a matter of principle, are genuine goods; far from corrupting our ability to take moral responsibility for the physical and biophysical structures of humanity and the cosmos, they enable us to enhance it (cf. §50, 1, a–b and [*m*]).

English theologian Robert Murray has developed these cosmological and anthropological reflections on a firm foundation of biblical theology. Ancient Near East literature, Jewish ritual, the Jewish Scriptures as a whole, early and later Christian tradition, as well as Christian ritual culminating in the Eucharist (cf. §78, 3–5; §90, 6) place humanity in a position of royal prerogative in the cosmos. But this is predicated on an interpretation of the world as a precious domain divinely entrusted to human "guardianship." This reveals an awareness of a divine ordering of creation antecedent to any notion of "salvation history." Murray's book reminds us that salvation history has all too frequently served as a means to glorify humanity, in a short-sighted fashion, at the expense of the cosmos; this is tantamount to doing an injustice not only to the theological cosmology of the great Tradition, but also to its anthropology, and thus, in the long run, to humanity itself (cf. §9, 1, [*I*]). As Murray puts it, "to say the least, wanton destruction of what we do not understand is not worthy of beings created in the image of our common Creator."[22]

[11] Our reflections have led us back to the opening theme of this section: natural evil. Given its position in the cosmos, humanity is required to understand what natural evil is, to identify occurrences of it, and to take action in order to contend with them; but it is also required to do so in a discerning fashion, by recourse to integrally *anthropological* criteria. These include an appropriate respect for the wisdom of such cosmic processes and structures which, while only very dimly understood by science, have nonetheless supported, and continue to support the emergence, survival, and fulfillment of humanity. Put differently, humanity itself, being the culminating configuration produced by the cosmic process, is also the point of vantage from which the essential goodness of Nature is established. In fact, Nature *as we know it* is no longer a raw, purely "natural" given appealing to human intelligence and the human penchant for development; in countless ways, it already bears the imprint of past human efforts at understanding and civilization. On both counts it presents itself to responsible human judgment; on both counts, too, if offers itself to human resourcefulness, to be evaluated and put to appropriate purposes.

[a] This valuing and putting to good or superior purpose is a matter of *oikonomia* or sound housekeeping; that is, it is transactional and in that sense collaborative; in *oikonomia*, persons and things, subjectivity and objectivity meet; when the encounter comes off, freedom is tempered by respect for otherness, and otherness liberated from

the limited conditions of its particularity (cf. §8, 2–4) [n]. For, if cultural and moral achievements are to be truly valuable, they must result neither from objective cosmic givens alone (including the given, cosmic structures of humanity itself) nor simply from the transcendence that sets humanity apart and enables it to understand and judge things cosmic and to enjoy, manipulate, exploit, manage, and transform them. Rather, lasting cultural values are attained in the context of qualitative relationships between, on the one hand, objective givens ("things") that naturally are so configured and arranged in the cosmos as to offer themselves for value judgments and development, and, on the other hand, human subjects and communities endowed with superior purpose and with the ability to discern and choose things in such a way as to do justice to the way they are "naturally" configured and arranged. Things and processes that so offer themselves we call "objectively good" because we know them to be real bearers of value—that is, intrinsically "value-able." But by the same token, within the range of value-able things, we will find ourselves deciding that some things and processes are inherently inferior and less constructive (and hence, less desirable) than others. Occasionally, we will find ourselves coming to the conclusion that there are things and processes which, when interpreted in the context of humanity and the cosmos as a whole (as far as we can responsibly discern them), are best evaluated as "naturally evil" [o].

[b] Summing up, a consistently cosmological and anthropological theory of values and valuing ("axiology") will not be reluctant to

---

[n] This is the central thesis of Max Scheler's monumental protest, in *Der Formalismus in der Ethik und die materiale Wertethik* (ET *Formalism in Ethics and Non-Formal Ethics of Values*) against the Kantian conception of ethics as a matter of pure intentionality. It is also at the heart of the encyclical *Veritatis Splendor* (1993), written by Scheler's long-time admirer, Pope John Paul II. Not surprisingly, Dietrich Bonhoeffer's *Ethik* (ET *Ethics*) struggles with the same agenda.

[o] Incidentally but not unimportantly, let us recall that our discernments and judgments arise not from any position of pure transcendence over things cosmic on our part, but by virtue of *both* our capacity to know and judge *and* our participation in the cosmos (cf. §115, 6). In other words, we arrive at value judgments about matters cosmic by *participative knowledge* (§63). Accordingly, these judgments are *interpretative, discretionary*, and *affective*. That is to say, we know things as valuable long before we can *argue*, with the detached objectivity of rational knowledge, that they are valuable, and why. Needless to say, this has two consequences. Firstly, it sharply limits the role that experts of whatever stripe must be allowed to play in the making of human, moral decisions (cf. H.-G. Gadamer, *Über die Verborgenheit der Gesundheit*, esp. pp. 11–49, 149–58). Secondly, participation in the cosmos accounts for the fact that our moral sense is liable to change and develop; this implies that it is capable of both refinement and degeneracy (cf. §105; §113, 2, a).

identify, with due caution and on genuine, integrally anthropological grounds, in an imperfect but "good" world, natural evils—that is, instances of cosmic combinations that destabilize the matrices of humanity's emergence and development, and hence, genuinely harmful to humanity's integral well-being as well as out of harmony with humanity's legitimate purposes. Various consequences of this important conclusion will be explored later on in this chapter (§120); for the moment, however, one fundamental implication of our conclusion—one of formidable moral significance—demands our attention.

[§116] NATURAL EVIL AND HUMAN LIFE

[1] Humanity, it has been argued, is intellectually equipped to discern and identify natural evil by recourse to integrally *anthropological* norms. But humanity is also divinely called to *act*, in such a way as to enhance itself as well as the cosmos, and to lead both to higher, ultimately transcendent purpose (§115, 10). In conjunction, these two propositions lead to an obvious conclusion: humanity is morally justified in correcting, resisting, and controlling natural evil, and even in combating it, provided it does so in a genuinely intelligent, understanding, discerning fashion.

However, humanity's license to take on natural evil becomes self-contradictory (and hence, completely incoherent) if it is not taken to presuppose the bioethical ground rule: *innocent human life never qualifies as natural evil.* That is, biophysical human life that [a] offers no present, *deliberate* threat, either to other biophysical human life, whether emergent or existing, or to the human community, [b] is not detrimental to *integral* human well-being, and [c] does not thwart legitimate human purpose) is to be held sacred, unconditionally. Accordingly, making innocent human life the object of intentional ("direct") efforts to subdue or destroy is intrinsically inhuman, and hence, immoral.[23] This important thesis requires careful analysis and understanding.

[a] In an illuminating essay entitled "Manuals and rule books," the English Dominican Herbert McCabe has offered a critical commentary on some aspects of Pope John Paul II's 1993 encyclical *Veritatis Splendor.* McCabe thoroughly agrees with the encyclical's insistence on the crucial significance and indeed the unconditional nature of the bioethical ground rule just formulated; but he also argues that we need a more precise understanding of just where both its signifi-

cance and its unconditional character lie. To make his point, he resorts to an analogy taken from the world of team sports.

McCabe begins by distinguishing between two kinds of "rules": "directives for players" and "basic rules of the game." Directives that coaches give to players typically consist in specific, often compelling orders detailing *how* players are to play the game, and in reasons stating *why* such orders are apt to get them to play well; explicitly or implicitly, the orders usually also direct the players how to avoid playing the game poorly. Such directives are useful and even indispensable, yet they always remain rather general and in that sense theoretical; players must indeed carry out the directives, but they must do so flexibly, by *applying* them as play situations demand. Specific moral rules and precepts are analogous to such directives. They lay down, in the form of general, often compelling rules, how human beings and communities, faced with moral issues, are to play the game of morality well and why, and how and why they are to avoid playing it poorly. Such precepts, in other words, enable human persons and communities to learn how to live morally *in practice*— which is, of course, what counts.

By contrast, fundamental moral rules are analogous to "basic rules of the game." Basic rules of the game lay down the difference, not between the game being played well or poorly, but between the game being played *and its not being played at all.* Soccer, for example, ceases to be soccer if all players and not just goalies are permitted to play the ball with their arms and hands, just as baseball ceases to be baseball when the bats may be used to hit not only the ball but other players as well. Basic rules of the game, therefore, do not give players any guidance as to how to play the game well, but how to play it, period. The same applies to fundamental moral rules, and in particular, to the bioethical ground rule just formulated. The rule "innocent human life must never become the object of direct efforts to subdue or destroy it" does not give anybody any *specific* guidance as to how to act morally and avoid acting immorally in *particular* situations where human life is at stake. Its value (and it is considerable) lies elsewhere: it lays down, in regard to the respect due to human life *as a matter of principle*, the *radical* difference between the game of morality being played (whether well or poorly) *and its not being played at all.*

In team sports, when a rule of the game is broken, the play itself ceases, interrupted by the referee; it is resumed only after appropriate penalties have been imposed by the referees, whose function it is to decide, *not* whether the game is being *played well*, but whether it is being *played at all*. In the same way, moral ground rules mark the boundary where responsible (if never perfect) moral engagement simply disintegrates, to give way to the jungle where human beings stop acting morally at all—a situation that obviously calls for strong moral judgments.

[b] A caution. In *Evangelium Vitae*, the bioethical ground rule is proposed as an "exceptionless precept."[24] This expression *can* be misleading, for this reason: the ground rule is not so much a positive moral precept as an unconditional boundary marker. Positive precepts or "moral laws," while conveying real imperatives for the good life, always remain somewhat general. They give essential guidance to the moral life, but they must be *applied in practice*, obediently and generously, but also discerningly and prudently; in that sense, they never apply unconditionally or automatically or without exception. By contrast, ground rules like the one just formulated are absolute; to consider oneself under certain circumstances absolved from them is tantamount to rejecting them. In the words of Pope John Paul II, they "indicate the minimum which [free individuals] must respect and from which they must start out to say yes over and over again."[25] In other words, they are made not for flexible application, but for fundamental acceptance, since they mark the divide between the human and the definitively non-human (that is, morally speaking, the positively "inhuman"). Thus, if they are absolute (and they are), they are so in the sense (and only in the sense) that they tell the difference between the moral and the unequivocally immoral. Accordingly, they serve to keep alive the realization that we need a fundamental, unconditional commitment if we are to lead a human (that is, moral) life at all; in that sense, they give guidance as to how human persons and communities should *approach* moral issues *in every case*. But, once again, they give no immediate, *practical* guidance as to how to proceed in concrete instances.[26]

Let us change the metaphor. Moral ground rules become part neither of the action of the morality play, nor of its performance, nor of its stage directions. What they do do is positively create the stage on which the play is to be performed. Without that stage, the play is *not performed at all*. This explains why the phrasing of ground rules of is so often *negative*—a point noted by Pope John Paul II, who explains that "the no . . . makes clear the absolute limit beneath which free individuals cannot lower themselves."[27]

In light of all this, we can now phrase the bioethical ground rule negatively, but in the service of entirely positive purpose, as follows. *It is always wrong to engage in the direct harming or taking of innocent human life—that is, human life that offers no threat to the common good.* Pope John Paul II takes a comparable approach, where he writes: "*I declare that direct abortion, that is, abortion willed as an end or as a means, always constitutes a grave moral disorder,*" and: "*I confirm that euthanasia is a grave violation of the law of God.*"[28]

[2] The bioethical ground rule, we have argued, is crucial in that it tells the difference between morality and its opposite. However, it differs from other, comparable ground rules in one respect: it tells the difference the moral and the unequivocally immoral from *a unique vantage point.* For it establishes the *baseline* where human life (that is, human life as a moral project) *first emerges,* by disengaging itself from infra-human evolutionary process and its achievements. Let us put this in reverse. The rule, when disregarded, marks the boundary crossing at which human beings stop acting in a distinctively human fashion, and begin to act as if they were merely cosmic, infra-human, sentient (that is, animal) agents, except that, unlike animal agents, they do so not instinctively and innocently, but deliberately.

Thus we have encountered once again, but at the most basic level, what we have called the inherent self-contradiction of moral evil (§113, 3). By treating innocent human life as if it were a natural evil, human beings seeking to ensure the fundamental value inherent in human life by turning against it. This is important enough to warrant clarification and elaboration, by means of a precise theoretical analysis.

[3] Cosmic existents range from the highly unstable and practically non-viable to the practically (if never perfectly or permanently) viable and stable; cosmic processes range from the equivalenty random to the highly (if never perfectly) coordinated. What distinguishes human beings among all cosmic existents is that they are only inadequately accounted for by reference either to their place on the viability range of cosmic existents or to the degree of their vulnerability to cosmic processes. For all human beings, the emergent as well as the mature, the robust as well as the tenuous, *enjoy transcendence*—that is, an immediate and inalienable relatedness to God as well as to all that is. In other words, much as human beings participate, by dint of mutuality, in the physical, biophysical, and psychophysical processes at work in the cosmos, their physical and biophysical being supports a reality of

higher significance. Human bodiliness is the material matrix of an immanently spiritual existence of transcendent value. To understand and formulate this transcendent value of every human being, the tradition has availed itself of the term "soul" (§115, 9; cf. §109, 9, c, [z]).

Humanity's distinctive difference in the cosmos (or, "the human soul") is manifested in *action*. Human beings and communities, in other words, have the capacity to act in ways unavailable to infra-human cosmic agents. This requires elaboration.

For purposes of present argument, let us prescind from the kind of cosmic incidents which strike us as large-scale mishaps. We can think of volcanic eruptions and devastating flood waves; while due to known or at least knowable factors (and hence, not simply haphazard), they are equivalently random; consequently, in practice they are indiscriminate and unsystematic, both in their occurrence and their effects. Instead, let us concentrate on the particular activities of specific cosmic existents of appreciable stability, and hence, readily identifiable: sophisticated physical, biophysical, and sentient configurations.

Cosmic existents are coherent structures—*systems*. Accordingly, their interaction with other cosmic existents is systemic, too; in relation to other cosmic existents, they function in a discriminating manner. Subatomic processes (or at least many of them) and chemical bonding, for instance, are not random, but systemic. Living organisms spontaneously discriminate between what suits their organic growth and well-being and what does not. Sentient organisms discriminate even across distances and over time: locomotion (or at least some form of it), sense perception, and memory combine to enable animals to overcome obstacles, pursue clues, and learn. This enables them to seek out, actively and with results that suggest purpose, what suits their own survival as well as the continuation of the species; it also enables them to avoid or even attack whatever threatens these essential benefits.

Yet all these forms of discrimination remain instinctive at best. Even at their most precipitate, proactive and spontaneous, infra-human existents, whether inanimate, organic, or sentient, stay within the bounds of cosmic process; they will normally settle for balance vis-à-vis their environment; at most, they aim at a convenient advantage, often quite ingeniously, but never wholly innovatively. In other words, what infra-human cosmic existents have in common is this: they do not (since they cannot) treat other cosmic existents (including human beings) as moral entities—that is, as entities of immanent worth and transcendent finality, and hence, as worthy of unconditional regard. That is to say, infra-human cosmic existents, not even the higher animals, do not *rise above and transcend* what suits themselves or at least the species; they cannot make *choices* between, on the one hand, their own survival and interests and, on the other hand, the survival and interests of cosmic existents outside the fixed ambits set by their own survival and interests. This is the same as saying that infra-human cosmic existents cannot genuinely work toward the fully common good. They neither make nor recognize moral claims; they neither make moral choices, nor do they make moral demands on each other. While certainly discriminating and sometimes even resourceful within the sphere of their involvement with other cosmic existents, and while certainly altruistic within the compass of their species and even in regard to their partners in symbiosis (cf. §122, 1, g), they do not discriminate freely and consciously; they communicate, but not by habitually rising above the situation by virtue of articulate speech and formal manners; they signal, but neither converse nor deliberate (cf. §130, 1). Accordingly, they are incapable of doing what we have argued human beings can and should do in order to identify natural evil: determine the goodness of things by the standard of their compatibility with humanity—its emergence and development, its integral well-being, and its legitimate, transcendent purposes.

Why can we be so confident that the engagement of infra-human cosmic agents is indeed wholly cosmic, and hence, a-moral? The answer is not far to seek. As human beings, *we* are radically cosmic ourselves. Accordingly, we are intimately familiar with cosmic involvement, by dint of participation (cf. §115, 6; cf. also §63). Much human activity occurs at the physical and biophysical (that is, the a-moral, or rather, the pre-moral) level (§115, 2, [a]). This experience of cosmicity is precisely what enables *all* human beings, in principle, to tell the difference between merely biophysical, instinctive, involuntary involvement and deliberate (that is, moral) action and interaction. In other words, it is *in the experience of human life itself*— whether of the emergent or the mature variety—that human beings discover the difference between moral humanity and a-moral (or rather, pre-moral) humanity. This insight can be further clarified and developed in the direction of its moral and theological consequences, as follows.

[4] In the cosmos, things that human beings regard as *right* are often frustrated by chance and the play of large numbers. But in addition to such fairly random mishaps, what is right from the human point of view is regularly damaged and even defeated by cosmic agents that are not just viable, but positively powerful and often (as in the case of

animals and many micro-organisms) very resourceful. This is typical of cosmic existents, both at the sentient level and below it; they exercise *power*. They wield inherent forces of self-maintenance and self-assertion; they are active by dint of persistence in being (*conatus essendi*: cf. §107, 5, c, [*n*]).

It follows that in the cosmos, to live is by and large to survive by dint of pushing for survival; and to survive is in practice tantamount to being among the fittest and (especially at the sentient level) the more resourceful. No wonder the universe, beautiful and undomesticated and intricate and imposing as it is, can strike us as morally unintelligible (cf. §117, 2). For while it is the fertile and protective and nurturing womb of all that is, the cosmos also wreaks devastation and death on its own as a matter of course (§128, 3)—a fact that can put the faith of those who believe in divine Providence to a severe test (cf. §118). Set against this cosmic backdrop, *deliberate regard for innocent human life becomes the most basic way in which humanity can and must distinguish itself from the infra-human cosmos and transcend it.*

Human beings transcend the cosmos. In the last resort this means that they are intrinsically attuned to the living God. No wonder the ban on the direct harming or taking of innocent human life is such an elemental moral rule in the Jewish and Christian traditions, which draw their understanding of moral responsibility from their understanding of God as the sole Creator of all that is (§98, 5).

[5] All of this can in turn be elaborated negatively as well. The rule demanding that innocent human life be unconditionally respected implicitly also states where the misery of miseries starts, namely, at the point where human beings first deliberately abuse the gift of transcendence which makes them human. Transcendence sets them apart from the cosmos at large and its processes. It enables them both to refine the cosmos and humanity, and to attain their own true identity, and thus to bring both themselves and the cosmos home to God. Now what happens is this. Miserably, in the interest of their self-maintenance and self-assertion, human beings turn their transcendence over cosmic process into acts of naked power directed against other, innocent human beings. Transcendence thus turns into self-serving domination. What is most precious in humanity thus becomes the instrument of sinful degeneracy, and specifically, at this elemental, cosmological level, of sinful *violence* (cf. Gen 6, 11; cf. §129, 1; §130, 8–9). For at this fateful juncture human beings cease being just involuntary participants in the inescapable round of natural vicissitude and failure;

they *deliberately* turn themselves into a menace to human life, vulnerable as it already is. This is where human transcendence over the cosmos is first put to the task of inflicting on humanity something that not even the beastliest, most merciless, most destructive infra-human cosmic agents, being blind to moral claims and incapable of moral activity, are capable of inflicting: *moral evil.*

What this amounts to can be expressed as follows. To a precarious cosmos, already laced with the scourge of natural evil, violent human beings add not only their unavoidable share of natural evil, but also moral evil at its most primitive and elemental: the subduing and taking of vulnerable, innocent human life. They do the very thing that is the core of the definition of natural evil. In so doing, humanity not only turns into a deadly danger to itself; it also becomes a deliberate menace to the cosmic environment that supports it, and which is hardly less vulnerable than humanity itself.

The moral rule that prohibits the taking of innocent human life, therefore, identifies the borderline where, at humanity's own hands, humanity and the natural world with which it is continuous lose their pristine innocence. They have never been the same. Small wonder the Genesis account of creation as we know it is hardly underway when Cain murders Abel and, enslaved for life by fear of death (cf. Heb 2, 15), begins to roam the earth, looking for a place away from God (Gen 4, 8–16). For in the world in which we live, the only way to live a human life left to us is to live on blood-soaked soil, fearful because forever in danger of our lives, and habitually running away from God's presence, in a landscape so darkened by violent death that even "natural" death is now apt to look like a defeat.

This raises a question. Could it be that in making this discovery, we have discovered the root of that basic conviction, shared not only by the whole biblical tradition, but also by the great tradition of patristic and scholastic theology, namely, that sin and death are connected at base, inseparably? Could it be that this is also the reason why the Fourth Gospel can have Jesus call the devil "murderous from the beginning" (Jn 8, 44)?

[a] A caution. While it is philosophically and theologically sound to recognize the moral horror that the deliberate taking of innocent human life provokes, it remains essential to remember that biophysical human life is not humanity's highest good, let alone an absolute. Most civilized traditions have given evidence of this conviction by treating the life of the human community, ensured by a reliable

order of justice, as a higher good than the right to life of individuals, especially of those who seriously harm or jeopardize that order. Even more importantly, such civilizations have, in a variety of ways, regarded the voluntary, self-sacrificial surrender of one's life in the service of a superior good not as an offense against human life, but as an act of high virtue and a sublime form of human living. In fact, the Christian tradition, taking its cue from such prophetic Jewish themes as second Isaiah's suffering servant (Is 53) and the God-fearing just man driven to death for no reason other than his own righteousness (Wisd 2), has insisted that life interpreted and pursued as if it were a good to be held on to for its own sake becomes, in fact, a lost cause. For cosmic life becomes true life only according as it is transcended—that is, freely given up (Mk 8, 35, parr.; Mt 10, 39 par. Lk 17, 33; Jn 12, 25), for others. If it stays caught in self-absorption, it will turn into an addiction which will force those enslaved to it to maintain and defend life by dealing death to others; thus human life becomes an unholy threat—in fact, the root form of sin.

This lethal form of human life is precisely what (so the Christian communities will proclaim) has been redeemed and transformed, in the only fashion in which anything can be genuinely redeemed and transformed, namely, from inside, by participation. For in his free and conscious obedience to his Father, the Son of God, having taken on human life, has gone against the purely cosmic grain, by freely accepting a violent death unjustly inflicted on him; in thus giving up his life in behalf of those he loved and loves, he has renewed human life in his own person, by taking it on again, transforming it into a life for God, for good (cf. Jn 10, 14–18; Rom 6, 10).

[b] Some recent christologies have rightly emphasized that the historical Jesus' life of freedom in the name of God, prophetic confrontation with the powers that be, association with the poor, and table fellowship with the marginal, has saving significance. In the process, however, the traditional affirmation of the saving significance of his violent *death* by crucifixion has more than once been presented as little more than a forced Christian attempt to put a positive theological construction on an event that can only be called pointless, unjust, and morally repugnant.

William Frazier has registered a provocative protest against this tendency, by stating, in uncompromising terms, that if Jesus had failed to meet, in a violent and unjust death, the deadly dynamic inherent in human life as we know it, there would be no salvation.

He explains: "Without death, in its many shapes and sizes, and without the hurtful ways people defend themselves against it there would simply be no need for deliverance by way of the cross. This, however, is only halfway into the problem. For life itself works malignantly beneath the surface . . . whenever running from death reaches destructive proportions. *Life in this sense, given to defeating death by escaping death, is the engine of our fallen world*".[29]

[c] Theological issues like these, of course, will have to come up for careful and nuanced reflection later on, in the context of christology and soteriology. For now, the points just made serve merely to show that it is a mistake, even in a world so insensitive to the sanctity of human life as ours, to allow ourselves to get so fascinated by the intrinsic value of human life that we end up not only idealizing life in a naive fashion [*p*], but also downplaying the profound religious significance which death, even unjust and violent death, has always had in the Jewish and Christian traditions: "The souls of the righteous are in the hand of God, and no torment will ever touch them" (Wisd 3, 1). This should help keep us from getting so preoccupied with the defense of defenseless human life as to withdraw from responsible bioethical debate (for instance, by declaring that biophysical human life in and of itself demands that it be maintained at all costs and by every means: cf. §124, 3, a, [*w*]).

[d] These central pieces of Christian theology, therefore, provide us with yet another reason why it is important to understand that *the unconditional ban on the direct killing of innocent human life does not tell the whole bioethical story*. Again, the ban is a moral rule; *it is not a positive precept*. Unlike precepts, the prohibition articulated in the rule does not illuminate, let alone settle, any of the many concrete moral issues that arise in the area of bioethics; it only fixes the lower limit of what is moral. But in so doing, the rule does achieve something utterly crucial: it *opens* all particular bioethical issues to careful, intel-

---

[*p*] Namely, by neglecting to take into account the basic ambivalence inherent in human life. Human life shares this ambivalence, of course, with all things cosmic. To enjoy biophysical life means being significantly immersed in mutuality; as a result, the life of everyone naturally involves, one way or another, the life and death of every other. Given both the ineluctability of cosmic mutuality and humanity's transcendence over it, human beings find themselves confronted, simply by virtue of being physically alive, with urgent questions. How is the human spirit to deal with the claims of the unavoidable other? How is human spirit to turn cosmic life into a required apprenticeship in the school of deliberation and (ultimately) self-abandon? These themes are to be explored, under the rubric of *alienation*, in the next chapter (§122, 1, a–f).

ligent, and responsible exploration, judgment, and moral decision-making.

The addresses on the subject by Cardinal Joseph Bernardin, collected (along with a number of essays by others) under the title *Consistent Ethic of Life*, provide a good instance of this attitude. Cardinal Bernardin insists that, in the interest of *consistency*, the bioethical ground rule be steadfastly honored; but he also insists that on that firm basis the discussion of important moral and public policy issues touching on the preservation of human life can afford to be *reasonable*. Thus he demonstrates that it is an error of both moral theory and moral judgment to cast doubts on careful discussion and casuistry in bioethical matters, as if both were no more than devious "liberal" attempts to undermine the sanctity of human life. This is entirely consistent with the catholic tradition. That tradition does not regard the natural law as a series of dictates to be fanatically proclaimed, heartlessly enforced, and blindly complied with; rather, it trusts human reason, enlightened by faith, to operate in a discerning fashion. Reason thus understood is moral humanity's prime instrument in the discovery and understanding of what is involved in the natural law, and this conviction becomes more, not less, important according as the moral issues in hand become more delicate and neuralgic [*q*].

[e] Two passages in the *Summa theologiae* suggest that the positions just rehearsed and developed can claim the support of Thomas Aquinas.

Our first passage points in the direction of the bioethical ground rule. Toward the end of the *prima secundae*,[30] Aquinas raises the question as to whether the natural law is one and the same, and thus universal. In a lengthy response he explains that all human beings without exception naturally know, by virtue of practical reason, the

---

[*q*] Incidentally, it may not be irrelevant here to mention a separate, yet not wholly unrelated issue. The inviolability of innocent human life as a *moral* issue must be distinguished from its inviolability as a *legal* issue; for example, legal decriminalization of abortion is not the same as its moral justification. In the catholic tradition, this creates a margin of freedom for Christians, especially legislators and judges, and even for Christian churches and their leaders, to accept , as a lesser evil and without encouragement, laws permitting, say, abortion in specified cases, provided they are enacted by competent civil authority and not selectively enforced. At the same time, the distinction should not be exaggerated. Our contention that respect for innocent human life is morality's baseline implies that there are very good reasons for both public servants and the bearers of office in the Christian churches to insist that *humanity itself* (and not just the Christian or Catholic tradition in a narrow sense) is at stake here. On these issues, cf. Pope John Paul II's *Evangelium Vitæ*, 73–74.

first and fundamental precept of the moral law: "What is good should be practiced and pursued and what is evil should be avoided." In that sense the natural law is one and the same. But then the question arises how this goodness can be discerned. In reply, Aquinas explains that reason allows us to perceive the tendencies *naturally* resident in things (cf. §80, 2); these tendencies reveal which way goodness lies. In the case of humanity, he continues, these natural tendencies occur in a threefold hierarchy of natural values; this reveals that the moral life must respect *basic, essential goodness* at three ascending levels [r].

In this hierarchy, the first and utterly basic good is revealed by a tendency that humanity has in common with all cosmic existents: it endeavors to continue in being. Now in the case of living organisms, being alive is not something incidental or additional to their being, but their very being itself;[31] consequently, in the case of humanity, striving for continuation in being is the same as safeguarding biophysical life. A second, higher, more particular level of basic goodness is involved in what human beings share with the animal kingdom; Aquinas notes, by way of an example, that human beings have this in common with many animals that they are natively inclined to seek sexual union and to care for their offspring. Accordingly, if humanity is to live well, the proper exercise of these highly constructive, instinctive tendencies toward altruism must be safeguarded. The third, highest basic human good is distinctively human. (Incidentally, in other passages Aquinas repeatedly intimates that it is the most tenuous as well.) This characteristically human good is mani-

---

[r] Incidentally, Aquinas' position implies that the one natural law lives and subsists in multiple moral laws. This multiplicity implies that not all *positive* moral precepts are equally stringent or fundamental, equally obvious at all times and in all places, or arrived at by way of equally compelling reasonings. Life in accordance with the natural law, in other words, is to a significant extent a matter of shared discretionary judgments (as well as personal ones), in which delicacy of public or personal conscience (or the lack of it) plays a considerable role. No wonder shared moral judgments vary according to civilizations and circumstances, and change over time in small ways, as manners and customs change, and hence, as new moral issues arise. John Henry Newman's distinction between the sense of duty (which is invariable) and the moral sense (which is not) makes the same point (§105, 3). For all these reasons it is sometimes said, in a fetching paradox, that the natural law is "simply immutable and multifariously mutable." Dramatic instances of change in the Catholic natural law tradition can be seen in the areas of usury, slavery, religious liberty, and divorce, as John T. Noonan, Jr., the author of widely accepted, reliable monographs on banking and usury (1951, 1957), contraception (1965), abortion (1970, 1979), the dissolubility of Christian marriage (1972), and bribery (1984), has insisted, with increasing firmness and clarity. Cf. his more recent "Development in Moral Doctrine."

fested by the tendencies that create the preconditions for the life of the human spirit proper: the human desire to know (and most of all, to know God) and the human knack for social structures; accordingly, the fully moral life begins with the removal of ignorance and the cultivation of constructive habits of living together.

These three basic levels of natural inclination toward goodness, it must be recalled, are in the nature of natural *inclinations and predispositions*; they describe, *not* moral maturity or perfection, but baselines—the natural takeoff points for mature, discretionary moral judgments and behaviors. While absolutely vital and unconditionally normative, they define only the lower limits of three levels of goodness—the minimal but essential preconditions for the pursuit and attainment of, respectively, (1) the disciplined life, (2) the responsible life, and (3) the life of selfless love [s].

The "continuation in being," which Aquinas regards as the first of humanity's three basic natural goods, clearly corresponds to what the bioethical ground rule means to affirm, namely, that human life must be regarded as in and of itself entitled, by natural law, to respect and the assurance of continuance. Obviously, it is in the nature of the case that human beings can jeopardize this entitlement and even forfeit it, namely, by inhumanly lowering themselves to the infra-human level, where they become a deliberate threat to the continuity in being of innocent human life other than their own.

---

[s] Aquinas' account of the basic goods, with its progression cosmology → anthropology → theology, is another instance of the persistence of the trichotomy in his thought (cf. §102, 10, a–b). In due course the reader will discover that both the trichotomy and Aquinas' order of basic goods will recur in the three levels of moral maturity and sinful degeneracy, to be developed, respectively, in chapters 15, 16, and 17. At the lowest, *cosmological* level, only to the extent that biophysical life is substantially safeguarded can the disciplining of passion and power become a moral issue; conversely, if passion and power are allowed free play, biophysical survival itself will be in jeopardy (§§127–130). At the second, distinctively *anthropological* level, only to the extent that the disciplined life (in which the passions are appropriately restrained to make room for altruism) is substantially established is it possible for the deliberate life—the life of justice and the pursuit of the common good—to become a truly moral issue; conversely, if injustice and mere expediency are allowed to be the order of the day, discipline and control of the passions will break down and give way to moral anarchy, to be curbed only by the iron fist of tyranny (§§131–137). Finally, at the fully *theological* level, only if appreciation of knowledge, civility, and considerateness are substantially guaranteed, and vice, ignorance, and anarchy consistently discredited, can natural human self-transcendence be transformed into faith and hope and the love of God and into the self-sacrificial love of others; conversely, if loss of the sense of God, disbelief in the possibility of self-transcending love, and self-righteousness are allowed to carry the day, human intelligence and civilization are bound to decay.

Aquinas deals with this situation in a second passage from the *secunda secundæ*—one that we must briefly consider as well. Earlier on, it was stated that what we have called the bioethical ground rule is rooted in humanity's transcendence over the cosmos; this means, in the last analysis, that it is rooted in humanity's attunement to God (cf. §116, 4). This fully theological approach is the one Aquinas adopts when he turns to the killing of human beings as a moral issue.

The context differs substantially from the context of the passage just discussed. At issue here is not the philosophical issue of *emergent humanity*'s universal search for basic canons of essential moral goodness, but the *specific moral issue* involved in the deliberate taking of the life of certain human beings. Accordingly, Aquinas approaches the serious question not from the angle of humanity's survival in the cosmos, but from its most distinctive feature: its being made in the image of God. Not surprisingly, he begins by declaring that it befits human beings (*secundum se*) that they should never be put to death; "the nature God made" (which is scholastic shorthand for "the nature made in God's image and likeness") deserves unconditional respect, even in sinners. But there is an addition. Human nature demands that individual human beings should be considered in relation to others; consequently, just as the *natural* well-being of a body makes the amputation, by a competent physician, of a sick member morally licit, so, if certain individuals should pose a grave *moral* danger to the community and the common good (which, Aquinas adds, "is compromised by sin"), it is morally licit for the legitimately constituted authorities to deprive them of life. Obviously, no such excuse could ever exist in the case of just people, since by their very lives they precisely preserve and promote the common good. This second argument, therefore, equally results in an absolute ban on the taking of innocent human life, except that in this case the fundamental reason is strictly theological, both in regard to the duty to respect human life and in regard to the licence to take it. For, in regard to the latter, Aquinas is simply heir to the Jewish-Christian tradition which holds that sin involves separation from God, the Author of life, and hence, death. In allowing the punishing of sinful crimes against the common good, Aquinas is merely permitting human judgment (which must always model itself after the divine Wisdom) to do justice "within the limits of its ability" (*pro posse*). Still, it is to be noted that Aquinas stops short of *obliging* human tribunals to inflict capital punishment.[32]

Quite recently, Aquinas' position was retrieved, surprisingly but quite consistently, by Pope John Paul II in his encyclical *Evangelium vitæ*. The Pope limits capital punishment to "cases of absolute necessity," which, "as a result of steady improvements in the organization of the penal system, . . . are very rare if not practically non-existent."[33]

[f] A final note in the interest of balance. Later on in this volume, it will be argued that systemic forms of evil occurring at the higher (*i.e.*, the properly anthropological and theological) levels of human existence have a fateful way of suggesting that moral wrongs can be effectively righted only by cosmological means—that is, by power, by force, and, if necessary, by violence (§130, 6, [*n*]; §134, 10; 12–14). In other words, it will be argued that unwarranted violence is often the desperate, immoral response to those "higher" forms of immorality that are all the more infuriating for being subtle. This has consequences for the human and Christian response to the unwarranted jeopardizing and violent taking of innocent human life, not only by abortion and active euthanasia, but also by premeditated attacks on defenseless civilians in armed conflicts (§129, 7, a, [*j*]); by culpable failure, on the part of whole communities, to provide food and shelter to the hapless, the weak, and the marginal; and by the execution of criminals where incarceration is a viable and available alternative. In his encyclical *Evangelium Vitae* Pope John Paul II surprised the Catholic as well as the non-Catholic world by arguing the last of these points.[34]

Moral revulsion at immoral forms of forcefulness is understandable and indignation is often appropriate. Still, neither dispenses from reflection. Much as violence against human life must be denounced, denunciation remains morally incomplete if it is not accompanied by a commitment to search for the hidden catalysts of these dreadful feats of inhumanity. For, while there is little doubt that overt violence against human life is frequently committed by identifiable, irresponsible (and even depraved) human individuals and groups of individuals, the roots of this inhumanity are often systemic. Pope John Paul II's encyclical *Evangelium Vitae* explicitly recognizes this. It acknowledges that mothers often resort to abortion because they see no alternative.[35] It also pointedly places the responsibility for the contemporary assaults on innocent human life squarely on systems and prevalent sinful cultural assumptions and prejudices rather than on individuals.

[g] If any general conclusion can be drawn from the reflections contained in this section, it has to be this: only where human life *as such* is prized, not just as an instrumental value but as an inherent one, can natural evil be reliably corrected. It follows that, given the fact that basic respect for innocent human life is far from assured in the world we live in, humanity's ability to deal with natural evil is precarious at best. Let us return, then, to this latter theme, admittedly less pressing than the one just treated; but this time, let us treat it in an explicitly theological perspective.

COSMOLOGY, ANTHROPOLOGY, THEOLOGY

[§117] SUBJECTION, RESPONSIBILITY, AND ABANDON

[1] Earlier on (§115, 5), it was observed that humanity is about as vulnerable to "destabilizing natural occurrences" as comparable biophysical configurations. Clearly, the same cosmic process that has produced the combinations favorable to humanity's emergence and endurance has also produced combinations detrimental to them. What is more, this is likely to continue in the future: new adverse combinations will imperil us. Intelligent and dexterous humanity has many admirable ways of coping with them and even controlling them; still, there is no guarantee, from a cosmological point of view, that the struggle will forever be successful.

We have defined cosmic factors unfavorable to humanity's well-being as "natural evil." What entitled us to do so? The answer was: our understanding and acceptance of humanity as the most advanced (and indeed, qualitatively superior) fruit of cosmic process. In other words, in the last resort natural evil must be defined anthropologically (§115, 11). Accordingly, humanity is that being among all the beings that make up the cosmos whose distinctive capacity (and indeed, duty) it is to do the *valuing* of everything in the universe. Natural evil, therefore, is whatever jeopardizes humanity's integral well-being—its emergence, its continuance, its authentic growth and development.

[2] Still, now that cosmology has once again referred us back to anthropology, a caution is in order. While it is appropriate not only to define natural evil, but also to identify instances of it, by recourse to anthropology, that anthropology should reflect humanity *in its integrity*. That is, it should be predicated not only on humanity's subjec-

tion to cosmic process and its precarious participation in it, but also on its transcendence over the cosmos.

The former—humanity's subjection to, and participation in cosmic process—has meant and still means that countless human individuals and communities have been, and still are, the hapless and often inno-cent victims of uncontrollable violence inflicted by "a beautiful but morally unintelligible universe" (cf. §115, 2).[36] This constitutes a gen-uine moral challenge (cf. §120, 2): deadly natural failures simply must persuade humanity's native powers of rational objectivity and technical resourcefulness to attempt to counter and control, in a focused fash-ion, a largely intractable cosmos—a cosmos that resists full subservi-ence to, and integration into, human life and well-being, and hence, one that invites (and in cases demands) the use of a certain amount of manipulation and forcefulness.[37]

Such attempts at control will, of course, not always be successful. Many human persons and communities will continue to find them-selves in the predicament of Job, whom God, out of the whirlwind, overwhelms with a torrent of questions (Job 38–41) to which there is no reasonable answer (as, incidentally, Job had anticipated God would: Job 9, 16–20).[38] That is, there will always continue to be ex-tremities and hardship in which the only form of transcendence over the cosmos available to human beings is submission, resignation, the acknowledgment of the mystery of existence, and (in cases) repen-tance at the presumption involved in calling God's wisdom and justice into question. Still, in the normal course of events, whenever humani-ty and its position of transcendence are threatened by cosmic process, human intelligence must and often will take the form of some sort of ingenuity aimed at deliberate control from a position of superiority. In this sense, the cosmos must truly be "subjected" (cf. Gen 1, 28) so that humanity may truly live and prosper. There is no doubt that, in this perspective, modern scientific achievements are among the finest demonstrations of human transcendence over cosmic process.

However, the authority legitimately seized by *homo faber* to exercise control over the cosmos will lead to responsible human behavior only if two essential truths are appreciated.

First of all, since it is often the *inadvertent associate* of natural evil, humanity cannot justify the application of raw power and control by pleading helplessness in the face of cosmic might. Both human indi-viduals and communities find themselves habitually tempted to live by the dynamics of cosmic mutuality alone; they tend to give in to an in-stinctive, nervous urge to survive; that is, both humanity's conduct of itself and its management of the cosmos is liable to remain thought-less. Whenever this has taken place, humanity has become a menace not only to the environment, but also to the precarious balance that enables human individuals and communities to survive. That is, it has become a menace to itself.

But, secondly, as has been pointed out at length, there is something far more disturbing (and only here do we reach the fully anthropologi-cal level, where humanity's continuity with the cosmos gives way to the decisive element of discontinuity). Purely visceral instinct has often succeeded in putting the very instruments of human *transcendence* that is, intelligence and will—to the service of raw control and domination. Whenever this has happened, a crucial boundary has been crossed: humanity has appealed to the blind forces of mutuality that connect it with the material cosmos to justify the use of violence and even the deliberate inflicting of positive damage. In so doing, humanity has become the *deliberate, moral accomplice* of the natural evil that threatens, in a merely *a-moral* fashion, not only the environment, but also human individuals and communities. In sum, much as we may be justified in stating that natural evil jeopardizes humanity's well-being, it would be peevish and immature to make this statement *from a position of presumed defenselessness, let alone innocence, on humanity's part.* For part of the human propensity to sin is precisely this: human beings tend to forget that the infra-human cosmos has *rights*. Why does it have rights? *Not* because it is in the same boat as humanity, for purely cosmologically speaking, neither humanity nor the cosmos have rights; they just have to accept cosmic process as it comes. The infra-human cosmos has rights only because *humanity* is capable of appreciating it as the pre-condition for the emergence, the continuance, and the integral well-being of humanity itself. Humanity, in other words, is capable of mor-al discernment and moral behavior, not only in regard to itself but also in regard to the cosmos. The infra-human cosmos has no such capac-ity; it depends on humanity to receive the respect and the cultivation it deserves on account of its crucial significance for the emergence, the continuance, and the integral well-being of moral humanity.

[3] Here, then, lies a deeper, more fully anthropological reason why we find the concept of purely natural evil so hard to bear. Natural evil does indeed hurt humanity. It hinders the full deployment of our human potential. It puts our faith in a good God to a painful test. But that is not all, for in doing so, natural evil nettles a fundamental weakness in us—the one the Bible calls "the flesh"—our natural pre-

cariousness insofar as it is the potential source of our estrangement from God (cf. §112, 4, [d]). Natural evil, in other words, can provoke, in human persons and communities, outbursts of *irrational self-defense* against cosmic mishap and violence; it even tempts them to resort to responses that involve *deliberate violence.*

That is, we know from embarrassing experience that both the always-impending threat of natural evil and the actual occurrence of it can (and often will) stir up in us that embarrassing trepidation—the anxiety that is the negative shape of the awareness of our finitude. Natural evil is capable of triggering in us the ontological uneasiness that lurks at the core of our being (cf. §113, 1, [e]). The combination of the onrush of existential anxiety and the natural evil that arouses it is precisely what lies at the heart of the temptation to respond to the cosmos in ways which we *feel* may settle and secure us, yet which we *know* may be neither right nor constructive in the long run.

Thus the very thought of natural evil kindles in us what we would much rather keep quiet, namely, the unsettling sense of our proven inclination toward estrangement, degeneracy, and decay, and of our concupiscence—all those deep-seated forces of chaos that have impelled human beings to treat the cosmos around them not just as imperfect or dangerous, but as positively hostile, and not just the cosmos, but other human beings as well (CF. §115, 2–3).

No wonder natural evil pricks the human and Christian conscience. However unavoidable and blind and impersonal natural evil may be from a cosmological point of view, we sense its affinity with another form of evil inflicted on humanity and the world: the evil we know *could* have been, and *should* have been, and *can* be avoided—the evil we know whom to hold responsible for: sinful human persons like ourselves. Clearly, sin is first and foremost the deep injury humanity inflicts on itself and its relatedness to God; but it also deeply impairs its ability to take moral responsibility for the cosmos (cf. §114, 5).

[a] The realizations just developed are a most compelling reason why the cool acceptance of natural evil proposed by the rational theodicies characteristic of the modern age fails to persuade. Rational as they are, they overlook *the moral impact natural evil has on moral creatures.* From Leibniz on (cf. §115, 4, b), rational theodicies have often succeeded in making a tolerable *cosmological* case for the compatibility of the existence of an omnipotent God with the existence of imperfection in a finite universe. However, dedicated to ob-

jectivity and geometrical method as they have typically been (cf. §7,

1, a; §56, 12, a), they have tended to treat God in almost wholly cosmological terms (§103, 2); accordingly, they have treated the material cosmos, as well as humanity's relationship to it, as *morally neutral.* One important side-effect of this approach is the tendency to consider humanity the helpless (that is, a-moral) victim of natural evil —a position which implies that God alone bears moral responsibility for it. This, of course, favors a religiosity both narrow and immature, and hence, very vulnerable to a typical resentment response:dogmatic atheism (cf. §99) [*t*].

[b] Here, therefore, lies the parting of the ways. In having to respond to natural evil, we are faced with an alternative. Either we remain immaturely tied to a narrowly cosmological world view [*u*]. Or we allow ourselves to be morally tempted, tested, and stimulated. In the latter case we are apt to realize that the occurrence of natural evil may render faith implausible; and by this brush with atheism we may find both our faith and our humanity deepened. In Emmanuel Lévinas' words, we may come to realize that "the adult person's God reveals himself precisely in the emptiness of the child's heaven."

[*t*] Anthropologically speaking, it is perhaps possible to believe in, and live in awe of, a remote deity regarded as omnipotent (cf. §107, 5, c and [*n*]) and thus, as solely responsible for the world's real imperfections. But such a deity can be recognized as benevolent and worshiped and loved only in the most general of ways, and only as long as human persons and communities, in a childlike manner, acquiesce in natural evil as either unavoidable or deserved. However, once human beings begin to wake up *morally* (as they should), the reality of undeserved suffering is bound to become a huge challenge to faith in God. This marks the end of the "rather elementary god, who awarded prizes, imposed sanctions, or pardoned mistakes, and who, in his goodness, treated people like perpetual children" (Emmanuel Lévinas, "To Love the Torah More than God," in F. J. van Beeck, *Loving the Torah More than God?* p. 37).

[*u*] Often, this world view inspires fights against cosmic evil with every available scientific and technological means. Theologically, it matters little whether such fights are motivated by an atheistic protest against God (as in the case of Dr. Rieux in Albert Camus' *The Plague*), or by an eagerness to prove that we are "on God's side" in the fight against antagonistic forces in the world (as in the cases of "wars" waged on disease and undesirable ideologies, or of the undiscerning use of every possible medical technology to "save life"). Both stances are humanly and morally inadequate, on two grounds. Firstly, humanity is *not* innocent, and fighting evil with every weapon and with the best of intentions will not make it so (as Tarrou in *The Plague* realizes). Secondly, humanity's integral relatedness to God is a matter, not just of cosmology (that is, of *dependence* on divine omnipotence undergirding natural process) but also of anthropology and natural theology (that is, of *participation* in God's attributes and of *aspiration* to seek the most high God in and above all created things; cf. §102, 10; §103, 1). The consciousness of the former impels us to be discerning and to make free *choices*, as God's responsible partners in the world; the latter disposes us, ultimately, to *abandon* ourselves to God's care, and thus to accept everything, whether good *or evil*, as a possible way to God.

Seen in this perspective, unbelief sparked by cosmic mishap has a positive prognosis: it can be an occasion for the development of "the full maturity of the integrally responsible person," capable of stewardship in both action and endurance, and prepared to "feel, on his shoulders, all of God's responsibilities."[39] Such a seasoned faith in God implies the burden of responsibility; still, far from being an affront to human dignity, the burden is a privilege—one that enhances human maturity and hence, one that demands that those relatively mature in faith help bear the burdens of the less mature.

[c] We have argued that there is a real continuity between the blind violence wielded by the cosmic play of large numbers to which humanity has been exposed since its emergence, and the irresponsible, merciless loss of moral vision involved in humanity's historic violations of human dignity. Yet in integrally anthropological terms, we have argued, there is a decisive discontinuity in all of this as well: in human sin, blind violence is not just something passively undergone but something positively adopted, in various degrees of deliberation and intentionality. In light of this insight, we can better appreciate a positively Christian, theological affirmation. Both cosmic disaster and human sinfulness culminate in an historic feat of blind violence (violence all the blinder for being premeditated and all the more violent for having no resistance to overcome) inflicted on humanity at its most sensitive, aware, attractive, and innocent: the harassment and execution of Jesus, who had "done nothing wrong" (Lk 23, 41; cf. §113, 3, j) [v].

---

[v] In insisting on a *history of sin* as the context for the understanding of original sin, Piet Schoonenberg has also been one of the first Catholic theologians to suggest, in a seminal book of enduring importance, that the historical rejection of Jesus is a better paradigm of sin than Adam's sin (cf. *Man and Sin*, pp. 24, 101, 178–79, 195–96). This, incidentally, is consistent with the fact that the central significance that Paul accords to Adam's sin (a theme unknown in the Jewish Scriptures) is dependent on his conception of Christ as the new Adam. In this context it is gratifying to note that the *Catechism of the Catholic Church* does not hesitate to call the execution of Jesus "the greatest moral evil ever committed"—an affirmation which, to my knowledge, no previous magisterial document has ever made, or at least made so unequivocally. Interpreting Jesus' rejection as the culmination of sin may also help shake some Christians out of a self-indulgent habit: cherishing the suffering and death of Jesus' as gestures of God's redeeming love to the point where thankfulness for divine love perversely turns into a glorification of suffering and death. The harassment and execution of Jesus was and remains an appalling crime, made fruitful only by *his acceptance* of it, at our violent hands, in total self-abandon to a God who is greater than our sins. In this final, unconditional act of acceptance of the human condition, including humanity's inhumanity, Jesus truly becomes the embodiment of God's own compassionate embrace of us sinners, to be fully revealed in his resurrection. Consequently, any thankful Christian appreciation of God's mercy and compassion should lead not to

[4] Once again we have arrived at a point where cosmology and anthropology are turning into theology. On account of natural evil, humanity, along with all the human and religious values it embodies and promises, is in jeopardy, at least cosmologically speaking. Nevertheless, speaking both anthropologically and theologically, humanity is hardly entitled to complain about the risks involved in its cosmic existence. None of us are in a position to indulge in self-pity, let alone in self-justification. To be fully human (that is, fully true to God), we must take moral responsibility for an a-moral cosmos.

This is a daunting proposition when viewed in personal or even in communal terms, so much so that it may make us morally irresolute. But this is precisely where the great Jewish and Christian traditions can come to the rescue, for they embody and make habitually available to us the consciousness of cosmic responsibility understood as a high, if daunting, privilege. For they conceive of God as utterly transcendent over the universe, as well as wholly immanent in it. Thus, far from excusing humanity of moral responsibility, on God's behalf, for a world and a humanity charged with unresolved tension and the violence that springs from it, they also encourage the discerning, patient acceptance of an imperfect world (cf. §98, 4, a–d). And if this conception (not surprisingly) involves the recognition that humanity has failed, from time immemorial, to acquit itself fully of its responsibility, both cosmically and morally, the Jewish and Christian traditions have also recognized that God remains faithful as well as infinitely merciful.

This implies that humanity need not carry out its responsibility in its own regard and in regard to the cosmos by power and control alone— by the anxious wielding of technological might or by dint of mere action and reaction (that is, by blind, undiscerning action *against* rival forces, whether human or environmental). It can afford to work *with*

---

an immature, self-centered feeling of relief at our redemption, but to a mature awareness of the inhumanity of the crucifixion and to a conversion to compassion with all those who suffer violence. Sound Christian theology, in other words, offers no grounds for the idealization of human suffering as "salvific" in and of itself. Cf. F. J. van Beeck, *Loving the Torah More than God?* pp. 47–52, 75–77). It was argued earlier on that the recognition of Christ as the *Logos* Incarnate should make Christians more, not less, appreciative of wisdom and virtue as they occur among non-Christians (cf. §23, 3, a; §90, 5, c); analogously, awareness of the evil involved in Jesus' execution should make Christians feel more, not less, sensitive and responsive to evil and injustice in the world at large (and in particular, for the age-old injustices done to the Jews). Incidentally, on the subject of Jesus' sinlessness, John A.T.Robinson's treatment (*The Human Face of God*, pp. 88–98) remains one of the more convincing ones. For a listing of the New Testament evidence, cf. John P. Meier, *A Marginal Jew*, vol. 2, p. 184, n. 4.

things human and the cosmos, both of them interpreted in the light of responsible faith—that is, by searching for, and embracing, reasonable moral norms. These norms embody, proximately, the human transcendence over cosmic process; ultimately, they represent what is right by God's creative ordinance (§98, 5).

At this point, let us briefly pause to review our argument. We have found ourselves invited to interpret, first of all, natural evil in anthropological (that is, potentially moral) terms, and, secondly, natural *and* moral evil in theological terms. First of all, therefore, it is part of human maturity to perceive, both in natural disaster and in human violence and depravity, a call to discerning, responsible, and healing *participation* on behalf of God, whose representative humanity is. But, secondly, a fuller maturity invites us to adopt an even more radically theological stance: *compassion.* As we suffer the brunt of violence, we must learn how to discern, in and below the surface of both natural and moral evil, imperfect creation's and imperfect human beings' impotent yet ineradicable yearning for God—their anguished plea for unceasing growth and development, and for a definitive release from the welter of the forces of decomposition and entropy.

[5] Pierre Teilhard de Chardin's theological convictions are an imposing example of the kind of interpretation just suggested. His view of cosmic failure enables him, in the deeply moving appendix to *The Phenomenon of Man,* to recognize that the "evil of disorder and failure" is found everywhere in the universe, from the most basic levels of cosmic development right up to its pinnacle: self-conscious humanity. But he also succeeds in interpreting failure with the help of wholly anthropological criteria—that is, *as a threat to humanity and its highest aspirations.* Thus he can write:

We have seen that, right up into the realms of reflection, the World process unfolds by dint of chance, groping to find a way. Now just on this score alone, right up into the human domain (which is where, admittedly, the peril is best controlled): how many failures over against one success, — how many afflictions over against one delight, — how many sins over against one single saint . . . At the outset, there is the simple physical non-configuration or mis-configuration at the level of Matter; but right away, there is the suffering ingrafted upon the sentient Flesh; and even higher up, there is the malice or the torment of the Spirit, self-examining and making choices: statistically, at every degree of evolution, always and everywhere, there is Evil, inexorably fashioning and refashioning itself in us and around us! . . . This is the toll exacted, with no possibility of appeal, by the play of the large numbers operating at the heart of a Multiplicity that is in process of being organized.

And surveying, in a sweeping gesture of compassion, the precarious cosmic prehistory of humanity and its continuing struggle, not only for survival, but also for authentic growth and development, he takes another giant step and concludes:

One way or another, it is obvious, even to the gaze of a simple biologist, that nothing looks so much like a way of the Cross as the saga of humanity.[40]

In this second passage, Teilhard de Chardin takes a critical step. His interpretation of the cosmos does not stop at anthropology; it is fully theological as well as thoroughly Christian. If it suffers from anything, it suffers from the dramatic foreshortening that characterizes the intuitive and the visionary. In theological argument, we wisely take our steps a bit more deliberately—that is, more consecutively. Let us try.

[6] The central thesis of Teilhard's entire work is theological: the universe is marked by the person of Christ, both originally and definitively (Col 1, 15–17; cf. §59, 5–6); it is in and through the humanity of Jesus Christ that God is taking the universe to its final completion. But this has repercussions in anthropology and cosmology. The condition for the possibility of Christ's appearance is hominization—the emergence of humanity. In retrospect, therefore, on account of the painful emergence of humanity, the entire sweep of infra-human evolutionary process has been involved, however provisionally and indirectly, in a qualitatively different relationship with God. The distinctive dignity of the noosphere lies in its being *immediately* open, freely and consciously, to the transcendent creativity and graciousness of the living God. Now, through the mediation of humanity as a cosmic phenomenon, the entire infra-human cosmos turns out to be laboriously striving to gain access to, and thus to find its fulfillment in, a stability and harmony that are not naturally open to it. In this way, cosmic process, in and of itself purblind and only haphazardly coordinated, weighed down by entropy, and rife with failure and natural evil, is finding itself recognized, guided, embraced, and integrated into a transcendent destiny. Yet this destiny surpasses not just the mere chances of cosmic process, but even humanity's own precarious attempts at spiritual transcendence over cosmic process. The world's destiny is superhuman. It is strictly supernatural. It is beyond humanity from beginning to end; it is the gift that eludes human comprehension at the end of the way as much as the inner attunement to it has eluded human comprehension from the outset. It can only be accepted, and even the acceptance is gift. It is the living, infinitely good (that is, infinitely self-communicating)

God. Only in existing purely in praise of God does the cosmos find fulfillment.

Thus, quite strikingly, a consistently evolutionary world picture like Teilhard's enables us to retrieve, in a new fashion, the *all-encompassing eschatological vision* of Saint Paul. In his vision, mediated by the conception of a final justice that includes the resurrection of the flesh (cf. §39), anthropology and cosmology are reconciled in an ultimately theological perspective. The emancipation of the world from its inherent bondage to misarrangement and frustration has become inseparable from the liberating divinization extended by God to a sinfully misguided humanity beset by death and extinction. Having been wearied all too long by cosmic misery both inflicted and self-inflicted, and having suffered even more keenly from the fear that the effort and the trouble of the human spirit just might be pointless and of no avail, humanity has now, in the resurrection of Jesus Christ, been given grounds to live by a hope that embraces and outsuffers and outweighs all misery, purposelessness, and violence:

I judge that the afflictions of the present age do not compare with the glory whose revelation is to come upon us. For creation's eager longing is for the anticipated revealing of God's children; for creation was made subject to frustration, not willingly, but by the design of the One who thus subjected it, in the hope that creation itself will be set free, out of the bondage to decay, and into the freedom which is: the glory of God's children.

(Rom 8, 19–21)

[7] Here we have retrieved one of the central elements in the great Tradition. The Christian life, it was explained long ago, is essentially transitional (§76): the community of faith moves from a natural state which only God can originate to a fullness of grace that is only God's to bestow. The great Tradition cannot but be aware of the massive accidents and failures and sins that beset the journey's blessings; but it can travel under these discouraging conditions because it feels in its very soul the attraction of an embrace held out by a transcendent God who encompasses all. In fact, the promise of this embrace enables the Tradition to accept and cherish both the blessings and the failures, and to carry them along with itself, transformed by the very act of carrying, into the sanctuary, as the very stuff of the holiness to come (cf. §36, 3). Accordingly, Jewish-Christian eschatology does not pick and choose; it embraces all of humanity and the entire cosmos, along with all the good and all the evil they entail, for

the Church, to which we are all called in Christ in which we attain holiness by God's grace, will reach its completion only in the glory of heaven, when the time for the restoration of all things will come [cf. Acts 3, 21], and when, along with the human race, the whole world, too, which is intimately linked with humanity and attains its goal through it, will be perfectly established in Christ [cf. Eph 1, 10; Col 1, 20; 2 Pet 3, 10–13].

(LG 48)

This eschatology also sustains a theological position that lies at the heart of the great Tradition: the course of the universe, and of humanity in it, is reliably guided by *divine Providence*.

[§118] ABANDON TO DIVINE PROVIDENCE

[1] In adopting this position, the Christian community is carrying forward a Jewish conviction—one seasoned especially during the Exile. It holds that, if we entrust ourselves to a restless cosmos (and we do, under God) and take our responsibility amidst the bewildering course of world history (and we do, at God's word), we can do so only because all things are in the hands of a God who is unfathomable—that is to say, transcendently good. In professing this conviction, the great Tradition is also the heir of Platonic and Stoic exhortations to mature equanimity, based on the idea that the course of the universe, erratic as it may seem, is in the last resort good and meaningful.[41]

[2] The doctrine of divine Providence appeals directly to God's utter transcendence (which, of course, implies God's presence to everything that is). But for that very reason, it is intellectually and affectively coherent only if it is kept united with its attitudinal counterpart which is squarely mystical: the habit of *total abandon to God, and specifically to God's transcendent goodness, in all the contingencies of human life* [w]. In accordance with this, one of the earliest truly authoritative spiritual di-

---

[w] A deeply mature account of the conjunction between divine Providence and total abandon is a treatise by the saintly French Jesuit Jean Pierre de Caussade (d. 1751). It was put together by the sisters of the Convent of the Visitation at Nancy, on the basis of notes taken at de Caussade's conferences and quotations from his letters to the community's superior. Heavily edited to avert the charge of quietism, it was first published in 1861, by Henri Ramière, S.J., under the title *L'abandon à la providence divine* (ET *Abandonment to Divine Providence* or *The Sacrament of the Present Moment*); in 1966, Michel Olphe-Gailliard finally published the original text. De Caussade himself was occasionally suspect in his lifetime; in a book published anonymously ten years before his death, entitled *Instructions spirituelles en forme de dialogues sur les divers états d'oraison suivant la doctrine de M. Bossuet* (ET *Spiritual Instructions on the Various States of Prayer*), he carefully explains the difference between quietism and genuine abandon. For a capable short treatment of de Caussade, cf. Aelred Squire, *Asking the Fathers*, pp. 214–23.

rectors and teachers of prayer, Evagrius Ponticus (cf. §111, 5), can write:

What is good other than God? Then let us leave to Him everything that concerns us, and it will be well with us. For the One who is wholly good is also a giver of good gifts.[42]

[3] This total abandon to God, the Christian tradition claims, is a responsible and intellectually consistent attitude inspired by eschatological hope. Still, the question arises, What distinguishes total abandon from intellectual, moral, and spiritual laziness and irresponsibility?[43] The key to an answer to this question, it would seem, lies in the maturity of the discretionary stances that precede and undergird the total abandon. At an initial, fairly immature ("pistic") level of experience, it is both reasonable and responsible simply to *depend* on God as the transcendent Supporter of the ordinary dependability of the cosmos that supports us. However, in situations where cosmic structures prove to be hazardous or downright undependable, such simple abandon to divine intervention could well be not a gesture of faith, but an act of either presumption or despair.

In situations of ordinary distress, therefore, a maturer ("charismatic") faith in God demands that we live by the use of intelligence and will—the faculties by virtue of which we *participate in* God's spiritual perfections. Since these faculties enable us to be God's discerning and deliberate *partners*, we cannot mindlessly relinquish the task of enhancing and correcting the cosmos and the conditions of humanity when they turn out to be threatening.

[4] Still, in the final analysis neither cosmic process nor human responsibility will succeed in assuring us of divine Providence, on two counts. The first and fundamental reason is this: it may very well be that the infra-human cosmos' knack for meaningful and productive combination and humanity's gift of intelligent and careful management and foresight may point to a provident God. Still, even at their best they can only *suggest* the radical response of total self-abandon— they do not make it the clear and compelling option. Secondly, we have to acknowledge that the experience of the actual conditions of existence makes the case for abandon to divine Providence less, not more, persuasive. The cosmos as we have come to know it only too well is shot through with randomness, accidental mishap, and natural evil; indeed, humanity itself has been an embarrassing source of both cosmic violence and injury to itself. Under these conditions it is hard

to accept that a good, perfectly trustworthy God is reliably guiding the course of humanity and the cosmos, or at least that God is doing so in any readily observable way. No wonder the human spirit, worried and easily drawn into self-absorption at the best of times, finds itself positively dissuaded from the kind of abandon that would give unconditional glory to God in all things.

Before it can venture that final, decisive step into naked ("mystical") faith, therefore, the human spirit must come both to accept itself and to embrace the cosmos and humanity at every juncture *as they are*—that is to say, at once noble and attractive, and riddled with failure and sin. Only on that condition can it turn them as well as itself into a living offering to God. To do so, humanity must draw upon its own deepest potential: its transcendental attunement to the living God who remains hidden. This deep-seated, immanent attunement gently but persistently urges us to take that final step: willingly to entrust our integral selves, along with all that we and other human beings have ever understood and loved, and with all we and they have ever misunderstood and failed to love, to God's gracious care, on the strength of God's gracious promise alone. This is the ultimate step—the discerning step beyond all reason and the free step beyond all will. It is the step into the worshipful darkness of learned ignorance, selfless love, willingness to serve all others and the whole world solely in recognition of God's will, even if this should involve the acceptance of suffering and death. It is the self-abandonment that is capable of turning the appalling riddle of inevitable death into an appealing mystery. It is available only on the strength of the living God's paradoxical (as well as gracious) assurance that fullness of life and authentic identity are its reward. No wonder total abandonment to God never turns into a firm position, let alone a possession; it remains elusive—an endless gift [x].

[5] The classical doctrine of divine Providence has an immediate consequence for the Christian view of the mature life. The world and humanity are indeed made for both our self-actualization and our enjoyment: still, both self-actualization and enjoyment would be immature and incomplete if life were not also, at least in a substantial sense, a *paideusis*—a school of self-discipline in the service of obedience and total abandon to God.

---

[x] The attentive reader will have noticed that this analysis parallels the accounts of *docta ignorantia* in §§66–67 and of the mystical ascent in §107, 1; 4, and in §109, 10–12.

[a] Before the advent of Christianity, this had long been a central and widespread theme in Mediterranean antiquity, which contributed so strongly to the spirituality of Hellenistic Judaism. The latter distilled its conception of suffering as a form of divine education both from the classical Jewish idea that God uses suffering by way of correction of human waywardness (cf. Deut 8, 5; 2 Sam 7, 14; Prov 3, 11–12; Job 5, 17–18), and from the Greco-Roman notion that suffering serves to test the soul, and thus to refine and ennoble it. Understandably, the New Testament continues and expands this late Jewish tradition, especially in Paul's Letter to the Romans (Rom 5, 3–5), the Letter of James, the *prima Petri*, the Letter to the Hebrews (Heb 12, 4–12; cf. Rev 3, 19), and Luke–Acts. All of these writings, each in its own distinctive ways, interpret suffering as a necessary school of endurance: patient perseverance is an essential feature not only of the truly human life, but also, and especially, of the life of Jesus (Heb 5, 8), which Christians are called to imitate.[44]

[b] It comes as no surprise, therefore, that *paideusis* became a central feature in the spirituality of the ascetical communities from the late third century onward, critical of the comfortable, acculturated Christianity of the city churches. No amount of civilization, foresight, and care, so the Desert Fathers maintain, will completely eliminate natural evil, mishap, and human sin. But rather than getting inflated with indignant pride and putting the blame for our troubles on God or on other persons, and rather than afflicting ourselves and others by the waging of fruitless battles or the making of impossible demands, let us turn inward. There we will discover the root of our anguish: persistent, self-serving willfulness. To tame this immature and dangerous instinct for arrogant self-assertion, we must learn how to accept realistically, to embrace, and sometimes even to actively confront, the intractability of the elements and the afflictions of the flesh ("famine, plague, drought, diseases, wars"[45]). Life in a world of mishaps and misfortunes and among flawed human beings is a mixed blessing, affording plenty of occasions for *askēsis*—spiritual exercise. But for all that, nothing on earth is utterly and unequivocally bad, and so, "Life remains a blessing / Although you cannot bless."[46] Only God is wholly and simply good, and those who trust in this God cannot but believe that everything that happens to them is ordained to the good and for the benefit of their souls. In this perspective, we learn how to accept even the moral disarray of our own spirit; as we learn how to notice the embarrassing surges of

temptation inside our bodies and minds and to make our peace with them, we learn the humility and patience that will make us discerning, kind, and compassionate (cf. §54, 5, d, [o]; cf. also §90, 5, d). Thus we are enabled to turn the pangs of anxiety into growing-pains, and the temptation to self-centered unbelief into a test of mature faith.

[c] Curiously but fortunately as well, this central piece of desert asceticism was to find its way into the everyday life of the Christian community at large. In late antiquity in the West, the channels of this spirituality were (curiously) monks and ascetics. The desire for a more principled Christian life had driven their third- and fourth-century predecessors in the East out of the all too broad-minded city churches and into the monasteries; now their successors in the West came back with a vengeance, to become the preachers, teachers, the bishops of urban communities, starting in what is now Southern France.[47] Eventually, under the impulse first of the *Devotio Moderna*, and subsequently of the twin Jesuit ideals of "restraining the will" and "finding God in all things" [y], this ascetical tradition succeeded in producing such a thoroughly modern, winsome, deeply mortified gentleman-bishop as Saint François de Sales (1567–1622), to whom the Jesuit Jean Pierre de Caussade, a century later, was to be substantially indebted in turn. In his *Introduction to the Devout Life*, Saint François explains that the pursuit of holiness is open to all Christians of good will and holy desire; that it is self-defeating to fight the circumstances of one's life; that it is far more profitable to pick such devotions as will fit one's circumstances; that the presence of God can be found in everything—in every situation, and in good fortune as well as in adversity.

---

[y] The works of St. Dorotheus of Gaza occupy a strategic place in this transition from the desert to the modern city. Why? Of all the Desert Fathers, Dorotheus is the least impressed by bodily penances and austerities, and the most insistent on the restraining of self-will as the key to both union with God and kindness toward others. Thus he can write (Letter 2, §187, 11–16; *SC* 92, pp. 502–04): "Conquer yourself in everything and check your will, and once you have become, by the grace of Christ, routinely accustomed to checking it, you will continue to do it effortlessly and without stress, with the result that what happens will always agree with you. For you 'will not will things to happen as you want them to, but you will will them the way they happen,' and thus you will live peaceably with all." The quotation is almost literally taken from Epictetus, but Dorotheus has replaced the original's squarely Stoic conclusion "you will prosper" (*Manual*, 8; ed. Oldfather, vol. II, p. 490) by the Christian ideal of hope: seeking to be at peace with all. Incidentally, it is significant that St. Dorotheus was the only Desert Father Jesuit scholastics in the late sixteenth and early seventeenth centuries were allowed to read.

[6]   Trust in God's Providence, therefore, involves the principled refusal, based on responsible faith in God, to blame or try to punish either God or anybody or anything in the outside world for the occurrence of human inadequacy or human suffering, especially our own. That is, abandon to Providence involves the *acceptance of the cosmos and humanity itself* as good things shot through with evil, and hence, of the civilized, moral, human, Christian life as a pedagogy.

This position is difficult to accept today. We are part of a culture that insists, at every turn, on fixing, correcting, and combating what it considers imperfect or evil, often in technologically advanced ways. We will have to come back to this, both in this chapter and later on. But before we do so, let us at least briefly ponder, in explicit terms, a proposition about evil which has been tacitly assumed throughout this chapter. It is an encompassing one, for it matches the all-inclusiveness of Jewish-Christian eschatology. Equally importantly, it is supported, at least implicitly, by the common consent of humanity. It is this: *since the occurrence of failure is coextensive with the cosmos, evil is universal.*

[§119] THE UNIVERSALITY OF EVIL

[1]   It is Paul's explicit contention, in the Letter to the Romans, that moral evil (and hence, estrangement from God) enslaves both Jews and Gentiles, and hence all of humanity, whose sinful predicament, leading to death, is summed up in the figure of Adam (cf. esp. Rom 1, 18–2, 24; 5, 12. 15–21). This universalist vision of sin is matched by the universal offer of justification by faith in Jesus Christ, holding out the promise of everlasting emancipation from the power of death. In Paul's vision, this anthropological vision of salvation is set against a backdrop of cosmology: in its own way, all of creation is yearning for a liberation as definitive as humanity's. No wonder that Paul, when commending Abraham's exemplary faith, can adopt an anthropological-cosmological perspective and write that "the God in whom he believed" is the One "who makes the dead come to life and calls into being the things that do not exist" (Rom 4, 17; cf. Ps 33, 9).

[a]   A book like the Apocalypse offers a very different picture, yet one as universalistic as Paul. It evokes a solemn, heavenly victory liturgy of all those redeemed by Christ and gathered into the New Jerusalem, which takes place in the setting of "a new heaven and a new earth. " In this renewed creation (cf. Gen 1, 1), the forces of

chaos—the abysmal waters of Gen 1, 2—have vanished: "And the sea was no more" (Rev 21, 1).

[2] It would be easy to multiply biblical instances of this cosmic, all-encompassing vision of salvation, both from the Jewish Scriptures (especially Third Isaiah) and the New Testament. Nor is it surprising that this eschatology should be reflected in the great Creeds. As we have argued, the Christian profession of faith is compatible with, and indeed invites, a natural theology with a universalist appeal, on account not only of its profession of God's universal creatorship and its positive eschatology, but also of the fact that it addresses itself as a message of salvation to humanity and the world at large (§59, 4–6). The same can be said of the patristic doctrine of redemption, one of whose essential elements is the restoration of the integrity of the whole universe by Christ's victory over sin, death, and the powers of evil.[48]

[a] In the present context it is pertinent to recall an observation made long ago. Christianity and Judaism are not alone in claiming that their professions of faith match the objective world-order universally accessible to humanity (§61, 1). All the world's great religions make universalist claims, explicitly or implicitly. They all offer encompassing interpretations of human life in the world, and of the world itself. We must now add that both in the Jewish and Christian traditions and in the great religions this cosmic order is both marked and marred by the all-pervasive presence of evil as a power—an awareness especially prominent in Buddhism, which regards the universality of evil as the first of the "Four Noble Truths."

In the cosmographies of many religious cultures, evil involves the intense participation of invisible hierarchies of evil spiritual beings; but in most (if not all) of them, the picture is cosmological-anthropological: the visible cosmos, in and of itself, offers and obtrudes itself to human concupiscence and sinfulness to the point of positive seduction, while the human community, for its part, adulterates the pristine condition of the cosmos by dint of sin and transgression. Much as cosmic violence and human lawlessness are morally distinct, they are inextricably intertwined. This invites two short reflections.

[b] In *tribal* civilizations and "closed" societies, *outsiders* are typically regarded as the embodiment of most of what is wrong and contaminated in the world. Yet even there it is always somehow realized that human existence is made precarious by alien elements *within* the family or the tribe—a realization driven home by the occurrence of

sickness, suffering, unexpected death, ritual and moral transgression. Evil, therefore, exists not just among outsiders, but among insiders as well. Ominously, life at home contains a troubling ingredient of exile. Accordingly, no matter how much observances may uphold and celebrate such communities' identity and nobility in relation to its world and to the invisible powers that are part of it, the good life is experienced as perpetually threatened; it must be kept up and restored in the teeth of threats of invasion—overt in the form of cosmic violence and foreign enemies, and covert in the form of moral or ritual degeneracy at home. Part and parcel of these efforts at maintenance are prayers, sacrifices, and purification rituals practiced in deference to cosmic powers. "Primitive" religious observances, in other words, are often eloquent professions of an implicit belief in the universality of evil and cosmic malevolence [z].

[c] The evidence of firm convictions about the all-pervasiveness of evil in "open" civilizations, guided by universalist religious philosophies, is much more elusive, yet (upon reflection) far from absent. We can think here of classical Stoicism, but even more of the Enlightenment, to which modern Western culture remains so deeply indebted. The religious and philosophical point of departure of these non-tribal cultural systems is optimistic, universalist, and inclusivist. Still, this very world-view gives rise to a curious dynamic. For on the one hand, apprehensiveness about survival in the cosmos and worry about human evil and sin have been replaced by optimism and enlightened egalitarianism; the cosmos is intelligible and of one piece, and so is humanity. It is granted, of course, that there exist imperfections due to finitude; still, in the last resort, the world is good and the alien element in it is not overpowering. Leibniz' assurance that we are living in a world as perfect as any world can be is a typical instantiation of this mind-set; given the perfection and goodness of the Creator, it is a priori reasonable (and hence, universally acceptable) that the actual world, taken as a whole, is also "the best possible world."[49]

---

[z] These ridiculously sketchy remarks are meant to honor, not dismiss, a vast and important body of literature in comparative religion which I have not studied. But I did find Mircea Eliade's chapter on "Misfortune and History" in *The Myth of Eternal Return* (pp. 93–137), and his sobering interpretation of the relative irrelevance of the "Sky Gods" to daily life in *Patterns in Comparative Religion* (pp. 38–123) very stimulating. And last but far from least, I have found *The Symbolism of Evil*, by Paul Ricoeur (who *has* studied the pertinent materials) a treasure house of insight on the subject of the ubiquity of cosmic and human evil.

This cheerful understanding, however, is apt to raise problems of its own. Rationally sophisticated cultures typically tend to *idealize* uncultivated Nature and uncultured Natives; they are apt to regard civilization as an exercise in insincerity, pretense, and prejudice; they will decry it as unnatural and barbaric; the purely natural (so they will often suggest) put the civilized to shame. That darling of the Enlightenment, the noble savage, neither guilt-ridden nor evil-ridden—what a lesson he is for all of us, so estranged from the wholesomeness of Nature and the simple virtues of genuine Humanity!

In this way, optimism about the world and human nature turns around to attack those who have embraced it. The civilized turn out to be untrue to the faith they profess; the theme of evil reappears, with a vengeance. In the idealized world picture of cheerful enlightenment, evil (both of the cosmic and the ethical, human variety) becomes both persistent and (as a matter of intellectual principle) a meaningless, pointless "something that need not be." From there, of course, *il n'y a qu'un pas* to the self-defeating idea that natural evil and human failure "should not be," soon followed by the resentful thesis that they simply "should not have to be." At this point, evil is no longer acknowledged as just universal and all-pervasive; it has also become intrinsically unacceptable—an intolerable enemy that only spoils and contaminates the world and humanity as such. That is, *finite being itself* is now being experienced as *unacceptable*. In such an interpretative framework, "to exist" is apt to be experienced as "to be defeated by the nature of things cosmic as well as one's own nature," with death as the final defeat. The universality of evil, first denied by dint of naturalistic optimism, has, in the end, come home to roost in the form of discontent, not to say resentment.

[3] Let us sum up. *All* things cosmic, including human individuals and communities of relative innocence, are naturally unstable and precarious, and hence, susceptible to *cosmic* mishap—a fact that causes dreadful suffering in the human domain. But conversely, all things cosmic, innocent as they are, naturally lend themselves to involvement in, accession to, and complicity with humanity's own proven penchant for spiritual degeneracy and its positive sinfulness. Ever since humanity's emergence, things cosmic have naturally moved human desire, whether by appeal or repulsion; and since concupiscence is the shape of our desire, things cosmic have disturbed our balance and prompted us to go where, at least in our best moments, we did not really want to go. That is, things naturally good will always *tempt* us and natural evils

will always *test* us; and since natural good and natural evil are notoriously hard to tell apart, being tempted and being tested are too [*aa*].

In any case, the fact that genuine sin *can* occur at all in the world is rooted, ultimately, in natural finitude. On the cosmic side, the natural goodness of the world and everything in it is limited—shot through with natural evil both potential and actual. On the human side, in the world as we know it, both humanity's natural instability and its positive sinfulness will seize upon the finitude that it has in common with the world, to turn what is merely finite into the stuff of pointlessness and sin. Thus evil is universal: both the cosmos and humanity groan under the weight of frustration—both the impending threat of it and the actuality of it.

Evil, and especially evil of the persistent kind, puts the cosmos and humanity to a most severe test. Yet theologically speaking, this is no excuse for non-acceptance, condemnation, and rejection (cf. §113, 4). Let us close this chapter with an exploration of one aspect of this proposition that would seem particularly relevant to the culture we live in.

[§120] COSMIC VIOLENCE AS A CALL TO DISCERNING PATIENCE

[1] Père Teilhard's awareness of the hazards involved in cosmic process marks him as a modern scientist; his eschatological confidence marks him as a Christian. Still, at least as importantly, his keen awareness of the amount of human failure in the world (including moral failure) and of the suffering caused by it identify him as a child of the modern era. Our century has become aware of the extent to which the human quest for control of things both cosmic and human, whether accidentally or (more ominously) by design, has frustrated human aspiration and done violence to human well-being. Two world wars, the massacre of the Armenians, a Holocaust, two cities wiped out by atomic bombs, the threat of a nuclear holocaust, a murderous *Gulag* system and a *ditto* Cultural Revolution, the nagging intractability of global tension caused by blatant injustice, and ominous symptoms of worldwide ecological imbalance caused by human carelessness and inattention have helped unmask the nineteenth century's *Fortschrittsglaube*[50] as an illusion. Not surprisingly, suffering historically inflicted by *human* agency has made us more sensitive to the timeless human suffering caused by *cosmic* process.

[*aa*] Interestingly, both biblical Hebrew and biblical Greek have only one word for "test" and "temptation": *massāh* and *peirasmos*, respectively.

[2] Yet at the same time, we will do well to realize that our sensitivity to failure and suffering is the dark side of what is, and undeniably remains, a spectacular human accomplishment—one ultimately built upon that extraordinary evolutionary development known as hominization. If our knowledge of the physical and biophysical (and, increasingly, the subatomic, genetic, and psychophysical) structures of humanity and the cosmos is often off-balance and uncoordinated, it also has become deep and vast. If our skills in working with these structures and bending them to new purposes often drive us into thoughtlessness, they also have produced countless successes in the management and development of both the cosmos and the natural and social condition of humanity. As a result, and despite significant human failure, we are more persuaded than ever that *natural* failure and evil unquestionably engage humanity's *moral* responsibility. Something like this has, of course, always been the case; the human drive to transcend nature and achieve civilization has always been experienced as a moral imperative (cf. §117, 2). But, far less able to change the world than we are, past generations (and even today, communities less technologically advanced or even simply less interested in "progress") often give the impression of being more given to old-fashioned resignation or faith-abandon or fatalism (or, perhaps, an inextricable combination of all of them). In comparison with them, there is no doubt that the modern era has witnessed a startling and impressive increase in the awareness of humanity's moral responsibility on behalf of both itself and the cosmos—a development welcomed, with appropriate critical empathy, on almost every page of *Gaudium et Spes*, the Pastoral Constitution on the Church in the Modern World proclaimed by Vatican II.

The roots of this increase in moral sense are not far to seek: to a degree unimaginable in a pre-scientific and pre-technological civilization, science and technology have provided feasible and affordable alternatives to fatalism and resignation in the teeth of the forces of cosmic chaos and destruction. Consequently, when it comes to changing and developing the cosmos and humanity's natural and social condition in ways that befit the dignity of the human person, we moderns feel that the application of ever more advanced ingenuity and the deployment of ever more advanced engineering is incumbent on us as a moral and religious imperative. Negligence in remedying horrible natural evils and the human suffering they cause, or acquiescence in them, or even the appearance of failure to try to defend ourselves and others against them: all of these strike us moderns as sinfully irresponsible.

[3] The trouble is that not all zeal is enlightened (cf. Rom 10, 2). Not each and every movement of our moral conscience is a reliable guide (§113, 2). And besides, that most perplexing task, the development of authentic anthropological norms for responsible intervention in cosmic and human systems, is made even more confusing by the dynamics of *concupiscence* (§113, 3, b).

Why is the case? Firstly, natural good and natural evil are hard to tell apart (cf. §115, 5). The sheer multiplicity of combinations thrown at us by the cosmic play of large numbers so overwhelms us that we often merely reciprocate in kind. That is, instead of discerning patterns of coordination and harmony, we react to cosmic processes virtually blindly, whether by mere trial and error or by quick fixing, and not infrequently inspired by resentment and fury. However, to the extent that we do so we fall short of the transcendence that is the source of humanity's authentic mastery of the cosmos and its own destiny in it: our ability to discern and interpret deliberately, and take positions accordingly [*bb*].

Secondly, our own natural desires are not unaffected by history; they are scrambled by failure past and present, to the point where they often misdirect our desire to make responsible choices. In our self-absorption, both individual and social, and in the face of the chaotic features of the cosmos, we will often take our cues from our immediate need for self-maintenance and self-assertion (§112, 4) rather than from right reason—that is, from habits of discernment, realism, and a quiet sense of proportion (cf. 129, 7 and [*j*]). Our technology and the unstated imperatives that guide it tend to take their cue predominantly from *power*—both from the sheer might of cosmic power that faces us and from the nervous excitement that tricks human ingenuity into attempting to defeat it (cf. §107, 5, c, [*n*]). We are far too ready to presume that the generous application of trial-and-error and a certain swiftness of attack are proof of dedication. No wonder Hans-Georg Gadamer can be so critical of "the arrow-straight will," which he regards as characteristic of the scientific-technological mentality, with its faith in the "expert" approach to reality.[51] No wonder, either, that our scientific technological culture often uses fairly crude, compara-

---

[*bb*] There is an affinity between principled pluralism and the glorification of trial and error as a "method" for dealing with humanity and the world, both regarded as cosmic systems. In the name of this pluralism, many in North America will insist that human freedom and intellectual integrity are, in the long run, best warranted by *dispersal*—that is, by the availability of *the widest variety* of ways of thinking and living (cf. *God Encountered*, vol. 2/1, p. xiv).

tively a-moral, and sometimes quite violent strategies to correct the imbalances that necessarily beset the delicate systems that make up humanity and the cosmos. As a result of our faith in "the state of the art" as the most reliable guide to action, we often find ourselves creating, in short-sighted ways, new imbalances. Quite frequently, the latter will prove harder to correct than the ones that first threatened us, if only because accepting responsibility for the latest imbalance is hard: it hurts our pride. So, caught in this awkward predicament of our own devising we find ourselves excusing ourselves and pleading not guilty, because "we tried everything we could"—as if meaning well and trying hard absolves us from moral discernment and the kind of judgment that is the fruit of *phronēsis*: wisdom both acquired by careful practice and tested by it.[52]

[a] The ambiguities that beset the contemporary attitude vis-à-vis *human suffering* demonstrate both the complexity and the urgency of the issue just raised. Physical pain and mental distress may not be the most degrading form of human suffering; they certainly are very immediate ones—they clamor for attention as soon as they are felt or observed. We moderns are more capable than ever of relieving these kinds of suffering, as well as more eager to do so. It is hardly surprising, therefore, that we should have witnessed a widespread increase, especially in the affluent West, in sensitivity to physical and (increasingly also) mental pain. So far so good. The trouble is that suffering and pain, whether natural or induced by human agency, are now often simply regarded as *evil*—that is, as a form of *evil* in its own right (cf. Leibniz's classification of evil: §115, 4, b). And, regardless of this thoughtless identification of pain with evil, many tend to think (or rather feel) that at least what *causes* suffering and pain must be evil.

   J. H. van den Berg has attempted to account for this phenomenon. He has suggested that the modern intolerance of pain is a *historic* development, well documented by the recent history of anaesthesia. For we now not only avail ourselves of anaesthesia in order to be able to benefit from advanced medical and surgical procedures, which admittedly are quite often beneficial; we are also progressively becoming a civilization that kills pain because it simply will not tolerate it. In attempting to account for this latter phenomenon, van den Berg suggests that it is largely self-induced, and that the cultural factor operative in our diminished tolerance for pain is the experience of *sheer multiplicity*.

Van den Berg is not the first to have pointed in this direction. Not long after World War II, the sociologist David Riesman had shown, in a classic monograph entitled *The Lonely Crowd*, that the enormous variety of social demands that characterize modern American life have a disturbing impact on *character*. Life in modern society, van den Berg explains, is not a unified experience; it is riddled with multiplicity. Our daily experiences, especially at work, are juxtaposed rather than coordinated, at odds with each other rather than mutually enhancing—that is, in the terminology used by the great psychiatrist Harry Stack Sullivan, "parataxic" rather than "syntaxic."[53] Ever so many relatively unconnected objects, tasks, and personal affiliations (and, indeed, conflicting ones) habitually demand our simultaneous attention, forcing us to adopt a variety of different *personae* to deal with these multiple demands. This makes it hard for us to develop a firm sense of self and to rely on it habitually, independent of situations; in a situation of culturally induced stress, a personal sense of focus, concentration, and coherence is hard to sustain (cf. §112, 4–5). Now it is the case that modern life (especially modern urban life) simply presumes, on the part of all, a natural ability to live with the inner and outer dissociation and even dissipation brought about by incessant stress. This makes it hard, even in our day-to-day lives, to hang on to a focused understanding of our outside world and a vigorous inner sense of personal integration and identity. But the fact is that the latter two are precisely the necessary preconditions for the ability to put physical pain and mental anguish in perspective and thus to tolerate them in a mature fashion.

No wonder many modern people, pulled apart and distracted as they feel, cannot abide pain, whether in themselves or in others. Accordingly, their attitude in regard to pain remains unexamined; that is, it is predicated mainly on *sentiment*, and frequently detached from every kind of objectivity. But sentiment frequently takes the form not of compassion with others in real pain, but of an ill-focused sense of *pity*—of the kind that regards, in an unspecified fashion, all suffering as something painful and bothersome that simply should not be.[54]

One of the pioneers of psychosomatic medicine, the German physician Hans Müller-Eckhard, has identified this as an illness, whose central symptom is: the inability to be ill. At the heart of this illness, the author emphasizes in his book *Die Krankheit nicht krank sein zu können* ("The illness of not being able to be ill"), lies the refusal to take seriously the fact that human well-being is inseparably connected with human freedom, and hence, with the acceptance of a personal life destiny, with its inevitable ups and downs.

As a matter of fact, many of our contemporaries, their nerves worn thin, regard pain as positively evil—that is, as an unacceptable fact, which, like every other evil, we must do our best to rid ourselves of. They are puzzled (if not downright irritated) by the relative equanimity with which past generations appear to have accepted suffering. This implies that they regard patience as a cop-out. They seem to assume that the only thing needed to deal with the phenomenon of pain is quick, effective intervention; pain, in their minds, stands in no need of reflection, let alone integration or free acceptance. These are dangerous prejudices. They were unknown to a past age, which tended to combine a great tolerance of pain (especially unavoidable pain) with habits of *interpreting* it as an occasion to entertain things more fundamental.

Hans-Georg Gadamer writes of Viktor von Weizsäcker that he "always used to wonder: What does the sickness have to say to the sick person? Not: What does it have to say to the physician? Rather, what does it *want* to say to the sick person? Could it be that the sick person can find help in learning how to ask that question?"[55] Rather than killing pain at the shortest possible notice and at all costs, reflective people will *accept* it in a qualified manner, and thus try to alleviate it (or at least its mental repercussions) by *managing* it [*cc*].

[*cc*] The term "manage" is borrowed from the title of the late John J. Bonica's encyclopedic work *The Management of Pain*—a monument to the sophisticated anaesthesia practices that are part of modern medicine. The work demonstrates how the humane and reasonable response to pain is patient understanding and research; morally speaking, the two handsomely epitomize the search for the golden mean (§123, 2, a) between the indiscriminate, wholesale rejection of the phenomenon of pain as simply evil and unacceptable, and its idealization as a builder of character and a test of moral fibre, exemplified in the alleged stoicism of the noble savage. In regard to the latter, it must be remembered that civilizations proud of their impassiveness and their high tolerance of pain have often cultivated heartlessness and even appalling cruelty (especially in regard to women and outsiders) as if they were virtues. However, the technologically sophisticated West now tends to err in the opposite direction, intolerance of pain. H. B. Gibson's *Pain and its Conquest* (note the connotations of the title!) is a good example of this trend. While readable and interesting from the point of view of popular medicine, as well as expressive of a broadly humane sense of compassion, it provides telling instances of the modern irritation with the very idea of acceptable physical pain—an idea the author characterizes as barbaric and (of course) "medieval." As a result, Gibson's treatment of pain as a *human* issue is undifferentiated and philosophically thin; it reviews historical facts anecdotally rather than interpretatively; it is marred by an annoying and ignorant insistence that Christianity commends and idealizes pain and perversely opposes its alleviation. By contrast, F.J.J. Buytendijk's *Over de pijn* (ET *Pain*) opens with a critical account of the modern intolerance of pain in all its forms, and proceeds to offer a

This management includes, of course, the task of surrounding those suffering pain with care both expert and tender, in hopes of helping them derive wisdom from such pain as cannot be alleviated.

[b] Here we are faced with an ancient moral and religious problem, but one intensified by modernity.

On the one hand, configuration, decombination, and recombination of elements (and hence, physical integration, disintegration, and reintegration) are inherent in humanity's participation in cosmic process and its perpetual and ubiquitous odds. At the most basic level of cosmic mutuality (cf. §115, 8), pain is one very significant way in which we register that participation. Consequently, *living as part of the cosmos and as members of an embodied humanity involves living with pain*; in fact, pain and suffering often bond people together, for better, for worse.

Yet on the other hand, it is clearly a human responsibility to influence adverse cosmic occurrences and to bend them in the direction of meaningfulness (§115, 10). Consequently, *relieving pain is part of the human stewardship in regard to the cosmos and humanity.*

This is a serious dilemma, and one that has been intensified rather than eased by our increased scientific and technological ingenuity. How to deal with it? A few reflections.

[c] At the fundamental level, only the most careful discernment and interpretation will enable us to tell the difference between cosmic good and evil (§115, 5–6). This suggests, at the very least, that we will have to learn, in Gadamer's words, the "laborious task of restraining and directing that arrow-straight will."[56] For will and determination, especially when posturing as noble resolve and professional expertise, are often nothing but forms of hate and resentment in the face of a cosmos that does not readily accommodate our immature demands for immediate physical and mental comfort. Accordingly, those who impatiently refuse to suffer are liable to turn violent, as the German psychiatrist Horst Eberhard Richter has recently explained in a profoundly insightful book with the ominous title *Wer nicht leiden will, muß hassen: Zur Epidemie der Gewalt* ("Those who refuse to suffer can only hate: Notes on the epidemic of violence").

---

phenomenological treatment of pain both physiologically and psychologically informed and philosophically and theologically profound. In the process, it succeeds in developing scientifically responsible and humanly mature criteria for both the alleviation of pain and its acceptance.

All this suggests that, as a culture, we will have to learn how to *interpret* pain, and that we must do so in terms of *both good and evil*. That is, it suggests that *pain is not evil in and of itself* any more than enjoyment is good in and of itself. Equally fundamentally, any determination of natural good and evil must occur along integrally anthropological lines (§115, 10, b; 11). This suggests that, before we decide when and how to intervene, we must learn how to differentiate. We must learn to distinguish carefully between pain (whether mental or physical, inflicted from outside or arising from inside) that is unacceptable because it isolates and dehumanizes [*dd*] and pain that is acceptable because it is endurable, or even worth enduring [*ee*]. We may even have to learn (but here we enter the park of mysticism) how to discern pain that is capable of being voluntarily taken on, for the sake of others. And those others may very well be not just victims of violence, but also perpetrators of violence—people positively "ignorant and wayward" (Heb 5, 2). For pain (like enjoyment) is in and of itself capable of holding the promise of growth toward a fuller, more authentic, more communicative humanity. And mature humanity is governed, not by instantaneous, instinctive affects like sentiment and pity, but by affections that transcend the immediate situation, like fortitude and prudence and wisdom—virtues that are the fruit of the integration of painful (as well as joyful) experience.

And beyond this, there looms an even nobler vision: a humanity capable of transcending even the self-conscious, self-asserting ego. Its ruling affects are the varieties of loving self-abandon, such as soli-

---

[*dd*] There are two kinds of "dehumanizing pain": pain suffered and pain inflicted. Some forms of pain suffered, both of the involuntary (*e.g.*, continuing in a vegetative state) and the induced variety (*e.g.*, by harassment or torture) dehumanize those suffering it. But whenever human agents inflict pain without proportionate reason and good purpose (especially if the pain itself is the set purpose of the act of inflicting it, as in the case of harassment and torture), pain always dehumanizes those inflicting it, even if the victim should be an animal.

[*ee*] In view of widespread residual Jansenism and other forms of "dolorism" in some Catholic subcultures, let us point out at once that what has just been explained can be turned (and has been turned) into an irresponsible idealization of suffering as "redemptive" in and of itself, in a "mystical" way (cf. §117, 3, [*v*]). This response to suffering is so unhealthy because it authorizes observers to wish sufferers well in their pain while staying at a safe distance (cf. Jas 2, 15–16). Even worse, it allows detached onlookers to rationalize their refusal to be compassionate by piously pronouncing the sufferers blessed. The authentically Christian understanding of suffering is only available to those who truly believe and act on that belief. On that basis, they will *freely* help relieve such suffering as can be relieved, protest suffering unjustly inflicted on others, and embrace and share such suffering—their own and others'—as cannot be relieved. On this sensitive issue, cf. F. J. van Beeck, *Loving the Torah More than God?* pp. 47–52; 76–77.

darity and compassion, in which pain and love become inseparable. In fact, this vision, however dimly discerned, is an essential predisposition for the appreciation of the ultimate and central "Christian point" and paradox: by God's loving design "the Christ had to suffer these things" (Lk 24, 26).[57]

[4] A passage in Flannery O'Connor's *Introduction to a Memoir of Mary Ann* contains a pointed protest against the modern, largely sentimental intolerance of suffering and pain as unacceptable and evil. Not surprisingly, the protest is based on the specifically Jewish-Christian recognition that *both* the causes of joy *and* the causes of suffering are givens; that both are offered to us for our acceptance, and hence, that both are capable of being interpreted as gifts (cf. §112, 2). What is important, ultimately, is the *meaning* of whatever suffering may occur in a human, Christian life—a life positively devoted, as a whole, to the imitation of Christ, including his voluntary suffering:

The creative action of the Christian's life is to prepare his death in Christ. It is a continuous action in which this world's goods are utilized to the fullest, *both positive gifts and what Père Teilhard de Chardin calls "passive diminishments."*[58]

On this basis she can write, with her customary candor:

One of the tendencies of our age is to use the suffering of children to discredit the goodness of God, and once you have discredited His goodness, you are done with Him. The Aylmers whom Hawthorne saw as a menace have multiplied. Busy cutting down human imperfection, they are making headway also on the raw material of good. Ivan Karamazov cannot believe, as long as one child is in torment; Camus' hero cannot accept the divinity of Christ, because of the massacre of the innocents. *In this popular pity, we mark our gain in sensibility and our loss in vision.* If other ages felt less, they saw more, even though they saw with the blind, prophetical, unsentimental eye of acceptance, which is to say, of faith. In the absence of this faith now, we govern by tenderness. It is a tenderness which, long since cut off from the person of Christ, is wrapped in theory.

And in a rabid overstatement, she takes the measure, both of the appalling mood-swings that human sentiment, left to itself and untempered by objectivity, is capable of, and of the rationalizations which human beings are capable of mustering up in support of such mood-swings:

When tenderness is detached from the source of tenderness, its logical outcome is terror. It ends in forced labor camps and in the fumes of the gas chamber.[59]

[5] All of this tests our new-found sense of moral urgency in the face of cosmic process and the suffering caused by it. It suggests that we should rise to a level of quiet intellectual and moral sophistication proportionate to our vastly increased and differentiated ingenuity in taking on and managing humanity and the cosmos. Precisely because of our superior understanding and powers of control, we can afford to *accept* the given structures of humanity and the cosmos, so as to let them test our fortitude and thus educate us. After all, a humanity that must find its authentic self in the cosmos from which it has emerged (§115, 8–10) must agree to an appropriate measure of cosmic pedagogy [*ff*].

Our very resourcefulness, therefore, now faces us with a fundamental moral choice. *Either* we continue to use our ingenuity immaturely and largely impulsively, as the instrument of our anxious need to exert and assert ourselves in the immediacy of trying cosmic situations, desperately trying to defeat whatever appears to threaten or inconvenience us. *Or* we attempt to avail ourselves of our ingenuity and experience to broaden our vision, and thus to become less anxious, more fearless, more accepting, more patient, and thus, far more focused and deliberate. That is, either we will find ourselves adding much random violence to a world already replete with it, or we will learn habits of interpretation against broader horizons allowing us to decide, in particular instances of natural evil, *whether* to act and *how* to act in a truly humane fashion (cf. §115, 10).

[a] Hans-Georg Gadamer has set forth his ideas on this issue in a collection of essays entitled *Über die Verborgenheit der Gesundheit* ("On the Hiddenness of Health"). He writes with the authority of one who has experienced both serious illness, especially when young, and remarkable health, especially in old age. He also writes with the wisdom gained from lifelong habits of philosophical reflection.

One recurrent theme in his reflections is the distinction between the Greek words *metron* (Gm. *Maß*: "measure") and *metrion* (Gm. *das Angemessene*: "what is fitting"). Objective scientific tests operate by objective assessment; if and when successful, they can *identify illness* by recourse to scientifically established, standard measurements. Still, they can only *approximate* the sense of well-being ("fittingness") that is the sign of health; *they cannot diagnose health*, and even less define it. In this sense health is "hidden"; it is a matter not of clinical

---

[*ff*] One relevant part of this pedagogy could very well be: a patient dialogue between faith and science, and between theology and technology.

observation and measurement, but of an inner sense of well-being, experienced as balance, and expressed in ease of energetic communication with both the world of things and with other persons. Health can no more be reduced to scientific measurements than riding a bicycle with ease and dexterity can be acquired by scientific method.

But if health is not readily measurable and thus hidden, then there is more to pain and disease and illness than meets the scientific eye, and if it is a matter of balance, then healing is only in a very limited sense the product of medical intervention. For there exists no illness apart from some form of health; only the experience of wholeness qualifies us to identify illness. Healing, therefore, is not the *replacement* of illness by health, but the *recovery* of wholeness—a wholeness which, of course, is and remains liable to be thrown off-balance again.

Our civilization is to an appreciable extent the product of the division of labor. The spectacular accomplishments of modern, scientific medicine (where knowledge is taken to be a matter of control) are liable to lead both the physician and the patient to indulge in an overdose of specialized intervention. This, however, will blind both the physician and the patient to the wider, deeper dimension of healing and recovery (which invites the kind of knowledge which is called understanding). Accordingly, in the teeth of a scientific-technological civilization with a tendency to make totalitarian claims and to have a fixation on illness, physicians must first acknowledge the gap between science and genuine *praxis* (which focuses on wholeness), and then proceed to act in such a way as to bridge it. That is, they must learn how to relate their scientific mastery to the patient as a person, by exercising it in the wider context of *conversation* ("Gespräch"). And for their part, patients (and who is not one?) must learn not simply to surrender passively to medical science; they must do so both by cooperating with the healing process. That is, they must take responsibility for their integral health by appropriate ("fitting") habits of self-care. In all of this, what remains fundamental is the Platonic insight that all particular efforts at healing must be embedded in the healer's ability to understand both the whole and the deeper harmonies that inform the whole. That is to say, any healing ability includes the ability to understand the patient as a whole, as well as the environment that is integral to the patient's sense of well-being.[60]

[6] It is time to return to theology in the narrower sense of the term. Failure to appreciate the whole (that is, failure to go beyond the particular) opens unsettling perspectives. Proximately, in the cosmological realm, if we lose sight of the whole, we will find ourselves shortsightedly compounding the natural evil already rife in the cosmos to which we owe our emergence. But beyond it, in the anthropological realm, we will find ourselves procuring the decay of our authenticity as persons; we are natively capable of finding our true selves only to the extent that we attempt to be true both to each other and to the cosmos in which we exist and communicate so gloriously yet so precariously. But most of all, theologically speaking, failure to go beyond the particular forces an appalling perspective upon us. The quotation that opened this chapter must be read in its entirety:

Is there anything more familiar and self-evident (whether explicitly or implicitly) to the self-aware human spirit than this: the wordless questioning that extends beyond all the things already conquered and mastered; the humble, loving sense (that sole origin of wisdom) of having more questions than answers? Down deep, there is nothing we know better than this: our knowledge (that is, what in our everyday lives we call knowledge) is but a small island in a measureless ocean of elements not traversed; it is a floating island, and much as we are more familiar with it than with this ocean, in the last resort it is carried; and only because it is carried can it carry at all. Thus the existential question, put to all those who have knowledge, is this. Which will they love more: the little island of their so-called knowledge, or the sea of measureless mystery? Is the little lantern (we call it science or learning) by whose light they explore this island really going to have to be an endless light, which will forever (but that would be Hell) shine for them?[61]

In this riveting image, Rahner is but conveying, in a contemporary idiom, what the great Tradition has called *sin*, and what the Christian West, in a classical phrase, has defined as *aversio a Deo et conversio ad creaturam*: dissociating oneself from God in the act of (unduly) associating oneself with something created—that is, with something quite particular. This chapter must close with an exploration of this celebrated definition.

AUGUSTINE'S DEFINITION OF SIN

[§121] WILLFULLY TURNING TO CHANGING GOODS, AWAY FROM GOD

[1] Like so many key theological conceptions of the Christian West, the definition just quoted hails from Augustine. It first occurs, fully

orchestrated, in his treatise on free will, *De libero arbitrio*, completed in 391 A.D., the year of his ordination to the presbyterate.

And so it is [Augustine writes] that neither the good things which are the object of sinners' appetites are in any way evil, nor is free will itself, since, we have determined, it is to be accounted one of the indifferent goods [*in bonis ... mediis numerandam*]. But evil [*malum*] consists in the latter's turning away from the unchanging good [*auersio eius ab incommutabili bono*] and its turning toward changing goods [*conuersio ad mutabilia bona*]; however, since this turning away and turning toward is not forced but voluntary, its direct consequence is punishment both just and fitting: misery [*gg*].[62]

The central issue in this forceful statement is the question how it is at all possible for moral evil to result from the combination of two things that are at least relatively good—things made and willed by God: a world full of good creatures and that precious (if precarious) endowment of humanity, free will. Augustine's answer is that human beings *freely and deliberately* choose good things in such a way as (miserably) to estrange themselves from God, whose goodness is undeviating, who made the world good, and who endowed humanity with the capacity for free choice.

So this is moral evil: deliberately choosing to do what is wrong by turning to realities that are unstable and impermanent, away from God, who remains steadfastly faithful, forever. It is a definition that is bewildering in its very clarity. Much later on, in the four chapters of the next installment of this second volume, we will have to explore the *dynamics* left unstated by this definition. At this point, before embark-

---

[gg] I suspect that in this passage Augustine is borrowing from that generally accepted source of public ethics in late Antiquity, Stoicism. Accordingly, I regard the word *medius* as the Latin equivalent of Gk. *mesos*, a synonym of *adiaphoros*, meaning "indifferent" (cf. Diogenes Laertius, *Lives* VII, 102ff. [Zeno]). However, Augustine is also drawing upon a theme of Neo-Platonist origin, namely, the notion that there prevails a permanent tension between what is unchanging and what is changing. While this latter theme is of frequent occurrence in Augustine's works, his definition of evil itself, surprisingly, is not. It was in the later tradition that it gained an acceptance so wide and deep that someone like Aquinas can treat the definition as universally known: he frequently uses it, without hardly ever quoting it as an *auctoritas* from Augustine. Some examples, out of a great many that could be cited, are: *In II Sent.* 30, 1, 3, *in c.*; 42, 1, 3, *ad 5*; *In IV Sent.* 18, 1, 2, *ad 3am, in c.*; *S. Th.* I–II, 73, 3, *ad 2*; II–II, 20, 1, *ad 1*; 162, 6, *in c.*; III, 86, 4, *in c.* and *ad 1*; *Q. D. de Malo* 2, 9, *ad 10*; 13, 2, *ad 6*. Augustine's definition lent itself to fruitful elaborations as well. Aquinas uses it, for instance, to point out that the turning away from God is the *formal*, constitutive element in sin, while the turning toward creatures is the *material* element. The former, of course, is not always fully intentional, while the latter has a broad range of possibilities of varying seriousness; between them, Aquinas often explains, these two insights add up to the distinction between mortal and venial sin.

ing on the next chapter, which will deal with human life understood as a process of being exposed to testing and temptation, let us, by way of general preparation, simply review three passages from Augustine's writings, taken from among many other possible ones. All of them have this in common that they refine his definition of evil and sin, by making explicit some important implications.

[2] In the year 396, the young bishop Augustine wrote a series of replies to questions posed to him by someone many years his senior, Simplicianus, a presbyter in Milan. Many years before, in Rome, Simplicianus had been Ambrose's tutor; when, in 374, his pupil, still a catechumen, had been elected bishop of Milan, he had moved there to become his spiritual advisor. Now aged and much respected, Simplicianus was about to become, upon Ambrose's death in 397, his successor in the see of Milan.

In the course of one of his answers, Augustine explains how he understands the phrase "turning away from the unchanging good." He writes:

The essence of human sin is lack of order amounting to perversion, for it consists in a turning away from the more eminent [*præstantiore*] Creator and a turning toward lesser [*inferiora*] creatures.[63]

To appreciate Augustine's point, we must notice the two comparatives in the text. They are to be interpreted, not statically, but dynamically—that is, as meaning "ever-more-eminent" and "ever-lesser." Augustine uses them to convey the ceaseless dynamics of morality and immorality. This can be developed in two ways.

[a] Unlike any and all creatures, God is transcendently and undeviatingly good. Accordingly, Godself is and remains the abiding principle and point of reference of any moral order that may prevail or be made to prevail in the world. Accordingly, Augustine must not be taken to regard sin as a straightforward choice *between*, on the one hand, the utterly transcendent God regarded as the highest good offered to our free choice, and, on the other hand, one or more of the countless created goods regarded as forbidden, or at least of lower rank [*hh*].

[*hh*] This conception would also be quite primitive theologically; if our choice were *between* the one unchanging God and the many changing goods, this would imply that God and created things can be treated as *comparable* goods. Augustine's point is precisely that treating God and created things as comparable entities lies at the

Rather, what Augustine means is this. God is transcendent—that is, always greater (cf. §96, 6). Accordingly, our awareness of, and duty toward, God puts *all* our choices of relative, changing goods in a moral perspective. That is to say, right choices are choices that respect and enhance the order inherent in the world and humanity, as well as their orientation to the transcendent God; in freely making these choices, we will find ourselves turning toward God. Choices that disregard the order inherent in the world and humanity, as well as their orientation to God, are perverse choices; in making them we will find ourselves turning away from the One who alone is and remains worthy of unqualified devotion: God.

Now it is the case that we humans live and grow toward maturity in a world of created things, and the fact that all of them should somehow appeal to our desire is only natural and God-given and consequently good. The problem is that, given the fact of concupiscence (§113, 3, b), we are prone to *disorderliness* in relation to created things, both those we find attractive and those that repulse us. And for their part, created things, including other human beings, cannot be counted on to positively resist misuse and abuse; in fact, they lend themselves to both. This means that we find ourselves tempted as well as tested by them (cf. §119, 3). This in turn puts pressure on our choices; it often skews them; it also makes the avoidance of sin a matter of our being constantly, vigilantly, and obediently attuned to the will of God: we must let no creature, whether noble or abhorrent, attractive or repulsive, naturally good or naturally evil, draw us into consciously and deliberately disproportionate responses — that is, choices out of harmony with the will of God discernible in the order of the world. This God is the transcendent source of the moral order, and consequently, beyond compare; God is always greater—ever more eminent than any created good. Consequently, God's will is forever to be preferred in all things and to all things.

[b] Augustine is implying something else as well. In the experience of saints and sinners alike, both moral choices and immoral ones are habit-forming. All choices, that is, are set in a dynamic perspective. Every single good choice will incline the chooser to further good choices, as well as to a deeper awareness of God's transcendent holiness; in other words, every good choice refines and deepens our moral conscience and gives us a taste and a desire for

---

heart of sin. Cf. §102, 4, c.

even better choices (cf. §105, 5–6). By contrast, every time we settle for something less than good, or positively opt for it, we also predispose ourselves to settle or opt for other, even lesser goods. This is because all human persons are born with a dynamic attunement to the ever-greater God; accordingly, no human life (that is, no moral life: §115, 2, [v]) can be a matter of assured stability. Either we will find ourselves made holier, as we make choices that move us in the direction of an increased awareness of the transcendent God, or we become worse sinners, as we lapse and slip further away from God, increasingly losing touch with our native sense of God as well.

[3] Another passage that is often quoted when Augustine's conception of sin is discussed occurs in the fourteenth book of *The City of God*, the ambitious work on Christianity and classical culture that Augustine started in 413, and which occupied him until 425, five years before his death. The passage serves to confirm the dynamic interpretation of the difference between right choices and wrong choices just proposed.

As Augustine grows older he continues to do what he did in the *Confessions* : he looks back to understand what is happening now. Only his purview is considerably broadened. He now understands that in his own lifetime he has watched two civilizations vying for humanity's favor. He characterizes them by characterizing their deepest motivations. The two civilizations have this in common: they are moved by a deep preference or *dilectio*. At the same time, however, they differ altogether in regard to the *objects* of their *dilectio*.

On the one hand, there is the ancient civilization of Rome. Despite the recent revival of fashionable forms of neo-paganism, Augustine realizes that this culture has now for some time been receding into the past, under the pressure not just of Christianity, but also, and more immediately, of the onslaughts of the barbarians. Still, in its heyday, the *terrena civitas* of Rome had proudly as well as successfully aspired to being a truly cosmopolitan society—a creation of human autonomy. Augustine knows that he is himself a product of its polite culture, as he is at pains to show in *De Civitate Dei*—indeed at every turn.[64]

On the other hand, Augustine sees a new commonwealth being laboriously forged. It is being decisively influenced by Christianity. In fact, Augustine himself is a prime witness of the birth pangs of this new world order. The new civilization, he explains, is motivated by a dynamic love fundamentally at odds with the dynamic love that informed the old, and what makes the difference is the living God. Happily, autonomy is yielding to theonomy.

So it is that two commonwealths have been shaped by two kinds of love [*amores duo*]: the earthly one by love of self, carried to the point of disregard of God [*amor sui usque ad contemptum Dei*], the heavenly one by love of God, carried to the point of disregard of self [*amor Dei usque ad contemptum sui*]. In the last resort, the former glories in itself, the latter in the Lord [cf. 2 Cor 10, 17; 1 Cor 1, 31]. For the former looks to human beings for glory [cf. 1 Thess 2, 6]; the latter's greatest glory is God, who attests to its conscience [cf. 2 Cor 1, 12]. The former, full of its own glory, lifts up its own head; the latter says to its God: "My glory, and the one who lift up my head" [Ps 3, 4 Vg]. For the former, power is the thing, embodied in its rulers, yet also in the nations brought to heel by lust for power; the latter lives by mutual service in charity —leaders have the best interests at heart and subjects comply. The former, in cherishing its commanding figures, cherishes its own strength; the latter says to God: "I will cherish you, Lord, my strength" [Ps 18, 1; 17, 2 Vg].[65]

[4] Finally, in a long letter of uncertain date to a friend in Carthage, Honoratus, known as "The Book on the Grace of the New Testament," we have Augustine's explanation of how he understands the "misery" he mentions at the end of his definition of evil in *De libero arbitrio*. To make his point, he draws humanity's native desire for *beatitudo*—that is, total fulfillment in God (cf. §67, 1)—into the picture:

Creatures endowed with reason [*rationalis creatura*] . . . are thus constituted: they are unable to be unto themselves the good by virtue of which they can become happy, but they do become happy if their changing selves turn to the unchanging good. Hence, if they should turn away from it, they are miserable.[66]

Again, Augustine's conception is clear. Sustained in being by God, and made in the divine image in a sense decisively surpassing the infra-human cosmos, human persons are ineradicably endowed with a free and conscious (though largely unthematic) desire for God as their total fulfillment (cf. §67, 1). Consequently, whenever they sin, they at least implicitly betray *themselves* as well. But this means that, in the very act of sinning against God, sinners are being self-contradictory and self-defeating: they "hurt themselves, to their own shame" (Jer 7, 19). Accordingly, their punishment is not so much something they pull down upon themselves from elsewhere—a penalty justly inflicted upon them from outside. Rather, in sinning they bring about an immanent, inherent misery in their own selves. Much as in making immoral choices we may be first and foremost turning away from God, as well as doing an injustice to others and to the world around us, we also, and fundamentally, act against the desire for fulfillment that lies at the core of our own being. In that sense, just as the virtuous person's virtue is its own reward, the sinner's sin is its own punishment. "Our deeds judge us even as we perform them," as Ambrose puts it. And Augustine can say: "When God punishes sinners, he does not inflict an evil of his own making on them, but sets them loose amid their own evils."[67]

[5] Augustine's analyses of sin encompass several important elements. First there is the insight that human sin is failure to relate to the created universe in a theologically appropriate way—that is, in accordance with the requirements of humanity's fundamental and distinctive attunement to God. Then there is the recognition that this failure is not accidental but freely and consciously chosen. Finally, there is the awareness that sin inherently involves not only a failure to do the right thing "out there," but also—at the very least implicitly—a disturbing perversion of human integrity and identity "in here"; *sin is the deterioration of authentic human self-definition, or even its total breakdown* [*ii*].

[6] This failure, or (frequently) this positive refusal, on the part of free and responsible human beings, to relate to the cosmos and to humanity itself in a morally responsible fashion, to do justice to their innermost selves, and thus, to embrace their relatedness to God which is their lifeline, takes countless forms. Yet all of them have this strictly theological drift in common: they lead into the park of misery, death, and the absence of God.

[7] The next chapter must begin to explore these themes. It will do so only in a preliminary manner. For, in preparation of a full-fledged theological treatment of sin later on, we must attempt a fundamental theological understanding of humanity's *moral* predicament—an understanding both sound from the point of view of theological anthropology and consonant with the great Tradition of Christian doctrine, East and West. The elements that loom large in Augustine's conception of sin—the world, human integrity, and God—will be central themes in this endeavor. They already were central themes in the exploration, conducted in the previous chapter, of the basic dynamics

---

[*ii*] There is a widespread opinion that Augustine, dependent on Neo-Platonism as he was, took a dim view of *matter*, and hence, that he practically identified matter, and especially the body, with sin (cf. §79, 6, [*ff*]). Since there is some (but not very much) truth in the first half of the assertion, it is important to observe that there is no truth whatsoever in the second. The present context clearly demonstrates how Augustine squarely attributes evil not to matter, but to something *spiritual*: misguided human freedom of choice. His understanding of sin, in other words, shows no trace of the kind of dualism that would equate the spiritual with truth and goodness, and materiality with deceit and evil.

of humanity's *cosmic* predicament: its existence as part of a cosmos in process. They are also central themes in the stirring passage that brings to a climax the introductory section of *Gaudium et Spes*, the Pastoral Constitution on the Church in the Modern World issued by Vatican II:

Indeed, the imbalances under which the modern world labors are linked with that more fundamental imbalance rooted in the human heart. For in human persons themselves many elements are at war with each other. Thus, on the one hand, as creatures, they experience, in a multitude of ways, that they are limited. On the other, they are aware of themselves as boundless in their desires and summoned to a higher life. Pulled by many attractions, they are constantly compelled to choose among them, and to renounce some. In fact, being weak and sinful, they often do what they do not want to do, and fail to do what they would wish to do [cf. Rom 7, 14ff.]. Hence they suffer from being inwardly divided, and this leads to so many and such great conflicts in society. All too numerous are those, of course, who turn their eyes away from a clear realization of this kind of dramatic situation, since their lives are infected with practical materialism; others are prevented even from giving the matter any thought, being oppressed by misery. Many think they find composure in the great variety of interpretations of reality that are proposed. Others again look to human effort alone for the genuine and total emancipation of humanity, convinced that humanity's future dominion over the earth will fulfill every desire of the human heart. There are even those who, having despaired of finding meaning in life, praise the boldness of those who think that human existence has no inherent meaning, and hence do everything to confer an encompassing meaning on it by their own ingenuity alone. However, in the face of the modern development of the world, an ever-increasing number of people are raising the most fundamental questions or experiencing them with a new intensity: what is Man? What is this sense of sorrow, of evil, of death—things that continue to exist despite so much progress? What is the purpose of these victories, purchased at so high a cost? What can one offer to society, what can one expect from it? What comes after this earthly life?

(GS 10)

These are fundamental questions. Some of them have already been raised in past chapters; we shall have to revert to them. Some of them remain to be explored; we shall have to take them up.

CHAPTER 14

"Blessed are Those who Endure the Test" (Jas 1, 12)

IDENTITY IN ALIENATION: PROMISES AND AMBIGUITIES

[§122] "SUBJECTED IN HOPE" (ROM 8, 20)

[1] Humanity's transcendental attunement to all that is (which is also the repository of each person's fundamental sense of identity) is in the nature of a *dynamism*; we are natively predisposed to *action*—to engagement with the world we live in (cf. §87, 2, a). Like the attunement itself, this predisposition to action is a *given*; it, too, therefore, presents itself to us for our acceptance (cf. §112, 2). Only by dint of sustained engagement, both of the spontaneous and the deliberate kind, does human self-actualization occur; the latter, therefore, takes the shape of a history of *interaction*—of meeting the invitations and challenges posed by the infra-human cosmos as we find it and, in that setting, by other persons as we encounter them [a]. *Reditus* lives by the grace of *exitus*. Only according as we go out into the world of otherness and engage it, whether individually or communally, can we grow toward fulfillment and come home to our authentic selves as well as to the human communities in which we learn how to communicate and in which we find other human persons to communicate with. And in the process, we are ultimately and most of all invited, knowingly or tacitly, to seek and find the God who dwells in all that is, and come home to the God who dwells in us and makes us who and what we are. In all of this we are to grow in the very authenticity we aspire to exercise: only

---

[a] The vehicle (or rather, organ) of this self-actualization is, of course, *bodiliness*; cf. §115, 8 and [h]. Aquinas can write: "the lower spiritual substances, I mean [human] souls, have an existential affinity with the body [*habent esse affine corpori*], inasmuch as they are the forms of their bodies; and hence, by reason of their very mode of existing, it is fitting that they should acquire their spiritual perfection [*perfectionem intelligibilem*] from their bodies and by way of their bodies; otherwise being united with their bodies would be pointless" (*S. Th.* I, 55, 2, *in c.*).

to the extent that we go out into the world of otherness will our selves
and the human communities we come home to grow in authenticity
and identity, and hence, in actual resemblance to God. An early
Christian document like the *Epistle of Barnabas* puts it quite forcefully:

Do not stand aside and keep yourselves aloof, as if God had already declared
you holy, but get together and search for the common good.[1]

Let us put this in rather more philosophical terms. Only by virtue
of "alienation" and "de-alienation" (or "exteriorization" and "interiori-
zation") do human beings, whether personally or communally, grow
into their authentic identity.[2]

The alternative to such a life of freely chosen *exitus* is a life of isolation, uninvolvement, aloofness, indecision, relative inaction, apathy,
even withdrawal. But such a half-life is tantamount to an unnatural
failure to act either authentically or responsibly. After all, our native,
essential ability to live as responsive and responsible human beings
drives home an existential duty. What we most deeply *are* is also what
we *ought to be*. The indicative harbors an imperative. Natively and by
reason of our very nature, we are responsible (§98, 5): we must mediate between God and creation, and we do so by taking responsibility
for humanity and the world. Here if anywhere what becomes clear is
both the attractiveness of human authenticity and its precariousness.
Either we step out into the open, or we shrivel and decay; as a matter
of principle, there is neither maturity nor goodness nor religiosity in
unresponsiveness or inaction [b].

[a] In this context, it is appropriate to offer some philosophical and
fundamental-theological observations on *alienation*. First of all, however, let us clarify an important *terminological* issue. The treatment
of humanity's life in the world of otherness about to be offered will
use the term *alienation* without any negative connotations. Both in
the present context and throughout *God Encountered*, "alienation"
functions as the equivalent of Hegel's *Entäußerung*, in the sense of
"[self-]exteriorization." "Alienation," therefore, is *neutral*: it simply

---

[b] This, incidentally, has consequences for the practice of Christian *theology*, and
specifically for its relationships with the wider culture. It was stated long ago that
theology is the human mind's active mediation between God and the world, in the
form of disciplined thought (§2, 1). We can now add that humanity's condition of
alienation makes engagement with the world and the culture at large an integral part
of Christian theology. Only if actively engaged with otherness can theology achieve
maturity and become a genuinely humane (that is to say, moral) pursuit (cf. §14, 4).

denotes the fact that human beings must, by virtue of natural necessity, relate to otherness. Through the medium of their bodiliness,
all human beings participate in the material cosmos, and in humanity in particular. This brings otherness, and other human beings in
particular, home to them as part of themselves; it also impels them
to develop and express and "objectify" their growing, evolving selves
in the world of otherness, in the form of cultural creations of one
kind or another (cf. §115, 8, [h]).

By contrast, current English idiom almost consistently uses the
term "alienation" in a negative sense, as the equivalent of the term
"estrangement" (in Hegel's idiom, *Entfremdung*). This usage reflects
a painful human experience, namely, that human persons and even
human communities can lose themselves in otherness, especially
when, having expressed and objectified themselves in the world of
otherness, they no longer succeed in recognizing themselves in their
own objective creations.[3]

The present treatment will agree with current English idiom in
that it proposes to use the term *estrangement* to convey this negative
experience. "Estrangement," therefore, signifies alienation insofar
as it implies that otherness is experienced as foreign and even positively hostile to human integrity and identity. If and when and to
the extent that our inevitable (and always precarious) involvement
with otherness threatens to frustrate, or has succeeded in frustrating,
our human authenticity and identity, we labor under the burden of
"estrangement," whether personally or communally or both.

With the usage and terminology on the issue of alienation laid
down, let us move on to its substance.

[b] The life of *exitus* is marked (and to an appreciable degree even
determined) by our ontological status as beings contingent and cosmic. This latter feature—our cosmicity—defines our alienation.
Being cosmic, we cannot be what we truly are unless we become
what we are not, yet are meant to be; and we cannot discover (let
alone become) what we are meant to be *unless we turn to what we are
not*: the other. Being inherently cosmic, therefore, means being
compelled to forge identity out of alienation; for growth in identity,
human beings are essentially constituted by their *dependence on, and
in that sense subjection to, involvement with otherness*. "Is there anything
other at all that is not the other of our own selves? At any rate no
one who is another—who, too, is a human being" (Hans-Georg
Gadamer).[4]

[c] Still, while cosmic existence draws human beings, as a matter of ontological necessity, into radical involvement with otherness, the human *exitus* is not *just* a matter of cosmic necessity. True, none of us can ever effectively opt for total independence from other cosmic beings. But our being involved with otherness does not mean that we are engulfed in, and at the mercy of, randomness or undifferentiated cosmic process. For the cosmos in which we participate is *coherent and structured*; so are its processes. Quite obviously, as living organisms, we have this in common with plants and animals that we enjoy a real measure not only of immanence and self-sufficiency, but also of transcendence and freedom, in relation to the specific, structured environments and habitats that we feed on and live and thrive in (cf. §115, 8). Moreover (and far more decisively), our human, *spiritual* immanence and transcendence allow us, within the situations we live in, to make relatively free *choices* just as to whom or what we will depend on, and all the more so as we grow and mature. That is, though we cannot help turning to the other *in some way* in order to become ourselves, no single *particular* other is simply integral to our identity, nor does even our most radical dependence on other *particular* human and infra-human beings ever amount to *total* dependence [c].

Committing ourselves to the life of *exitus*, therefore, is not just an instance of our being subjected to ontological (*i.e.*, in this case, *cosmological*) necessity, nor is it just a matter of our being driven by

---

[c] In this light, it is easy to see why *human birth* should be so widely recognized as an occasion for congratulation. Physiologically and anthropologically, birth is an individual's first irrepressible, public move out into the open, away from deep dependence on otherness, and in the direction of the exercise of such independence and authenticity as befits human persons. No wonder we observe birthdays; in commemorating them, we symbolically take the measure of the maturity and transcendence we have attained in our lives so far. In light of the human individual's inherent potential for personal independence and initiative, first successfully demonstrated at birth and soon to be spectacularly evident in early development, most cultures have found it hard or even impossible to interpret the human embryo as a *totally* dependent entity. In this regard, pre-scientific ancient and medieval notions about ensoulment ("animation") some time *after* conception (cf. M. Canévet, "L'humanité de l'embryon selon Grégoire de Nysse"; Aquinas, *S. Th.* I, 118, 2, *ad* 2; *DTC*, I, 1305–20) agree with modern (since ± 1850 A.D.) physiological and philosophical theories on "the establishment of personhood" *at* fertilization or at least very soon after: both bear witness to the underlying awareness that no human being is ever to be thought of as so dependent on others—even its mother—as to be reducible to being a mere function of them. This awareness is further supported by the more recent discovery that the embryo is from the outset physiologically and (even more importantly) genetically distinct from its mother.

animal instinct. It is also an elementary exercise of our transcendental *freedom*. After all, human beings are not only cosmic but also
properly spiritual. This is an *anthropological* given; we are natively
predisposed to making choices about *how* we go out of ourselves so
as to actualize the authenticity and capacity for freedom implanted
in us. In fact, according to Jan van Ruusbroec, there are sound as
well as properly *theological* grounds for thinking that this transcendental freedom of ours to go out and "externalize" ourselves in a
deliberate fashion is more fundamental than the cosmological necessity that inexorably pushes us toward involvement with otherness.
For, Ruusbroec explains, the "outflowing" life is at bottom something deeply positive: it is our participation in the creative activity by
which God freely establishes the universe as truly other (cf. §90,
3–5) [d].

[d] If our going out to otherness is more deeply a matter of capacity
for spiritual freedom and love than of subjection to cosmic determination and necessity, this affects the complexion of our cosmic
alienation—of our *having to* go out to otherness. The more we come
to appreciate and cherish our native freedom, therefore, the less our
alienation is liable to turn into estrangement; rather, it will become
something deeply positive: a required apprenticeship to train us by
cosmic mutuality freely undertaken, by self-transcending creativity,
and most of all, by other-regarding love [e]. True, it is by no choice

---

[d] Philosophically speaking, therefore, to the extent that human beings fail to live
a life of chosen, self-initiated *exitus* they fail to live freely and creatively—that is, in
according with the divine image and likeness. This can be shown as follows. Creation is a continuing divine act of transcendently free, wholly self-initiated generosity,
intended to share the divine Self freely with otherness—that is, with the world and
humanity. In other words, in creating, God is not compelled by a need to enhance
the divine Self by means of involvement with otherness. Nor does God become creation's slave once it is a given. God is and remains forever free, as the sole initiator
of any process by which the world and humanity are brought about, enhanced, and
fulfilled to capacity, and beyond, brought home to the divine Self (cf. §82, 3, b).

[e] One characteristic intimation of what is proposed here is the widespread human
tendency to interpret the infra-human cosmos in anthropological terms. Many phenomena in the earth's atmosphere, and even more, the myriad, dynamic organisms
in the biosphere strike us as governed by living freedom rather than dead determin-
ism. This is, of course, an instance of projection: we *know* that the weather does not
choose itself, and that the "options" of plants and even of animals are severely limited
(cf. §115, 8). Yet the sheer profusion of atmospheric phenomena and the plethora
of forms and instinctive behaviors in the plant and animal realms, and especially the
fact that so many of these seem to defy the forces of inertia and gravity (as well as
calculating reason), strike the human imagination as displays of *freedom*—a freedom
all the more appealing (at least at first blush) by reason of the unfeigned *innocence*
suggested by the regularity that is so characteristic of the atmosphere and the bio-

of our own that we *enter* upon the processes of alienation inherent in humanity as a cosmic phenomenon; but once we find ourselves involved with otherness, and especially with other persons, it is not surprising that we *also* find ourselves inwardly invited, and indeed morally compelled, to respond (§95, 4–5 and esp. [*ll*]). If we are fortunate, we will even find ourselves wonderfully surprised and attracted by otherness, and especially by the self-communication freely initiated by mature and generous other persons; consequently, we will in turn find ourselves (if we use our good fortune to good purpose) freely taking the initiative in going out to other persons and things (cf. §95, 6–9).

All this is to say that the experience of alienation is meant to be a school of the responsive, creatively responsible life—a point nowadays often, and quite appropriately, made by feminist theologians, especially in ethical contexts.[5] Even more importantly, it will be (in Jan van Ruusbroec's vision) an experience of life in union with the "fecund nature" of the triune God.[6] For created activity is the finite reflection of the everlasting Trinitarian life; hence, going out of ourselves ultimately means: drawing upon, and participating in, and aspiring to, the eternal dynamism by which the Father, in the all-embracing Love of the Spirit, is freely and ecstatically fecund in generating the *Logos*, in whom the whole creation pre-exists spiritually as truly other (cf. §60, 2).[7]

[e] If existence in alienation is not the equivalent of being mired in estrangement and inauthenticity, it follows that not every experience of ourselves as *divided* should conjure up the unsettling specter of existential estrangement [*f*].[8]

---

sphere. No wonder the poets of Psalm 104 and of the song of the three boys in the fiery furnace (Dan 3, 52–90 LXX), not to mention Saint Francis of Assisi in his *Cantico delle creature*, can take their cues from cosmic phenomena to sing the praise of God—a praise offered far more nobly, of course, in the free and conscious self-actualization, for all the world to see, of human persons and communities.

[*f*] In fact, the very fact that I consciously experience myself as torn and divided testifies to the fundamental, if largely implicit, *unity* of my self-experience as a "person"! This point is here made in studied criticism of all pessimist, existentialist, and anti-cosmological attempts to put a theologically and anthropologically negative construction on humanity's participation in the world of otherness, and especially in the world of *things* (cf. §10, 1, a; §104, 1, a). This negative interpretation of alienation is often proposed with an appeal to Hegel—a mistake, for Hegel always carefully distinguishes between alienation as self-exteriorization (which is the precondition for positive human self-realization in the world of otherness) and alienation understood as estrangement, as Louis Dupré has explained with great clarity (*Marx's Social Critique of Culture*, pp. 18–23.) By contrast, Paul Tillich's systematic theology affords an example of the consistent interpretation of the alienation naturally inherent in the

In this life, it is true, we do feel stretched and pulled apart (cf. §134, 1), and even "worried" and "divided" (1 Cor 7, 33–34). For on the one hand we are radically involved with otherness, and on the other hand, we feel the inner attraction of authentic identity, no matter how elusive and precarious it may be (§112, 3–5). Yet the latter, our implicit sense of identity, does quietly enable us, in principle and quite often in practice, to transcend both cosmic realities and our sense of being pulled apart by them; thus it allows us to turn alienation to good use and enjoyment. And one decisive form this transcendence must take (and ordinarily does take) is this: that we freely *accept* our inexorable involvement in the alienating mutualities of cosmic process in such a way as to endeavor, freely, to turn them to constructive ends (§115, 8–9), especially by *integrating* them into genuinely human relationships and purposes. True, the interior worlds where we are at home (at least in principle, or as long as we enjoy mental health) and the world of otherness where we find ourselves involved as relative strangers are indeed different; but this is quite appropriate—interiority and exteriority are *meant* to differ. The two can even quite appropriately be at odds, even to the point, at times, of mutual near-intractability.

Consequently, while the alienation inherent in cosmic existence does involve entering upon crises and putting our authentic selves at risk, these crises and risks have, *by nature*, a positive prognosis. By dint of attraction, negotiation, involvement, encounter, contest, standoff, confrontation, skirmish, and even outright conflict, the inside of us and the outside of us—our original, immanent selves and our situated selves—get dialectically engaged. And whenever the engagement comes off, both get enhanced—like difficult, demanding friends loyally determined to forge a stable relationship out of stubborn lopsidedness. It is by dint of endurance we come to experience integration and to find a new, maturer sense of identity. And as the world outside increasingly becomes the life-space in

---

human existential predicament in a negative sense, as the ontological equivalent of the Fall. Rather than acknowledging that finitude/alienation and concupiscence/inauthenticity/sin are *connected* (which is obvious), Tillich tends to regard them as *identical*. In doing so, however, he forgets that, more basically, alienation is humanity's inherent invitation to growth in authenticity. (But then again, this is to some extent compensated by the fact that Tillich, quite rightly, views *culture* not as an expression of estrangement but as a victory over it.) Even the Catholic Bernard Häring, in *Sin in the Secular Age* (pp. 37–105) uses the term alienation in an exclusively negative sense. The position adopted in the present treatment is more balanced (as well as more typically Catholic).

whose familiar furnishings our restless, growing personal identities can settle, our ability to seek out fresh encounters with otherness—encounters ever more freely and creatively undertaken—is intensified: our taste for expanded horizons is enhanced (cf. §95, 8 and [*ss*]). And as our effective encounters with the outside world and, most especially, with other persons leave our imprint on them, they, too, in their very otherness, become more settled, more civilized, more personalized, more capable of growth, more human and humane, more capable of constructive engagement with otherness, and hence, more deeply identified [*g*]. In this way, by dint of careful human mediation, some of purblind, precarious cosmic process is steadily being integrated into significant purpose freely adopted and executed—that is, transformed into meaningful human and cosmic history (cf. §87, 2, d, esp. [*gg*]).

[f] In all of this, it need hardly be added, acceptance of our subjection to alienation (and of the potential for both meaningful growth and baffling frustration which this subjection entails) is predicated on a basic attitude of *hope* (cf. Rom 8, 20). Where does the anthropological warrant for this hope lie? Let us try.

Human integrity combines two moments, identity and alienation, which exist in mutual interpenetration or *perichōrēsis* (cf. §26, 3; §23, 4, b; §57, 3, d; §100, 1). Yet, as in other instances of *perichōrēsis*, the mutuality is not complete. The relationship between identity and alienation (or between the I-as-developing-self and the I-as-situated-by-otherness) is one of *asymmetry*; both are essential to human integrity, even though in and of itself identity transcends alienation [*h*]. Otherness does indeed hold untold potential in comparison with

---

[*g*] Max Scheler's whole *oeuvre*, but especially his *Wesen und Formen der Sympathie* (ET *The Nature of Sympathy*), remains a profound study of alienation understood in a positive, constructive sense—as potential for both identity and communication rather than estrangement and isolation. Human togetherness experienced as "herd" (*Herde*) involves intimate participation in the organic, physical, instinctive, and emotional dynamics characteristic of the infra-human cosmos. But knack for self-transcendence (already noticeable in higher animals) impels humanity to avail itself of these cosmic dynamics as the matrix out of which it can fashion the rational, operational, world-shaping structures characteristic of "society" (*Gesellschaft*). And this self-transcendence serves, ultimately, as the basis for the development of forms of genuine "communion of persons" (*Personengemeinschaft*) of the spiritual (that is, freely other-directed, compassionate) kind: accepting and embracing both humanity as herd and humanity as society, communions of persons are capable of integrating both of them and bringing them to fulfillment.

[*h*] This is a restatement of the classical Christian conviction that, while the human soul's engagement with the body (and the cosmos) is real and immediate, its "substance" is not exhausted by this engagement. Cf. §109, 9, c, [z].

our native identity (or "immanence"), which in this life is forever emergent and never complete. Still, otherness is not so much initiating as expectant. By contrast, our *given* identity harbors our native capacity for genuine transcendence (and hence, for actual dynamic initiative). Only by taking initiatives, therefore, can we hope to find our true selves; we must rely on our capacity for transcendence if we are to turn otherness, including its inevitable cosmic entanglements, into profitable, constructive experience. Yet on the other hand, given this native capacity, it is only by virtue of constructive engagement with *otherness* that our original identity can grow into mature selfhood. Thus, in the "perichoretic" dialectic between the two components of our being, interiority and exteriority, identity and alienation, we are to actualize that most touching of all things open to human beings: mature enjoyment of the world, and authentic encounters, not only with other human selves, but also, ultimately, in and through and beyond them, with the living God—the kind of encounters that are the very stuff of our "responsive identity" as true persons (cf. §95, 4 and [*ll*]; 6–7; 10–11; cf. §35, 1; §49, 1; also, §87, 3; §97, 3; §100, 1; §109, 8; §113, 3, F; §124, 12, D; §139, 7–8).⁹

[g] Needless to say, therefore, our understanding of alienation has important consequences for our theological understanding of *love* as the "form" of the virtuous life (§139, 1, b–d)—a subject to which we must come back at length. But one important point can at least be made. In an elegant and lucid monograph entitled *The Evolution of Altruism and the Ordering of Love*, Stephen J. Pope has observed that recent trends in Catholic moral theology have favored wholly altruistic, "disinterested" love as the central inspiration and principal norm of Christian conduct. Such positions are understandable; they have been framed mostly to correct and counteract the excessively legalistic, "biologistic," and even downright minimalistic tendencies found in the preconciliar, neo-scholastic manuals of moral theology. No wonder modern Catholic ethicists are often inspired by personalism of the existentialist variety (as in the case of Bernard Häring), or by the preferential option for the poor (as in the case of liberation theologians). By contrast, however, Aquinas had insisted that responsible love must be *rightly ordered* before it can become a matter of wholly disinterested choice; he had also pointed out that the phenomenology of biophysical and psychophysical life (for which he depended on Aristotle's authority) provides reliable cues to this ordering of love. Pope rightly contends that theories of love that fail

to follow Aquinas in taking the data of physical science seriously will end up commending wholly selfless love at the expense of those forms of love that lay bare humanity's rootedness in the world of otherness, to which they remain permanently indebted. As a result, Pope argues, recent trends in Catholic moral theology have tended to belittle natural love, such as love of parents, love of one's children, love of next of kin. In this way, he might have added, modern moral theology has called into question, at least indirectly, the integrity of the vast majority of Christians, who live by this kind of ordered love (if seldom exclusively). If modern moralists were to pay attention (as, in imitation of Aquinas, they should) to evolutionary theories of altruism developed by modern biologists, they would realize that tendencies toward altruism are inherent in many sentient life forms. This would also help them point out that the great Tradition has consistently held that wholly gracious and other-regarding love (*agapē*, or charity) *integrates* and *ennobles* natural love (*erōs*), just as grace presupposes nature and perfects it (§80, 2–4; cf. §26, 2, a; §23, 3). Or, to use an expression used earlier in this book, the Tradition has insisted that alienation, far from being identical with estrangement, "has a positive prognosis" (§122, 1, e and [*f*]).

[2] At the risk of being repetitive, let us sum up. Truly to live involves coming into our authentic selves and becoming self-identified and self-possessed by dint of increasingly self-transcending, other-regarding engagements—that is, by making moves outside ourselves so as to take positions that involve otherness, affirmatively (§108, 1–2). Without affirmativeness and the commitments it entails, we would cease, both as persons and as communities of persons, to do justice, both to our own native potential for authentic, mature human identity, and to the invitations, appeals, and challenges that come to us from otherness, in the form of humanity and the outside world.

But this is precisely where the shoe pinches.

[3] Being spiritual, we are natively identified by a taste for all that is, and indeed, for infinity itself. Still, since we exist in alienation, we effectively live and move and exist within limited contexts, or, as we propose to term them, *situations*. It is true, of course, that we are never wholly submerged in situations; we naturally transcend them in a variety of partial ways (§115, 8), as well as decisively by virtue of the spiritual nature that is ours by birthright (§115, 9). But it is only by dint of confronting and negotiating *particular* situations that we can learn how to transcend *any situations at all*, and transcend them in such a

way as to find our true selves—to become more fully the persons who (as we discover, largely by hindsight) we are meant to be.

Situations, in other words, are far more pervasive and more especially invasive than the word suggests. The ground for this lies in us: *we* essentially participate in them. For, while we are never wholly submerged in any situation in which we find ourselves, no situation is ever completely extrinsic or foreign to us. As long as we are subject to the conditions of cosmic existence, neither our inner, God-given identity nor our transcendence, no matter how substantial and deep-seated, are complete or secure. This is a consequence of alienation: *being situated is integral to us as human persons* [*i*].

[4] Only *within* the confines of whatever situations we find ourselves in can we go out of ourselves and adopt positions. In doing so, we endeavor to integrate the two worlds that meet in us: our own "inside" world, where, precariously, we are natively disposed to grow into our *identity and integrity,* and the "outside" situation, which we are to engage in all its *otherness and multiplicity.* Not surprisingly, therefore, taking positions is a matter of judging and choosing, and no particular position we choose to adopt is ever going to be wholly unequivocal or even persuasive [*j*]. The reason for this is not only that any positions

---

[*i*] At the risk of running ahead of our argument, let us note that what has just been explained has significant consequences for our understanding of original sin. Original sin is inherent in us *by virtue of our being situated*; that is, it attaches to us through the medium of our alienation. And since alienation is not incidental (let alone foreign) to human nature but utterly integral to it, the doctrine of original sin declares that there is something really wrong with *us,* the way we really and substantially *are.* This, however, does *not* imply that we are wicked by virtue of our *essential nature,* which is God-given and knowable as such (cf. Aquinas, *S. Th.* I–II, 83, 1, *ad 4*). Realizations like these led Piet Schoonenberg, in developing his first intuitions about original sin (to which we will return in the next part), to revise and refine his understanding as well as his terminology. Initially, he had described original sin as the "situation" in which humanity finds itself—an expression that cast original sin in so extrinsic and accidental a mold as to be misleading. Only later on did he begin to emphasize that being-situated (cf. §125, 5) is an *essential* feature of humanity; accordingly, he came to view original sin and its transmission as effects of *our being situated,* ultimately, in a world shaped by an immemorially sinful humanity. Hence, we are *intrinsically* affected by sin as it has taken shape in a variety of sinful *social* structures (cf. James L. Connor, "Original Sin: Contemporary Approaches," pp. 229–30).

[*j*] In affirming positions like this, it remains important for us to remember that, much as we are *subject* to the conditions of alienation, we are not the *prisoners* of alienation any more than of finitude (cf. §112, 1). It is precisely our transcendental attunement to the absolute that enables us to realize that both the particular positions we adopt and the commitments we make in adopting them, while certainly determinative of further positions and commitments, are never definitive or conclusive.

we adopt, being finite, are intrinsically partial and hence, provisional; it is also that they are to an appreciable degree *unclear.*

After all, every position invariably has a margin of vagueness; positions implicitly connote counterpositions; that is, they inherently fall short of complete definition. This is because the only world in which we can adopt any positions at all is the world of otherness—that is, the world whose every determination is relative, and whose every structure is provisional. Consequently, the positions we adopt, both the moral ones and the immoral ones, are only *imperfectly distinct* from all conceivable other positions (cf. §108, 1–4; cf. esp. §115, 5, c, [e]; 8, [h]). Conversely, too, the world of otherness invades us. Parts of it are part of us, and not an entirely controllable part by any means; strangeness crowds in on us; we are never wholly in the clear about ourselves nor ever wholly free. Consequently, much as alienation may draw us into growth toward fulfillment by virtue of the positions we adopt, it also prevents us, willy-nilly, from fully controlling and defining either what we do or the choices implicit in what we do. Consequently, otherness prevents us (very importantly and often quite painfully) from fully controlling and defining *ourselves.* The destiny and the identity we seek to forge out of the positions we adopt and out of the personal development we experience as we adopt them remain inconclusive. Thus, paradoxically, as we take steps toward our fulfillment by venturing out of our unformed, unfulfilled selves, these very steps also remind us how unfinished and undefined we remain.

[5] These realizations lead to two series of consequences. The first of these (to be treated relatively briefly) concerns the *way* toward fulfillment, which is *the good life;* the second (which will require much more analysis) concerns the gateway to its *attainment,* which is *death.*

[§123] MORAL LIVING AS A CALL TO FAITH-COMMITMENT

[1] No matter how rich the promise the good life holds out to us, complete moral integrity in action and a wholly compelling sense of identity are never attained; alienation sees to it that both remain provisional as long as we live. The habitual acceptance of alienation as integral to ourselves implies the habitual acceptance of *particular choices* as the only way toward integrity and identity; moreover, the acceptance of our situatedness in the world also implies an acceptance of the *limits* of our choices, in respect to both availability (*i.e.,* the range of our choices is always limited), substance (*i.e.,* our choices will always be less

than perfect), and definition (*i.e.*, the object of our choices will always be to some extent unclear) [*k*]. Consequently, while the making of right choices releases our native aspiration to integrity and identity, it also puts restraints (and hence, strains) on it. Morality, while integral to our makeup, invariably leaves us curiously dissatisfied in practice. This deserves some elaboration.

[2] First of all, in the actual moral behavior by which we must come into our true selves, not only are we hobbled subjectively, by concupiscence (which keeps us unfulfilled and always somewhat at odds with ourselves: §113, 3, b; cf. §112, 5); we also have objective ambiguities to contend with. We aspire to total freedom, yet we exercise this aspiration only by *choosing* (not the absolute best, but) what we judge to be *better.*

Accordingly, Hans-Georg Gadamer can write:

> Here, in the final analysis, lies the last root of the freedom that makes humanity human: choice. Human beings have choices to make, and they know—and they know how to *state in words*—what in so doing they claim to be doing: selecting that which is better and (since they are the better being themselves) opting for the Good, the Right, and the Just. An enormous claim—and one which, in the end, is super-human. But human beings must make it, because they must choose.[10]

In this way we discover, however dimly, that there is far more to the good life than the deliberate making of responsible choices. Not for nothing has the great Tradition maintained that right at the heart of our every choice we are natively prompted to seek the Absolute Best— the "super-human." At the heart of the moral life lies, not the strenuous, conscious day-to-day exercise of autonomous moral integrity, but

---

[*k*] This implies that no particular position, choice, or commitment is absolute; this applies even to pledges made to God. The thirteenth-century beguine, poet, and mystic Hadewijch makes this point when she writes (*Brieven*, IV, 60–68; cf. *Complete Works.* p. 54 [60, 64]): "Error in the area of charity occurs when people serve in an undiscerning manner: they give out of inclination, regardless of need; they serve where there is no need; people hurt themselves needlessly. Much of what is called charity comes out of inclination. By observing rules of life, people worry about many things they could well do without; this is an error of reason. A soul that is of good will leads an interior life that is more attractive than all rules put together can devise." Saint Ignatius Loyola furnishes another example of this realization. In the *Formula Instituti*, the charter document of the Society of Jesus, he explains that all who join the community must "keep constantly before their eyes, first God, and then also the nature of this Institute, which is *some kind of way* [*via quædam*] to God" [1]. Failure to appreciate the relativity of particular commitments is, of course, also the core of self-righteousness and religious fanaticism.

the constant search for God, the Sovereign Good. In that sense, the Tradition has sided not with Kant (cf. §104, 2) but with Plato and Aristotle [*l*].

[a] On this basis, too, the Tradition has been content to teach, with the modesty and realism of Aristotle,[11] that the pursuit of the Good is, in actual practice, a balancing act between excess and defect. Even at our moral best, we can only do the best we can. Selecting the right thing is taking aim between alternatives and even extremes —a wearying task, especially since the difference between genuine moderation ("the golden mean") and tedious mediocrity is seldom obvious [*m*].

[3] This means that the virtuous life (that is, the fairly consistent moral life) is a bracing art at best and a parade of tolerable compromises at worst; in any case, it is a matter of continuous *discernment,* not of massive assurance. Our native desire for goodness never loses its reliance on habits of interpretation, discrimination, and moderation; ours is a life lived somewhere between stolid dedication to moral laws and lighthearted confidence in the obviousness and prevalence of natural goodness; the good life results neither from an ardent rush into morality nor from a sweet expectation that the good will somehow triumph. Most moral choices have discretionary and decisionary aspects to them; and (sobering and even disappointing though it may be) actual choices have this in common with positions (cf. §108, 1) that they are almost never completely separable, or even distinguishable, from different choices that are also morally appealing, or at least

---

[*l*] In this regard, a fine monograph by the contemporary Platonist Iris Murdoch, entitled *The Sovereignty of Good,* endorses the Christian tradition, despite its avowed atheism.

[*m*] Aquinas follows Aristotle (but significantly expands his conception) by explaining that moderation applies not only to the moral virtues, but also to the intellectual virtues (like truthfulness in thinking and speaking) and even, at least for our part, to the strictly theological virtues of faith, hope, and charity (*S. Th.* I–II, 64, 3–4). He holds, in other words, that in no position we adopt do we ever have access to unqualified, wholly assured virtuous behavior. This, of course, is not to deny that we do have access to real virtue as well as sufficient moral certainty about the goodness of our actions. The great Tradition has expressed this by acknowledging, in a variety of ways, that the morality of particular actions can be reliably assessed by recourse to fixed moral norms applied discerningly (not mechanically, let alone fanatically). Thus, at the pistic level, it has accepted such systems as probabiliorism and even probabilism, as well as the practice of casuistry, as useful tools to guide people to a differentiated notion of moral obligation; at the charismatic level, it has pointed to the indispensable function of prudence and wisdom; at the ascetical and mystical levels, it has commended discernment of spirits (cf. §79, 2, a).

defensible or even merely enticing, not to mention acceptable choices of lesser merit. Thus the good life in its day-to-day shape fails to provide a foothold in perfect moral assurance; it keeps us off-balance; in the actual life of virtue, even the most sturdily virtuous among us remain at least somewhat unsettled and irresolute; there is more to the good life, it turns out, than deliberate acts of goodness or even responsible habits of doing good things.

That is to say, the life of virtuous and responsible engagement with otherness, while sound and moral in its own right, is not self-sustaining or self-justifying; in the last resort, it must be rooted in something else. If it is to be habitually experienced as engaging and even enjoyable, it needs the support of a *fundamental* commitment—a deeper, more radical sense of duty, responsibility, dedication, and satisfaction, capable of giving substance and perspective and wider relevance to the partial values we affirm in the particular positions we choose to adopt day by day.

[4] Precisely because such an undergirding commitment runs deeper than any particular positions we adopt, it must in some fashion be distinguishable (and even, in cases, almost separable) from them. Consequently, we must be able to embrace broad yet specific commitments freely and consciously, even if we may not be able to give an adequate account of ourselves (or of the commitment) in doing so. For precisely because it is foundational, such a commitment is bound to exceed our grasp [n].

Speaking purely morally, therefore, we are neither self-sufficient nor self-supporting. Obviously, we must (and quite frequently do) lead good and responsible human lives on the strength of particular and deliberate acts and habits of moral virtue; in this way, we often succeed in building integrity and identity both in ourselves and in the world. Still, as we mature morally, we are liable to experience the need for

---

[n] This conclusion is liable to become especially pertinent when we find ourselves face to face with negative moral experience—our own and others'. We may, for instance, find ourselves burdened with a sense of moral immaturity; we may conclude, discouragingly, that we have deliberate past moral failure to confess and repent of; last but not least, we may realize that the world we live in is not very fussy about morality, and that success or (as it is often called in this context) "survival" practically demands that compromise, not moral commitment, be the basis for moral decision and action. Precisely in situations like these, if we wish to strengthen or renew our resolve to make the right moral choices, we need the resource of an identifiable (and in that sense "separate," even if not wholly articulate) fundamental moral commitment. Such commitments are most available to us in the form of reliable traditions of moral and religious narrative, as we shall see (§123, 7; §124, 10, a–b).

a deeper, more general abandon, which will enable us to live responsible lives in a manner that is more deeply satisfying [o].

[5] This leads to a second set of reflections. It is true that the life of purposeful moral action has deep roots in us; in fact, it is on its strength that we responsibly, maturely, and even delightfully engage the world. Still, a variety of anthropologically striking (if also curiously mixed) experiences suggests that habitual dedication to, and performance of, right acts does not adequately assure us of the integrity and identity we find ourselves natively impelled to develop in acting right. That is, we tend to discover (not without pain and inner conflict: §138, 2–3) that the abandon that must undergird the good life runs deeper than the moral domain.

[a] What comes to mind are developmental experiences like the following. It is part of maturity to discover that the exhilaration and the enjoyment brought on by self-actualization, self-expression, and creativity, whether of the visceral, the muscular, or the heady kind, are not lasting. Furthermore, in the responsible life, we are liable to become aware, somewhat wearily, of the sameness and the sheer toil of it all, and of the fact that the tasks involved in the moral life are never finished. Even if we are successful and happy in the responsible life (that is, not secretly resentful of the happiness of others perceptibly less moral than ourselves: cf. Ps 73!), we may find ourselves tiring of the taste of virtue, as we discern the chasm that separates duty and responsibility from enjoyment and fulfillment; we may even begin to wonder about our own deeper motives, as, for example, we find ourselves wondering if in being responsible we have not been merely self-assertive. In this way, with Qoheleth, we get a taste of the "vanity" that is inherent in all human effort (Eccles 1, 2. 8, 14, etc.), and we may, oddly, experience a positive desire for greater depth, coupled with an appreciation of the wealth than can be gained, not from effort, but from "letting be." This discovery is often connected with some loss of facility for strenuous, wide-ranging endeavor, or with the sense that some of our faculties are failing with age; yet only

---

[o] This can also be put in terms borrowed from Newman (cf. §105, 3–5). Our moral sense is neither free-standing nor self-justifying. To be truly conscientious, we have to rely on our sense of duty, which, in the last resort, involves a commitment that takes us beyond our merely moral selves, which reveals that we are rooted in God. The conceptions proposed here have, of course, far-reaching negative implications for the merely consensual or contractual varieties of professional ethics that unfortunately have become so popular of late, especially in North America.

seldom is the discovery entirely reducible to such forms of physical or mental decline.

[6] In this way, we find ourselves concurring, willy-nilly, with the emergence of more mature forms of responsible humanity within ourselves. Often this is development almost imperceptible, yet it never occurs merely automatically, without any decision or at least acquiescence on our part. As moral accomplishment and its rewards somehow cease to be the be-all and the end-all of our life, a fresh maturity helps us face and understand and even accept, as givens, the intractability of the world, and (yet more surprisingly) the indifference, immaturity, or uncooperativeness of others who have different conceptions of life's priorities. Most importantly, however, we find ourselves accepting that, yes, we are not the creators of our own fulfillment. Thus Ruusbroec can write:

for none are able to either satisfy or soothe themselves, either with themselves or with all the things they are able to do.[12]

Obviously, Augustine was right. We are clearly "unable to be unto [our-]selves the good by virtue of which [we] can become happy" (cf. §121, 4).

[7] Such intimations of a life beyond mere virtue may be the result of conscious decisions and studied growth in self-awareness; far more often, however, and more clearly among the less self-conscious, they originate in an almost spontaneous inner growth rooted in *formation* —that is, in the appropriation, with increasing willingness, appreciation, and interior freedom, of constructive traditions of commitment handed on to them (cf. §95, 8).

This suggests a thesis already alluded to (§123, 4, [*n*]), and one to which we will have occasion to come back repeatedly (§124, 10, a–b; §132, 1; §134, 1, [*e*]; 11, e; §142, 4 and a–b). In the Jewish and Christian traditions, moral and religious *narratives* (the biblical as well as the post-biblical, and not infrequently the hagiographical), and the *rituals* in which they are most appropriately rehearsed (cf. §41, 2), are indispensable equipment. For they are designed to enable us to experience, interpret, and structure life *as a whole*—that is, as a single project. As we meet the succession of particular ethical tasks life sets us, we are not so much guided by depressingly earnest *ad hoc* moral purpose as nourished by traditions cherished by the moral *and religious* communities we are part of. Such traditions are capable of integrating the vexing multiplicity of moral tasks into a wider, more inclusive moral vision. And in the last resort, narrative traditions will put the good life in the context of a lived sense of God and the shared moral values connected with it, and they will do so not just "after virtue" (that is, *after* we become morally mature), but right from the outset (that is, *as* we acquire moral maturity).

This is especially true if the narratives function appropriately, as *myths* (cf. §§39–41)—that is, if they are (as they tend to be in the Jewish and Christian traditions) kept alive by celebration, application, and reflection: enacted and re-enacted in liturgical worship, revisited and reappropriated as treasure houses of practical wisdom, and cherished and reinterpreted as classics worthy of studious attention, again and again [*p*].

[8] In this way, if we are fortunate enough to discover the good life, we are liable to find ourselves in due course drawn toward a new, mature, strangely non-self-centered experience of integrity and identity—one appreciative of habits of morality yet surpassing them (though often only in the long run). Virtue, even enjoyable virtue, has

---

[*p*] The themes touched on in these two paragraphs are unknown to the moral individualism and positivism which the Enlightenment has bequeathed to much of the West. They have been explored, with rare integrity and persuasiveness, by Alasdair McIntyre, in *After Virtue*, pp. 190–209. On a different front, the points here made do not mean to restrict the moral significance of narrative to the explicitly moral and religious narratives of the Jewish and Christian traditions. Anyone even slightly familiar with, say, the Buddhist *jatakas* and comparable cycles of animal fables, with the heroic narratives—*Ramayana* and *Mahabharata*—featured in Javanese *wayang*, and, closer to home, with the *Ovide moralisé* of the early and high Middle Ages or with the cycle of medieval narratives glorifying courtly love (cf. C. S. Lewis' classic *The Allegory of Love*), knows how essential narrative traditions can be to formation in moral growth and refinement of manners. Only outsiders will object that these narratives can be surprisingly a-moral and at times even objectively immoral. What really keeps them alive is not their literal, face-value meaning, but the (mostly oral and hence flexible) traditions of interpretation that draw on them for both entertainment and moral and religious example. The strong point of narratives thus interpreted is that they never separate the *formal* ingredients of the moral life from the material (cf. §131, 2, c). That is, they invariably present the values honored by the *shared* moral sense (that is, those that are considered the backbone of the common good) as characteristic of *conscientious individuals* with a magnanimous conception of moral duty. In other words, they never present moral autonomy as conflicting with generous, unselfish dedication to the common good (cf. §141, 3–4). – Incidentally, in the light of the observations just made, is it not illusory to persist in believing that popular television series of the narrative kind have little or no formative moral significance? Is it responsible or even realistic to suppose that, as long as *individual* responsibility in moral decision-making is appropriately commended at home and in school, human beings will stop being dependent on the moral world that is so graphically presented to them as appealing, in narratives offered by the media?

indeed given us *access* to our integrity and identity, but it turns out not to give us an assured foothold in their *attainment*. But at last the moral self-directedness that is necessarily involved in the responsible life of every day has begun to yield its deeper secret: if virtue is to lead to authentic identity and integrity, it must be somehow rooted in a basic, at least implicitly *religious* faith-commitment that awakens hope, assurance, and (especially) a deeper, more carefree, more subtly responsible inner freedom [*q*]. Thus the pursuit of right living raises (but does not unequivocally settle) the issue of faith in God as the source and final guarantor of the integrity and identity we implicitly seek in acting virtuously [*r*].

[§124] DYING INCOMPLETE AND UNFULFILLED AS A CALL TO FAITH

[1] The insights developed in the previous section become incomparably more pressing when we place the human pursuit of integrity and identity by means of engagement with otherness in the perspective of its termination: death.

In aspiring to the good life, we find ourselves *pursuing* integrity and identity, and attaining a certain maturity in the process. Still, not even

---

[*q*] This implies, of course, that the faith-commitment that underlies the moral life does not *divide* the responsibility for our moral actions *between* God and ourselves. In other words, *we* are to take real responsibility for our actions, yet at the same time, rather than becoming wholly absorbed by our own morality, we are to let ourselves be made inwardly free, by abandonment to God. This is the point of the famous *prima agendorum regula* ("first rule in doing things") attributed to Ignatius of Loyola in Gabriel Hevenesi's *Scintillæ Ignatianæ*: "So trust in God, as if the success of your undertakings depended entirely on you, and in no way on God; yet so put your entire effort to the tasks, as if you were going to do nothing, and God alone everything" (nr. 2, p. 2).

[*r*] Fundamental faith-commitments take on a variety of forms and structures, both personal and social. Examples of the former are habitual fidelity to one's fundamental option (§112, 3, [*b*]), regard for the integrity of one's conscience [cf. GS 16; DH 4316], and the practice of prayerful surrender to God's Providence in all the contingencies of life (cf. §118). Examples of the latter are respect for humanity's accumulated moral wisdom, and specifically for the Christian community, its Gospel, and its authoritative teachings. As for explicitly theological interpretations of the forms and structures of the responsible life, there is, first of all, Aquinas' profound interpretation of the fundamental commitment that undergirds it. Following Augustine, he appeals to the fundamental affinity of the soul and its faculties with the triune God: cf. *S. Th.* I, 93, 7, *ad 3, 4*. Rather more recently, some structures and forms of moral commitment have been capably discussed by H. Richard Niebuhr, in his classic monograph *The Responsible Self*, and even more recently, in a Catholic vein, by Stephen Happel and James J. Walter, in their careful and penetrating book *Conversion and Discipleship: A Christian Foundation for Ethics and Doctrine*. For an effort to put psychological observation to the task of appreciating moral and theological maturity, cf. James W. Fowler, *Stages of Faith* and the literature discussed there.

our most constructive, sustained moral engagement with humanity and the world will, in our lifetime, add up to integrity *attained,* or to the kind of identity that suggests *completion,* say, by the unconditional openness and total forgetfulness of self with which we relate to others [*s*]. Not even the most contented, seasoned, or saintly among us are wholly complete or fulfilled; boundless desire makes us natively incapable of resting in anything short of total fulfillment, yet total fulfillment eludes us in our lifetime. In fact, just what could it mean to call anyone alive or any human community "entirely fulfilled"? And even if a wholly perfect individual or some wholly moral or religious Utopia were alleged to exist, how would we be able to test the claim empirically, given the inadequacy of all the yardsticks available to us? Little wonder that, around the turn of the first millennium, Saint Symeon, known as "the New Theologian," who was the abbot of an important Byzantine monastery, could write, with the wisdom of the great Tradition:

The human spirit, while unable to gain definitive possession of what it desires, is [yet] incapable of putting a measure on its desire and on its love [of God]; rather, because it endeavors to attain and grasp the end-without-end, the desire it carries around in itself always remains endless and the love unfulfilled. . . . None of those who come to this point think they have laid bare in themselves the first principle of the desire or of the love of God; rather, being unable to lay hold on the fullness of love, they feel as if they do not love God. Hence, too, since they think of themselves as the last among all those who live in awe of God, they think of themselves, from the bottom of their hearts, as unworthy even of being saved.[13]

Ceaseless *aspiration* to fulfillment indeed lies at the core of our being; still, while we live in the world the *actuality* of fulfillment is available to us only in *docta ignorantia* and in a keen sense of our insufficiency before God: we sense, negatively, that present moral satisfaction is never

---

[*s*] The position here taken implies a disagreement with the distinguished psychotherapist and educator Carl Rogers. His requirement that the counselor or therapist practice *"unconditional* positive regard" (cf. *On Becoming a Person,* esp. pp. 283–84) is entirely acceptable as the characterization of a therapeutic and human *ideal.* However, it is not, in fact, humanly attainable. As a matter of fact, Rogers' conception is residually theological; since only the Transcendent God is *per se* capable of unconditional positive regard, whenever human persons actually show unconditional positive regard, this manifests the presence of God. According to the Christian faith, God actually offers this kind of regard to humanity, in the person of Jesus Christ. Accordingly, Christians are called to let themselves be so deeply touched by Christ's unqualified loving regard for all comers, including themselves, that they find themselves prompted to offer it to others.

fully satisfying. We keep falling short of the very thing we most dearly aspire to (cf. §67, 1–2) [*t*].

Something important immediately follows from the thesis that fulfillment eludes us as long as we live. When we actually die, no matter how mature, prepared, and even (in cases) desirous of death (and/or of God) we have become, we will fall short of the actualization of the potential we have harbored from the beginning; none of us die entirely fulfilled or in perfect enjoyment of our identity. That is, nobody dies ready for God.

[a] Those of us who enjoy both the affluence and the considerable freedom of the North American and West European culture of self-actualization should appreciate the immense extent of this claim. We can begin by calling to mind the deaths—especially the sudden or violent deaths—of human beings who never live to see their basic human needs satisfactorily met: innumerable children and countless caring, productive adults cut down in the flower of life by illness or mishap, or the deaths—untold except in the narrowest circles—of the congenitally impaired, the sickly, the uneducated, the under-developed, the hardly noticed, the nameless, the unborn. But this is not all. There are also the countless people who have died unfulfilled because they did not find the hand of human care extended, or because, when it was extended, they did not feel they could trust it: the inconsequential, the misunderstood, the stereotyped, the perpetually outclassed, the systemically marginalized and oppressed, and (downright scandalously) the poor who could have lived but have died, and continue to die, for sheer lack of access to available food and available means of food production.

But not even this is all. Lack of completion marks even the end of the significant, the distinguished, and the self-actualized. To appreciate this, we may begin by recalling that the dying never die without leaving at least some unfinished business behind; and since engagement with otherness is how we establish our integrity and identity, every item of unfinished business suggests that the dying have had to leave the task of responsible living in some way unfinished, and with it, their own selves as well. Moreover, if at the personal, rela-

---

[*t*] Wholeness and integrity being so deeply attractive, and the steps toward them being so appealing yet so unsatisfactory, it is not surprising that there is a pervasive element of *melancholy* in human existence—a test of faith that sometimes amounts to an ache for death. Taking his cues mainly from Søren Kierkegaard, Romano Guardini has given us, in *Vom Sinn der Schwermut*, an poignant analysis of this.

tional level, we experience the death of others as a separation that hurts us, we can at least surmise that in some way it must hurt the dying as well—including those who are anxious to let go and to be let go of, or even those positively prepared to sacrifice themselves. But this implies that we think of the dying as somehow still involved in engagement with otherness as they die, and accordingly, as somehow aware of their own lack of completion.

[2] Few natural experiences raise the issue of the meaning of human existence *as a whole* with so much urgency as the death of others, which drives home the certain prospect of death for each of us, who are still alive [*u*]. This realization must prompt us to explore and develop the theme of human non-fulfillment in a somewhat more contemplative, theoretical (though hardly less unsettling) fashion.

Life's termination—in Heidegger's idiom, its "end"—is part of the life process itself. Taken by itself, dying is as particular an occurrence as other particular occurrences in life; like the latter, therefore, it fails to bring about total fulfillment. As a matter of fact, taken by themselves, as particular incidents, dying and death seem nasty and devoid of sense. Thus not even the successful, the conscientious, the mature, the self-aware, the heroic, and the saintly among us attain total fulfillment simply by virtue of their dying. Their lives, often impressive or attractive, may lend to their deaths, sometimes quite admirable and dignified, a wider symbolic significance. For instance, their deaths may indirectly suggest that, in dying, they have passed on to a deeper fulfillment. This, however, does not entitle us to say that the event of their dying *as such* has brought about fulfillment, let alone that the process of dying has been an experience of fulfillment for the dying themselves [*v*]. For in and of itself, the event of death never clearly

---

[*u*] Readers of Martin Heidegger's *Sein und Zeit* (ET *Being and Time*) will recognize in the following analyses occasional echoes of his analysis of human existence as "being unto death" (§§46–53).

[*v*] This last sentence is partly written to take into account the many plausible accounts, by both adults and children, of "near-death experience." These accounts regularly mention out-of-body ecstasy and heightened awareness, in which the principal ingredients perceived are light, serenity, beauty, as well as love and persons loved; freedom from fear and loving devotion to others are reported to be common after-effects of such experiences. Typically, however, the accounts, while suggestive of a better world, stay clear of definitive assertions about the ultimate meaning of either life or death; in other words, near-death experience is not claimed to supply incontrovertible evidence of, or access to, total fulfillment. Cf. Raymond A. Moody's *Reflections on Life After Life* and *Life After Life*, David Lorimer's rather too far-flung *Whole in One* (but it does have a careful preface by Dr. Moody and a useful bibliography), Melvin Morse's *Closer to the Light*, and (despite its lack of simplicity and directness and its

manifests fulfillment to those who attend to the dying even as they die. Thus, by all verifiable accounts, death is even more of an equalizer than we often declare it to be: not only do we all die, *we all die incomplete, unfinished, and unfulfilled.*

[3] This realization is liable to deepen when we realize not only that dying is only one particular event, but also, more basically, that it is not a voluntary undertaking. Death comes to us; it imposes itself on us; it is something undergone—*suffered.* Taken by itself, therefore, dying is not the last of the series of positions we adopt in our lifetime; it is not the last particular, deliberate, moral act we accomplish. In fact, death unmasks humanity's fabulous resourcefulness in engaging in deliberate activity as limited. Humanity, astounding and ever-ingenious as it is (so the chorus sings, in the first *stasimon* of Sophocles' *Antigone*),

> meets no contingency
> helpless; death alone
> it has devised no way to escape.[14]

Accordingly, dying is not the deliberate accomplishing of a positive good, of the kind by which we actualize ourselves while we live; it is not a properly human act (cf. §115, 2, [*a*]). For when we die, we do not "do" so by virtue of our faculties of freedom and consciousness (that is, by exercising our transcendence). Quite the contrary, death happens to us by virtue of our involvement in otherness. In fact, we die owing to an excess of otherness.

Dying befalls us. Death puts a stop to us. The very otherness that is integral to our humanity now makes common cause with the cosmos at large and invades and overwhelms us as if it were an alien power (which, of course, is exactly what it is becoming). Thus dying is, essentially, a biophysical failure—an adverse cosmological occurrence that is happening to us from the "outside" and which we cannot ward off because it is at the same time inside us and part of us. For a lifetime (whether long or short), a balance of cosmic mutualities has enabled us to be relatively successful participants in the cosmos—in our environment, our habitats, our cultures (cf. §115, 8–9). Cosmic participation has supported our existence, both physical and spiritual, as effective human individuals or communities. Now a decisive shift—one not

---

frequent lapses into sermonizing, conceivably due to the influence of a co-author/ghostwriter/editor bent on effect) Betty J. Eady's *Embraced by the Light.*

infrequently some time in the making—gathers momentum. Balance gives way to imbalances so severe as to undo, slowly or swiftly, our bio-physical viability; cosmic process seeks a new equilibrium of factors and forces—one that excludes our continued biophysical selves; the press of otherness becomes too much for us; the dynamics of disinte-gration put an end to the ways in which, both unconsciously and delib-erately, we have for a long time been negotiating with cosmic process and enjoyed control over it, or at least, holding our own in the midst of it. Life may go on, but *our* death is setting in, and it proves to be non-negotiable. No wonder, anthropologically speaking, human death (whether of individuals or, as sometimes happens, of entire communities) habitually impresses us as intractable—unexpected, pre-mature, sudden, inexorable, or merciless, and always in some sense a natural evil, or at least a defeat.

[a] Consequently, as we move to death, such positions as our physi-cal condition may still allow us to adopt will be less and less cosmo-logical and increasingly anthropological in nature. They concern the choice of conditions and circumstances and the attitude we adopt with regard to the process of decline and dying, rather than the process of decline and dying itself. *From a strictly cosmological point of view*, therefore, the positions adopted by the dying are very limited in scope: in the very choices they still succeed in pulling off as they approach death they acknowledge and increasingly accept the basic fact that dying is precisely the diminishment and eventual cancellation of their capacity for choice and engagement. For, as they die, decision gives way to a passivity so overwhelming as to be final.

This means that in the last resort we find ourselves deprived even of the satisfaction that we are ending our life on a note of something noticeably well *done*. For dying is the forcible cessation of all efforts to engage the world of otherness—a cessation we may be able to ac-cept and even welcome *before* it overtakes us or perhaps even *as it be-gins* to overtake us, but no longer *when* it does. For the stop put to our trying to do things coincides with the stop put to our efforts to do the right thing; as such, life's cessation is not a moral matter [*w*].

[*w*] This being the case, the question arises if death and dying, being involuntary, can ever become a moral issue, and if so, how. Two points can be made. *Firstly*, hu-man life is a natural given; that is, it is something that offers itself for interpretation and acceptance, in faith, ultimately as a gift from God. It is part of human life that it should come to an end biophysically, and consequently also as a moral undertak-ing; death forces upon us the end of all meritorious engagement (cf. DH 1488). Ac-

Whatever else it may bring about, dying puts an end to all character-istically human (that is, moral) attempts at both living and living well. On that score, too, we die incomplete and unfinished.

[4] This means, once again, that, far from disclosing fulfillment, death appears to defeat that very notion [x]. In fact, the phenomenon

---

ceptance of this end is, both morally and theologically, far from inconsistent with either human dignity or moral responsibility. In fact it is incumbent on those facing death as well as on those attending them and those acting in their behalf. On princi-ple, therefore, there must be a point beyond which the fierce resolve to stay alive or the stubborn efforts to keep someone else alive begin to imply a refusal to accept that human life ends in death. In fact, this refusal may in cases be positively immoral. Thus it is morally incoherent to argue that biophysical life demands, in and of itself, that it be unconditionally supported even in the case of persons beyond all reason-able hope of recovery, or that the biophysical life of those irreversibly incapable of any response to others, or of any discernment of good or evil in regard to themselves, entirely becomes the moral responsibility of qualified others, whose unqualified duty it is *actively* to support it at all costs and with every available means (cf. §116, 5, a; c). There is a point, in other words, when the truly moral response to declining life is to support the dying with love and competent care and to ease their suffering, with-out placing any further obstacles in the way of the processes of decombination that lead to death. The determination of this point is a matter of discretionary judgment, and hence, very much a moral act. Like all moral acts, it must be justified practically —that is, by recourse to interpretation: when a human life can no longer be pre-served by reasonable and affordable care, or when it no longer holds out any hope for further responsible human living, but is so overwhelmed by virtually unbearable suffering that it has become a token and a portent only of dying and death, the deci-sion to end life support is neither suicidal nor homicidal, but moral (DH 4664–66). In fact, a human life forcibly and undiscerningly turned into a life of irremediable suffering or irreversible coma raises the troubling question whether such a life is not a monstrous human artifact, and thus in practice barely interpretable as a gift from God. This is often the point where the march toward the other extreme of the bio-ethical spectrum starts. So, *secondly*, it is also morally incoherent to argue that suicide and active euthanasia are to be considered part of the dying process. The reason is that the dying process consists in the *cosmic* processes that run their course, produc-ing, in the dying person's biophysical adjustment to the cosmos, imbalances so severe as to cause biophysical death. However, unlike the process of dying, suicide and active euthanasia (whether heedless, invited, or otherwise premeditated) are specific, elective interventions, deliberately designed to take human life, by adding to the death-dealing processes already being suffered. This is in and of itself morally in-defensible. Even if they should be inspired by the wish to undo a medically and mor-ally unwise decision to support life made in the past, it is by no means clear that suicide and euthanasia are morally justifiable, though persons in desperate condi-tions taking their own lives or begging for active euthanasia could well be exonerated from moral guilt for doing so (cf. DH 4660–62).
[x] This makes it wise for us not to anticipate an *experience* of fulfillment in dying, let alone to aim at one, or, for that matter, to hold out the promise of such an experi-ence to others. Real dying interrupts our self-centered dreams about a meaningful death, be they of the romantic or the heroic kind ("even if I surrender my body by way of a grand gesture": 1 Cor 13, 3). No wonder Qoheleth dismisses, with charac-teristic realism about the conclusiveness of death and dying, the expectation of any-thing grand or even positive in death; if there is any *ascertainable* hope, it is in staying

of death suggests that we will probably be doing quite well if we die without being simply routed by cosmic might or mishap, or overtaken by human inadvertence (or worse, by crass human purpose). And we will die uncommonly well if we get an occasion to surrender to the onset of death (or even accept or embrace it) in a reasonably deliberate fashion, at peace with ourselves and supported by persons we care for and trust, and who ease our final surrender by care and respectful love even as we approach it. For even at its best and most serene, death demands that we *abandon our selves as we have come to know and acknowledge them*—that is, such *limited* identities as it has been our responsibility and our privilege to actualize and communicate in life. Thus, when life runs out on us, we find ourselves not so much called upon to act well, as prompted, and indeed compelled, to resign our *unfinished* selves by surrendering to cosmic forces and purposes to which any further free and deliberate choice and activity have become irrelevant.

Those who attend to the dying (rather than to their property or to the positions of consequence they have occupied) find themselves forced to surrender to the same forces. For to the living, too, the onset of death opens a void upon which purposeful activity is lost for good. And once it has occurred, death declares to the living an emptiness only inadequately filled with what the dying have left of themselves, for others to bury, to cherish, to divide (whether discreetly or noisily), to carry forward, or (quite often) to quietly dispose of and forget. Death opens a vacuum that neither the harvest of a dying person's lifetime of dedicated endeavor nor, for that matter, the survivors' appreciation of that harvest can completely fill. All deathbeds, the peaceful as much as the fierce, are attended by might-have-beens, unfinished business, dreams unfulfilled, prayers unanswered. And even if, at the serene passing of a truly mature person, bystanders should discern the presence of a higher, invisible realm of being, and feel inspired to utter a few belated words of thankfulness and blessing for a life well lived, such words remain suspended, unverified:

> A Benediction whispered and belated
> Which has no fruit beyond a consecrated,
> A consecrated silence at the end.[15]

What death makes visible, therefore, is not the fulfillment attained through a lifetime of engagement, but rather, the closure imposed

---

alive, for "a live dog is better off than a dead lion" (Eccles 9, 4).

upon it—a closure underscored by a silence that drives home the end of all positive knowledge and all deliberate effort. Thank heaven, the event of death frequently carries intimations of transcendence and fulfillment, but it does not give clear, unequivocal assurances of it. In this sense, death is genuinely discontinuous, both with the actual, responsible pursuit of human integrity and identity, and with the native desire for the Transcendent that has undergirded the pursuit and inspired it. It puts an end to the pursuit while removing all discernible evidence of the desire. No wonder the discussion about the actual moment of death (and often, the long wait for it) has such a way of keeping us in suspense—of controlling the attention of both the dying themselves and the surviving (not to mention the members of the medical profession). In and of itself, death is a void; it brings on a loss of perspective; around the dying and the dead, space seems empty and time seems to come to a standstill. For the time being, every human death leaves a radical credibility gap to be bridged—bridged, not filled, for what in the world could fill it?

[5] Our examination, in the previous section, of the structure of the *way* toward fulfillment yielded the following conclusion: there is more satisfaction in the good life according as it is more deeply undergirded by a fundamental faith-commitment that inspires hope and assurance. That is to say, the life of responsible engagement commends to us (though it does not force upon us) a faith-commitment to God as the reliable source and ultimate guarantor of the integrity and identity we pursue, both for ourselves and for others and the world around us, by moral living (§123).

Our meditation on death and dying now turns out to yield an analogous conclusion, only far more pressingly. For in the effective moral *living* the need for a fundamental faith-commitment is at least *discernible* (even if hardly obvious). By contrast, the events of *dying and death*, in their cosmic starkness and intransigence, make the existence of life's deeper layers and the call of what is beyond life incomparably harder to discern. The reason for this is obvious: *dying and death obstruct discernment itself.*

[6] Death, therefore, is as definitive anthropologically as it is in biophysical, cosmological terms. The disintegration of our bodies puts an end to that most characteristically human, *spiritual* undertaking: conscious and free engagement with the world of otherness, in the constructive pursuit of truth and goodness—the pursuit that is also the

access-road to our own identity [y]. But even that is not all. For in obstructing engagement with otherness, dying and death also cut us off from the *conscious* religious awareness of the God to whom our evolving identities are ineradicably attuned. No wonder that even long-standing, reliable habits of deep prayer may give out for the terminally ill.[16] Speaking theologically, therefore, in cutting us off from any conscious sense of identity, death also marks the end of every *deliberate* faith-commitment. "For those going down into the Pit, there is no more trusting in your fidelity," as Hezekiah's prayer puts it bluntly (Is 38, 17).

Death, therefore, is the final impasse, cosmologically, anthropologically, and theologically. No wonder that even slight reminders of death can turn our trepidation at the precariousness of our being into fright. We find ourselves resisting death with the energy and vehemence of our entire cosmic and spiritual being, and the mere thought of its inevitability can evoke a consternation beyond words. No wonder, either, that the Second Vatican Council can write, with the candor of both existential humanism and authentic Jewish and Christian faith:

In the face of death the riddle of the human condition looms largest. . . . In the face of death all imagination fails.

(GS 18; DH 4318)

Death, that is, is the definitive test of faith. Faced with the prospect of death even while we are alive, then, we have, theologically speaking, three options [z].

[7] The first is *resistance and denial.* Shall we, dominated by fear of extinction, allow impending death to dictate the story of our life? That is, shall we find ourselves forcefully or even desperately turning life into a sustained battle against death and the countless forms its onset takes—a battle engaging every fiber of our being and every means at

---

[y] In the customary, practically normative language of Christian theology, this double impasse is expressed by saying: death is the "separation" of body and soul. This harsh idiom is rightly understood only on condition that the *unity* of body and soul in life is fully appreciated as *essential*, and hence, if the soul is understood to retain a continuing relatedness to the world of matter (cf. §124, 12, b, [*ii*]). Cf. Karl Rahner, *Zur Theologie des Todes*, pp. 17–26 (ET *On the Theology of Death*, pp. 16–26).

[z] These three options are the positive ones—the ones we can adopt with intellectual and moral integrity. Later on we will have to come back to the proposition that there are other, negative, unprincipled, and often sinful options vis-à-vis death as well. The feature they have in common is the attempt to escape from death by dint of anxious or violent self-assertion, at the expense of others (cf. §116, 5).

our disposal? Or, alternatively, since we realize that the war cannot be won, shall we disdain being enslaved by panic, and proceed to disown (or at least control) the vehemence and depth of our dread of death and of its countless premonitions? That is, shall we opt for a purposeful, dignified life, by concluding, impassively or perhaps wearily, that the one truly permanent (and in that sense, meaningful) feature of the cosmos is the coming and going of everything, like the sway of the waves of the sea? That the variety of the universe and of our own life in it, dazzling in its very transience, *is* its meaning? That "God" and "forever" are misconceptions? And consequently, that freedom and consciousness and the human spirit's unquenchable desire are splendid epiphenomena at best and painful illusions at worst? Are they nothing but fanciful reactions to mirages, displayed to ephemeral, fleeting human minds by a splendid but implacable cosmos? Could it be that the cosmos is simply forever gearing up and forever simply winding down, devouring all that it engenders? And therefore, could it be that the riddle of human life holds no lasting meaning that can be discerned? And thus, is any resistance to death no more than a brave pose before the curtain falls [*aa*]?

[8] The second is *suspense—epochē*. Shall we put our vital energy to the pursuit of restraint and thus remain disciplined agnostics? Shall we seek balance, control passion, and (despite all the pressure) live as nobly and attentively as we can, as aspirants and seekers permanently perplexed by the cosmos as well as by ourselves, so intensely cosmic and transitory, yet so endlessly aspiring to what lies beyond? Our selves, so inescapably self-conscious and conscious of an attunement to reality and beyond, yet so deeply precarious (cf. §112, 4–5)? Our selves, whose immortality our children seem to intuit so spontaneously, while we, responsible adults of all ages and places, find ourselves oh so easily calling it into question, especially when we attempt to articulate

---

[*aa*] Readers of Virginia Woolf's *The Waves* may have recognized the final paragraphs of the soliloquy that brings this splendid novel to its close. Bernard muses: "Day rises; ... the sun levels his beams straight at the sleeping house; the waves deepen their bars; they fling themselves on shore; back blows the spray; sweeping their waters they surround the boat and the sea-holly. The birds sing in chorus; deep tunnels run between the stalks of flowers; the house is whitened; the sleeper stretches; gradually all is astir. Light floods the room and drives shadow beyond shadow to where they hang in folds inscrutable. What does the central shadow hold? Something? Nothing? I do not know." And: "And in me too the wave rises. It swells; it arches its back. I am aware of a new desire ... What enemy do we know perceive advancing against us ... ? It is death. Death is the enemy. It is death against whom I ride" (pp. 291–92, 297).

the intuition? Does not death, once encountered, have a way of making us irresolute about our immortality even, in our maturity? In times of distress and lassitude, do we not find ourselves vacillating about life after death? When challenged to defend it, do we not tend to equivocate [*bb*]?

[9] The third is *acceptance*. With Socrates, we may (since "nobody knows what death is") want to entertain the possibility that it is "perhaps, the greatest good."[17] We could even go farther, and positively open ourselves to the realization that human beings

> have brought themselves, by both education and action, to such virtues as patience, self-discipline, and openness to restraint. [They do so] precisely because they are convinced that not until people act and think well do they live well, and that it must not be supposed that an immortal God should give life only in order that it might end in death, since it is inconceivable that a good giver should have made the experience of living so thoroughly delightful, only to have it rendered utterly dismal by the fear of death.[18]

Thus, shall we agree to having the riddle of human mortality and incompleteness turn into a holy mystery for us (cf. §112, 5; §113, 3, e)? Guided by life experience and religious traditions, shall we venture the ultimate option—the move beyond all moves [*cc*]? Shall we dare drink from the Source Invisible, whose waters, once we have taken them in faith, will turn out to well up in the deepest reaches of our own created selves (§89, 2)—reaches more deep-seated than the wellspring of our fears, and even of our joys (cf. §89, 2, [*jj*])? And so, shall we agree

---

[*bb*] On the human irresolution with regard to death and immortality as expressed in Greek poetry, cf. J.M.Bremer's fine essay "Death and Immortality in Some Greek Poems." On children's intuitions of immortality, cf. Roger Troisfontaines' quotation: «*L'enfant . . . se sait immortel avant de se savoir mortel. Longtemps avant.*» ("Children know they are immortal before they know they are mortal. Long before."). Cf. *Je ne meurs pas*, p. 28 (ET *I do not die*, p. 29).

[*cc*] A severely *radical* argument in favor this move, both in the face of death and as a guide to life, is Pascal's famous "wager." He writes: "Yes, but you must wager. It is not a matter of choice; you are in the boat. . . . Let us weigh gain and loss if we gamble that God exists. Let us consider these two: in case you win you win everything, and in case you lose you lose nothing; so gamble, without any hesitation, that he exists" (*Pensées* 418 [233]; *Oeuvres complètes*, pp. 550–51; quotation p. 550). This is an impressive argument, yet the trouble with it is obvious, especially when quoted out of context (as it usually is). In commending naked faith-abandon, Pascal seems to imply that faith-abandon to God is *unsupported by any other experience*, in typically seventeenth-century fashion (and probably also for the sake of argument, to drive into a corner those who insist on living by the spirit of geometry alone; cf. §96, 4), Pascal is prescinding almost entirely from the intimations, both moral and religious, of the divine presence that are ordinarily part of human life understood as an *integral* experience.

to treat our life (that is, at least indirectly, ourselves) as a poem—one that springs from an impulse deep inside us yet which is prompted from elsewhere? A poem which, in Paul Valéry's celebrated phrase, is never finished—it merely gets a stop put to it by the accident that sends it to its destination?[19] That is, shall we accept our incompleteness, leave ourselves be, and seek to surrender our fears and our preoccupation with self to the One who alone sustains the whole cosmos, fulfills every desire, allays all precariousness, reads crooked lines and even writes with them (cf. §95, 10)? The One who alone is capable of graciously filling the empty vessel of natural immortality with life overflowing? The One who can reveal us to ourselves more fully than we can imagine, in an encounter that will surprise us with the gift of an identity with which we had been only dimly familiar—one that was meant to be ours before we ever knew it (cf. §109, 9, c)? The One to whom the Psalmist can say:

> For better is your steadfast love than being alive;
>   my lips will be loud in singing your praise.
>
> (Ps 63, 4)

[10] Thus death and the anticipation of death drive home, like no other cosmic occurrence or consciously adopted human position, the issue of faith-commitment as the foundation of hopeful and meaningful living as well as dying. And it does so not just *when* it occurs or is about to occur, but *throughout life* (though in various degrees). For unlike plants and animals, which meet their end only as it meets them, human beings are natively attuned to transcendence. Hence, it is distinctive of them to go about their lives, not piecemeal, but intentionally, by way of a total project. Mature human self-awareness, in other words, includes the understanding of death as the horizon of life. This understanding both requires human maturity and is its source. As Martin Heidegger has so ardently explained to this century of pointless, violent death, awareness of certain and unpredictable death is an integral (if often frightful, painful, and ominous) ingredient of authentic (that is, meaningful) human living. And conversely, human living is an exercise in dying—regarded not as the peremptory end, or as the inescapable cosmic occurrence we share with plants and animals, but as the *lifelong* anthropological and fundamental-theological venture in self-abandon, deliberately undertaken (often anxiously, though sometimes also quite serenely and lovingly), in an attitude of faith.[20]

This faith in life beyond the clutches of death is as human as it is divine. It is divine because it is capable of habitually uniting the human spirit, precarious as it proceeds, with the God whom it natively mirrors and to whom it is natively attracted; it is human because it can reconcile us to our being tempted and tested by our participation in the cosmos we are part of—the very cosmos we also transcend (cf. §119, 3).

[a] Here let us interrupt ourselves to note that sustained faith-commitment in the face of death does not arise spontaneously or drop from the skies. Even more decisively than the sustained moral life (cf. §123, 7), it is dependent on formation by narrative traditions.

This issue is related to the question of explicit faith in life beyond death, but far from identical with it. For often (especially in the older layers of the Jewish Scriptures) the biblical narratives about Abraham, Isaac, and Jacob, and about the great believers, prophets, singers, and sufferers observe an unpretentious, sober silence about life beyond death. And never—not even in its more recent layers—does the Bible thematically treat the immortality of the soul as a hard, unquestionable fact. All of this is related to the fact that, throughout the Bible, anthropology defers to theology: any exploration of humanity's ontological constitution is parasitical on the biblical call to free and conscious encounter with the living God (cf. §109, 9, c), and to the shared life and the wisdom that are its fruits now, in the present. Thus, in the end, all the great believers of the biblical narratives are capable of looking, in faith, beyond suffering unto death as well as beyond death itself. For the gift of true life, they look to the same God whom Jesus will eventually call "the God, not of dead, but of living people" (Mk 12, 27). To this, Luke's Gospel will add the entirely pertinent gloss, "since for God all are alive" (Lk 20, 38).

[b] Still, this is not all. Later on in this volume, we will have to reflect thematically on the fact that both human death and the sufferings that lead up to it are often unnecessary or downright unjust; frequently, they are the effect of sinful human negligence, injustice, or even perversity. This means that the facts of human sinfulness often compound the natural human crisis of faith in the face of death, to the point of making it near-impossible to interpret human life and death as a gateway to everlasting life with God. Human indifference and malice lead many to despair and outright rejection of God.

The biblical traditions squarely recognize this most serious impasse. The Book of Psalms contains a number of dramatic monologues, in which just people surrounded by the forces of injustice turn to the God in whose image they are indelibly made with words like the following: "As for me, in my justice, I shall see your face; when I awake, I shall be fulfilled by the vision of your likeness" (Ps 17, 15). Likewise, the Bible contains numerous stories about the just being beset by sinful humanity, yet abandoning themselves to the living God and to God's promises despite the fact that the divine countenance is veiled [*dd*].

Not only has the Christian Church been inspired by this tradition of faith put to the test of unjust suffering; it has positively endorsed it, chiefly by interpreting Jesus' attitude toward his death as its culmination (cf. esp. Heb 11, 1–12, 3).[21] And of course, the Gospel accounts of Jesus' acceptance of unjust suffering and of his death-sentence in total abandon to God have in turn become a central theme in the tradition of formative Christian narrative. Patient acceptance of unjust treatment in imitation of Jesus is readily visible in the New Testament writings (cf., *e.g.*, Acts 6, 9–15; 7, 54–60; 1 Pet 2, 13–4, 6; 1 Tim 6, 11–16; Rev 7, 13–17; 14, 1–5), but the theme has proceeded to become a central and most characteristic topic in the spiritual literature of the Christian community [*ee*].

[*dd*] The figure of David is a case in point; cf. 1 Sam 16, 23; 24, 1–23; 26, 1–25; 2 Sam 1, 1–27; 4, 1–12; 6, 20–23; 16, 5–14; 19, 1–9. 16–24. Many psalms attributed to David and traditionally associated with critical events in his life add to this picture of David as the meek sufferer who, for all his insolence and ambition, puts all his trust in God when set upon by enemies: cf. Pss 3, 7, 17, 22, 34, 56, 69, 142. (J. Cheryl Exum's fascinating reading of David's life is far more suspicious than the one suggested here, but then again, she takes the David narrative entirely by itself, synchronically, regardless of its effective history in the tradition of the Hebrew Scriptures; cf. *Tragedy and Biblical Narrative*, pp. 16–42, 70–119.) Other biblical examples of believers variously driven at bay are Jeremiah (cf. Jer 1, 4–10. 17–19; 15, 10–21; 18, 18–23; 20, 7–14), Job (cf. esp. Job 1, 20–21; 19, 25–27; cf. Ez 14, 14), the harassed just man in the Book of Wisdom (Wisd 1, 1–3, 9), and the Maccabean martyrs (2 Macc 7, 1–41). For a contemporary Jewish example of an appeal to formative tradition as a support in enduring unbearable suffering in faith, cf. Emmanuel Lévinas, "Aimer la Thora plus que Dieu": "God veiling his countenance: I think this is neither a theologian's abstraction nor a poetic image. It is the hour when the just person has nowhere to go in the outside world; when no institution affords him protection; when even the comforting sense of the divine presence, experienced in a childlike person's piety, is withdrawn; when the only victory available to the individual lies in his conscience, which necessarily means: in suffering" (*Difficile liberté*, pp. 190–91). In this way, Lévinas explains, it is precisely in suffering that Jews find themselves being most proud to be Jews—that is, to have the traditions of the Torah to live by. Cf. F. J. van Beeck, *Loving the Torah More than God?*, pp. 37–39 (quotation pp. 37–38).

[*ee*] For a classic and influential example in the Christian West, cf. Thomas à Kempis' *On the Imitation of Christ*, II, 12: "On the Royal Road of the Cross."

[11] The start of the responsible life, it was argued in a previous chapter, faces us with the fundamental option to accept our emergent identity as a gift from God (§112, 2–3 and [b]). Our reflections on life's always-impending end now suggests that sooner or later, as the responsible life moves within view of its untidy end, we have an analogous option—an *optio finalis*. The prospect of death invites us to accept, in faith, that the selfhood we succeed in establishing in our lifetime will always be incomplete; this will encourage us not to make self-actualization the central endeavor of our lives; rather, we will find ourselves abandoning, in both faith and freedom, both our known, actualized self and our unknown, yet-to-be-actualized self to God, who is the Source of a fulfillment beyond every conceivable fulfillment, and, indeed, the very reality of it.[22]

Abandonment to God also lies at the heart of what is known, in ascetical theology, as *mortification*. This practice is as pertinent to authentic humanity as it is bewildering to the self-asserting ego. If the anticipation of death is part of authentic human living, it is also the school in which self-transcending, self-forgetful concern for others as well as self-sacrificing love grow and flourish; and for these very reasons it is also the school of the kind of self-abandon that lies at the core of naked faith (cf. §9). The willing acceptance of death's finality, therefore, is part of the highest, purely contemplative form of worship (cf. §67, 2–4), as well as the final answer to all our petitions. For worship and prayer patiently pursued will eventually lead us to the point where, in Ruusbroec's words (§109, 11),

we will unbecome and die, in God, to ourselves and to all that is ours. And in this dying we become God's hidden children, and we find a new life in us, and this is an everlasting life.

[12] A number of Christian doctrines and traditional catholic positions support and affirm the elaborate phenomenological explorations just offered. Let us detail some of them, in a series of rather more formal anthropological and theological observations and explanations [*ff*].

[a] First of all, our analyses have implied that *human death must be understood to affect, and affect decisively, not just human bodies, but integral human beings.* This means that, to be properly interpreted, it must

---

[*ff*] Some of the following explanations may be profitably compared with the *Letter on Certain Questions Concerning Eschatology*, a very careful document issued by the Congregation for the Doctrine of the Faith in 1979 (DH 4650–59).

be approached from the point of view of *both* integral components of human existence in the world: identity and alienation (cf. §122, 1, f)—or, in more traditional terms, soul and body.

Let us start with the latter. Death marks the end of effective engagement with the world of otherness. The Platonizers, idealizers, and romantics of all times are liable to hail this end as deliverance from the body and from estrangement, since they tend to regard the human spirit as the sole authentic constituent of humanity and as essentially self-identified. In doing so, however, they forget that death cuts us off from the very stuff through and in which we have emerged into being and consciousness and freedom, have learned to grow and find ourselves, and continue to pursue our fulfillment. They also tend to overlook that, far from restoring the spirit to its (allegedly) pristine flawlessness, death leaves us unfinished spiritually, and not just if we have turned out immature or miserable, but also if we have become seasoned and contented. Death, after all, disrupts the very desire that marks us as spiritual and attuned to the absolute; death, therefore, mocks spiritual completion, by positively attacking us in the way we most positively *experience* ourselves as infinitely desirous: in worthwhile engagement with otherness. Seen in this light, effective separation from otherness is an invitation to isolation and hopelessness: could it be that death unmasks human engagement and accomplishment as wholly transitory, and hence, human life as ultimately pointless? If ceaseless desire or *erōs* is at the heart of all of life's endeavors (as the Platonist tradition insists), is death not the human spirit's incapacitation at least as much as its liberation from the body?

This is not to say that the element of liberation is not real. Once we become reflectively aware that the desire that inspires all our particular engagements is and remains boundless, we become aware of its transcendence as well. We sense that our desire springs from the core of ourselves; no wonder we sense that these core "selves" of ours (or, as the Tradition has put it, our "souls") must somehow be transcendent and spiritual, along with the desire. Consequently, too, we sense that there must be more to the dead than what they have left behind for us to bury, be thankful for, treasure, divide, dispose of, or come to terms with [gg]. From experience we know that our ac-

---

[gg] It is not surprising that evidence of intentional burial is universally taken as evidence of human culture. Human beings perceive both others and themselves as memorable beyond death.

complishments in life are never final and our sense of identity never wholly compelling; this feeds the intuition that death is bound to set the human spirit free for the enjoyment of a permanent, substantially deeper and more luminous identity. And as for our own selves, we know from experience that we do attain a limited but real sense of identity; this makes it hard to believe that our deeper, "given" selves, which we take a lifetime to discover and accept and shape and make our own by engagement with otherness, are simply subject to disintegration or extinction. And by the same token (so we are apt to surmise in faith), death must somehow free us for the enjoyment of a life of decisively greater fullness of identity and immediacy of presence, not only, and above all, to the living God, but also to those left behind [hh].

[b] This realization also influences our conception of the human person's engagement after death. We know that the visible, palpable marks which most human beings leave on humanity and the cosmos are obliterated with the passing of time. Still, the fuller identities we believe they are enjoying beyond death remain inseparable from the engagements by dint of which they once acquired those very identities. For this reason, rather than regarding the soul beyond death as definitively freed and separated from the cosmos, contemporary eschatological thinking, inspired by contemporary cosmology and anthropology (cf. §115, 8, [h]), is insisting once again that the separated soul remains vitally related to the world [ii].

This is entirely consistent with the Jewish-Christian expectation of the resurrection of the flesh. Thus Paul can be at pains to reassure the Thessalonians, on the authority of the Lord's own word, that, in regard to the impending Judgment, those who have died in Christ

---

[hh] This leads to the thought that the dead (or at least the just among them, on account of the gift of grace that is theirs), while living in a state of suspense (and hence, cosmologically ineffective), are present to the living with whom they were once associated in the life of alienation. In fact, it is arguable that they are thus present to the living with a decisively greater *spiritual* immediacy than the latter, still bound by alienation, can be present to them. Cf. Aquinas' carefully stated positions in *S. Th.* I, 89, 4 and esp. 8. Origen had made a similar observation: cf. Brian E. Daley, *The Hope of the Early Church*, p. 56.

[ii] Aquinas' mature position on the *anima separata* suggests the same. The separated soul, he explains, retains a natural affinity with the body through which it has come to such perfection as it has attained. Consequently, it has an inclination toward union with the body. In other words, by virtue of the vision of God, the soul enjoys a happiness that is *intensively* perfect; yet it is still yearning for reunion with the body—that is, for a happiness that is more *extensive* (*S. Th.* I, 76, 1, *ad 6*; I–II, 4, 5, *ad 4, 5, 6*).

will be at no disadvantage in comparison with the living (1 Thess 4, 15). Similarly, the seer of the Apocalypse can call the dead blessed "from now on" (*ap' arti*); for, while they rest from their labors, their "labors" (*erga*) follow them into the beyond (Rev 14, 13). No wonder either that the liturgies of the dead, both East and West, do not tire of proclaiming that death is the natural preamble to the grace of the resurrection; catholic doctrine has followed suit by refusing to regard the souls of the dead as finished and fixed, and thus beyond the reach of intercession.

[c] Human death, therefore, while peremptory and in that sense final, intimates that there is a *life* beyond cosmic life, and not a bare, neutral existence. This implies that death is not the last word. Accordingly, the Jewish and Christian traditions interpret it as a radical anthropological crisis rather than as a dead end. Even more significantly, they regard it as a radical theological crisis. For while firmly professing the soul's immortality, neither late Judaism nor classical Christianity were willing to conceive of the soul as fundamentally self-sufficient and assured of life, as Renaissance humanism was first to suggest, and the Enlightenment and Romanticism were to propose with a vengeance. For Irenaeus, for example, genuine immortality is "clearly a gift from God, not a right of nature"; even Origen, who defends the natural immortality of the soul, does so only on the basis of its being *capax dei*.[23]

In the Jewish-Christian tradition, there have indeed been those who have understood the human soul as a pure spirit, inherently entitled to bliss and assured of it, upon serving a sentence of cosmic probation. Still, they have been marginal.. The mainstream tradition has constantly regarded the soul as the *locus*, not only of human persons' inalienable identity, but also, and primarily, of their relatedness to God (cf., again, §109, 9, c, [z]). According to this tradition, self-abandoning faith and hope in God when approaching the straits of death is the supreme exercise of this relatedness. For Christians, this self-abandon to God takes the shape of union with Christ's total self-abandon to the Father in life and death, and hence, of the imitation of Christ in his willing acceptance of death, which his Resurrection was to vindicate as his entry into imperishable life with God. No wonder Paul can think of death, even this side of the general resurrection, as the way to "be with Christ" (Phil 1, 23).

Gradually, therefore, the great Tradition has come to realize that death is the human person's transition to a state *both provisional and definitive.* Not surprisingly, it has not come to this realization without some fierce theological battles, especially between Eastern and Western Christianity. Some of these remain unresolved to this day.

Even today, the East generally favors a rather more thoroughly eschatological view of life after death, often with an appeal to Rev 6, 9–11. In this view, what is prominent is the element of provisionalness, not definitiveness: since the soul's *effective* union with unfinished humanity and the cosmos as a whole is in suspense, its predicament after death is impermanent; the soul must still live in the expectation of the general resurrection.

The Western teaching, on the other hand, is typically more concerned with individual salvation and hence, with the nature of afterlife. Its central affirmation is that, since the caliber of the individual person's relatedness to God is definitively established at death, death has consequences that must be thought of as everlasting. For in the light of God's presence, the soul finds itself revealed to itself, no longer in part (1 Cor 13, 9. 12) and by discernment, as it used to be while engaging the world of otherness, but fully, without mediation, "face to face" (1 Cor 13, 12) [*jj*].[24]

That is, the soul finds itself no longer temporarily tested (as it used to be while it was united with the body), but conclusively *judged.* This judgment, is administered, not forensically (that is, by God acting as judge in an external court of law),[25] but immanently—that is, by the

---

[*jj*] The ambivalence between provisionalness and definitiveness in the interpretation of the status of the *anima separata* accounts for that oddment in the history of the papal *magisterium*: the teaching of Pope John XXII (1316–1334) on the subject. John taught that not until the last day will the just duly enjoy the vision of God and the damned duly meet their eternal punishment. In teaching this, the Pope was reviving the traditional, undifferentiated position, which the theological consensus of the West had long come to regard as unsatisfactory. On the day before his death, under pressure from the assembled cardinals, John modified his opinion, but he still had the presence of mind to insist on a *proviso*. He conceded that separated souls enjoy the vision of God "clearly" (*clare*), but he maintained that they do so only "to the extent compatible with their state and condition" (*in quantum status et condicio compatitur animae separatae*; DH 990–91, quotation 991). This piece of papal theological acumen was accepted by the cardinals as a recantation of his error. Pope John's successor, Benedict XII, was the ascetical Jacques Fournier, who as bishop of Pamiers (1317–1326) had been responsible for a painstaking investigation of residual Albigensian heresy in the village of Montaillou—the subject of Emmanuel Le Roy Ladurie's brilliant *Montaillou: The Promised Land of Error*. Fournier, whom John XXII had respected as a hard-driving inquisitor, was also a learned theologian who had opposed Pope John on the fate of the souls after death; as Pope he hastened to set the record straight. He first published his predecessor's deathbed statement, and then, a little over a year later, in the dogmatic constitution *Benedictus Deus*, promulgated a pronouncement of his own, insisting on the full doctrinal development: the souls of the just enjoy the vision of God (DH 1000–02; CF 2305–07).

self-illumination prompted by the searching and revealing presence of the living God, now encountered without mediation. Thus, as our life and, consequently, such identity as we have succeeded in acquiring, come to light, we find ourselves individually assessed, in anticipation of the general judgment, by the only standard that is both definitive and just, since we were initially given it as authentically ours: our native, inalienable relatedness to a God both faithful and loving.

Without ever committing itself to a clear-cut position on the subject, the patristic literature is full of intimations to the effect that the individual soul wakes up from death (an awakening occasionally understood as the "first resurrection") to some kind of reward or punishment. This at least implies an acknowledgment of some form of individual judgment after death. But the judgment is understood to be provisional; it anticipates the general (or "second") Resurrection and the universal Judgment.[26] Everywhere in the West, this became known as the *particular judgment*. Augustine was the first to make a clear distinction between it and the general Judgment.[27] Strictly speaking, however, the particular judgment has never been taught by way of formal doctrine. Even in the West, it has been taught only by implication. In particular, the magisterium of the Latin church has been careful to emphasize that the encounter of the individual soul with God after death does not empty the doctrine of the General Judgment of its meaning (cf. DH 857–58; 1002; 1304–06; CF [2304]; 2307; 2308–09).

In fact, both the universal judgment and the particular judgment appeal to theological reason. The reality of the former is supported by the insight (cf. §138, 2) that in every particular situation, the story of human identity remains unfinished. As long as humanity and the cosmos are running their course in time and space, the actions of human beings, both individually and communally, are and remain part of a spatial and temporal network of moral (and immoral) endeavor which remains unfinished (and *a fortiori*, unrevealed). In that sense and to that extent, the moral status of all particular individuals and communities remains unrevealed, too. The Kingdom of God, after all, "is a collective reality, which is now achieved in individuals to varying degrees, but which will only be fulfilled at the end of human history." Even "the joy of Christ and his Apostles in the Kingdom is not yet full, 'as long as I remain in sin.'"[28]

As for the reality of the particular judgment, it is consonant with the insight that, while the full story of human responsibility and irresponsibility remains indeterminate, the caliber of each individual action, and hence, the fate of each individual, once sealed, lies open to divine scrutiny. This analysis calls for some further elaboration.

[d] In Christian theology, the attainment of responsive identity in encounter with God is consistently regarded as the fruit of two inseparable realities: grace and revelation. It involves grace, because authentic identity is not self-constituted, but responsive to God; it is prompted in us as we accept God's gracious self-communication in its fullness (§35, 1; 4; §49, 1; §87, 3).

Now it is precisely *in* divine self-communication that revelation takes shape (cf. §95, 4, [*ll*]; 5; 7; 10; §113, 3, f). Any *full* revelation of each and every person's given and acquired identity must include the whole network of the *relationships* that has contributed to their personal being. For that reason, this full revelation can only be eschatological—that is of ultimate divine grace. Not until all of humanity, along with the cosmos, reaches its definitive destiny can Christ be complete (cf. 1 Cor 15, 20–28; Col 1, 24; Jn 14, 2–3; cf. §126, 3) and fully revealed.[29] Only in that revelation, too, can the holiness of individual persons and their place in God's Kingdom become fully manifest [*kk*].

In the interim, the Christian community believes three things. First, the Christian fellowship of faith ("the Communion of Saints") reaches beyond the grave, in anticipation of the eschaton. Second, any person's definitive standing with God is a mystery shrouded by death [*ll*]. Third, the reward of eternal life shared with the living God is and remains a gift to be prayed for, not a right to be claimed. Hence, rather than thinking of the dead, fatalistically, as existing in a separate world of their own and as past all prayer, the mainstream Christian tradition, in commending itself to God's faithfulness and mercy, has also steadfastly commended to God its deceased mem-

---

[*kk*] This vision lies doubtlessly behind the classical practice of general, undifferentiated liturgical suffrages for the dead. The origin of this practice was rightly attributed to the Armenian Churches, but often meanly caricatured in the West by the suggestion that it meant to include the Blessed Virgin, the apostles, and other saints. As a result, the practice was understandably (if far too hastily) rejected by Pope Benedict XII in 1341 A. D. (DH 1010).

[*ll*] Consequently, the recognition of Saints and of their holiness results not from direct revelation, but from spiritual discernment; in the case of the Blessed Virgin Mary this discernment is part of the scriptural record. Canonization, in other words, is based on the interpretation of *signs*, chief among which is exceptional ("heroic") witness to the faith, but then also sustained, loving veneration by the faithful, supported by a proven reputation for uncommon virtue and creditable instances of effective intercession ("miracles").

bers—even those whom it has excommunicated here below; indeed, it has commended to God's mercy all the dead, "whose faith is known to You alone."[30] This has taken the shape of an age-old liturgical practice, which the Christian community inherited from late Judaism: *intercession in behalf of the dead* (cf. 2 Macc 12, 43b–45).

[e] This latter practice, along with the conception of the particular judgment, has given rise to the Catholic doctrine of *Purgatory*—a term that signifies the transitional state of the soul following death. The concept of purifying punishment after death, familiar in gnostic circles, goes back as far as Clement of Alexandria; it can be found in Origen, Gregory of Nyssa, Evagrius Ponticus, and, in the West, in Ambrose and especially in Augustine.[31] Much to the dismay of the Churches of the East, however, Purgatory became the object of much specialized doctrinal development, chiefly in the medieval Latin Church (cf. DH 854–57, 1000, 1304–5, 1820; CF [2304], 2305, 2308–09, 2310) [*mm*].

Still, the doctrine has a broad and solid base. Profound awe at God's holiness has always prevented the Jewish-Christian Tradition from thinking that anyone, let alone a sinner, can claim to be prepared to enter into God's presence (cf. §49, 1, a); the radiance of divine Wisdom does not admit of even the least defilement (cf. Wisd 7, 25), just as the fire that enhances the gold consumes all the dross (cf. 1 Cor 3, 12–15). Hence, none except the Blessed Mother of God will find themselves entering into the sanctuary without discovering that the kindly Light that welcomes them also embarrasses them painfully enough to reveal them as sinners and change them into supplicants. In fact, the embarrassment would undo them, if unconditional Love, with the inner touch of which only unconditional Love is capable, did not turn the surge of shame into a cleansing bath of penitence, the awareness of outstanding debt into the re-

---

[*mm*] In the matter of Purgatory, the oriental churches have constantly feared that affirmations about the eternal condition of the soul after death jeopardize traditional eschatology. Specifically, they worry that such affirmations jeopardize the general Judgment and the consequent eternal destiny of the just in Heaven and the reprobate in Hell. Medieval magisterial documents on Purgatory in the West are at pains to allay these fears. They explain, but do not insist on, the term *purgatorium*, to prove that the doctrine denotes a cleansing, not a punishment, and a *passage*, not a state. They also emphasize that the "fire" is only "transitory" (*transitorio igne*. DH 838), as well as effective only for lesser sins, and hence, in no way comparable to the fire of Hell, which is unique because it is eternal. Later magisterial texts of lesser importance treat the doctrine as simply established and add further refinements, but they are less meticulous in phrasing it: cf. DH 838, 1820, 1867; CF 2310, 35.

lief of unconditional acceptance, and any residual hardness of heart into total abandon: "Those who have died truly penitent in the love of God, without previously offering, by means of worthy fruits of penance, satisfaction for their sins of commission and omission . . . are cleansed after death" (DH 464; CF [2304]). Summing up, the Catholic doctrine of Purgatory is about *purification after death* (understood as an act of cleansing, graciously wrought in residually sinful souls turned repentant in the encounter with a merciful God and supported by the intercession of the Church), *and about nothing else* [nn].

[f] Few themes gave the intellectual restlessness of the Middle Ages (cf. §93, 5) more scope for imagination and creativity than Purgatory, starting with the twelfth-century wave of romantic humanism. In his evocative and provocative *La naissance du Purgatoire*, Jacques Le Goff has argued that the cultivation of Purgatory is rooted in the social order. In his view, it arose under the influence of the avid search for a society in which the painful vacuum between the uncouth wielders of undisputed feudal power and a backward peasantry would be filled with fairness and civilization. There is little doubt that the vivid imagery connected with purgatory supported the deployment of cultural potential and encouraged enterprising people to play their part on the inconstant stage of the world. It did so by promising them not only the reward for their labors as well as rest and *refrigerium* from toil, but also unwavering divine justice. Equally importantly, it held out to everyone the promise that God would forgive the various sins which are the unavoidable concomitant of feverish human effort. Unhappily, however, late medieval civilization lost itself in flamboyancy; as a result, Purgatory, ever more fantastically furnished, found itself increasingly at the center of the religious imagination, rather than at the margin where it belongs. This contributed not a little to the Reformation's harsh treatment of it.

[nn] In many traditional systematic theologies, Purgatory is treated in the context of the "Last Things": Death, Judgment, Heaven and Hell, and often clarified by means of comparisons with the latter two. This suggests that Purgatory is an intermediate state, if not, indeed, an actual place. This kind of treatment, mainly inspired by the superficial similarity between Purgatory and Hell, mostly at the level of images conveying punishment, is misleading. If anything, Purgatory is intermediate between Death and Heaven. Indeed, as soon as it is realized that Purgatory is *not eschatological* but transitional, any comparison with either Heaven or Hell becomes dubious. *God Encountered* will ponder the mysteries of eternal happiness and eternal reprobation at a much later point.

For indeed, like all highly specialized doctrines (cf. §23, 4, c; §72, 3; 4, c), the Catholic teaching on Purgatory is beset by hazards. The Oriental churches have always feared that too much interest in the state of the individual soul after death might lead to the loss of necessary religious reticence this side of the universal judgment. These fears have proved to be not wholly unfounded. Many images still current in the West vividly but misleadingly suggest that Purgatory is a permanent place and a fire reminiscent of Hell, thus associating it with fear rather than hope.[32]

Even worse, and downright tragically, in the later Middle Ages the doctrine of Purgatory, designed to convey God's merciful love of sinners and to encourage faith in the Communion of the Saints as well as Christian *pietas* shown in prayer for the dead, fell victim to a progressive degeneracy of a different sort. It occurred principally when access to the souls in Purgatory increasingly came to be considered the privilege of an inflated clerical establishment with too much social control, too much income from sacred functions, and too little understanding of the emergent laity and its aspirations. The fees payable to the clergy for indulgences applicable to the souls in purgatory and the stipends for private masses for the dead appeared to move the relevance of Christ's redemptive work more and more to the afterlife. The impression was created that the clergy had the power to assure the laity of efficacious solace after death and, in doing so, to excuse them from the life of virtue, faith, penitence, and eucharistic participation in their lifetime. (Dostoevsky's Grand Inquisitor was to call this, cynically, compassion shown by the clergy to the weak and the sinful.) This gave support to a penitential and sacrificial "system" which, while technically orthodox, was in fact abusive and un-Evangelical.[33] No wonder the Reformation, riding the crest of a wave of lay (and especially merchant) emancipation, lashed out at the system, and rejected Purgatory in the same gesture. No wonder either that the Second Vatican Council acknowledged, in passing, both intercession for the dead and the purgation of souls (LG 49–50; DH 4169–70), but otherwise left the matter untouched.

[g] However, the Catholic appreciation of Purgatory's authentic religious significance never quite disappeared. It is shown to best advantage in a handful of meditations on it (as well as defenses of it) written when the doctrine was at its most controversial: when the late-fifteenth- and sixteenth-century Church was struggling with serious abuses rationalized by means of appeals to the predicament of

the souls in Purgatory. Their authors are Catholic Christians of indubitable integrity: Saint Catherine of Genoa wrote the *Spiritual Dialogue on Purgation and Purgatory*, Saint Thomas More *The Supplication of Souls*, and Cardinal William Allen, the founder of the English College at Douai, *A Defense and Declaration of the Catholike Churchies Doctrine Touching Purgatory, and Prayers of the Souls Departed*. These tracts combine a deep, penitential profession of lack of readiness before the holiness of God with a profound trust in God's mercy.

[13]   Finally, few practices of asceticism bear out the fundamental Christian attitude toward death more clearly than an exercise as old as the ascetical movement itself, and commended from the outset by means of appeals, not only to Plato and the Stoa, but also to Paul (1 Cor 15, 31: "I die every day"). It is the practice of "living as if dying every day" (Athanasius),[34] of "keeping the memory of death every day before one's eyes" (Macarius the Great),[35] and thus, of "mak[ing] of our lives a practice for death" (Gregory Nazianzen).[36]

The thought of death turned into a guide to life not only serves to curb the passions of the moment; it is also an incentive to keep oneself from sin and to rise above disappointments and insults, as well as above the pain and resentment they may cause. But most of all, it is one distinctive way in which human beings can both experience and demonstrate, as a matter of habit, that they transcend the here and now, and hence, that they intend to undertake life as a total project, in the light of an expectation of life beyond life.

[a]   Two curious as well as memorable instances of this teaching are found in Evagrius Ponticus' *Praktikos* (cf. §103, 4, b). Evagrius is backed up by a long tradition. Pagan sages like Plato, Plotinus, and Porphyry had praised the practice of philosophic detachment; Clement of Alexandria[37] and Gregory Nazianzen had transformed this praise into a commendation of the ascetical life. Evagrius is now turning the latter into a commendation of the life of "withdrawal" (*anachōrēsis*)—taking one's distance from crowd and compromise. Without even a hint of an apology for his (or his mentors') reliance on pagan Platonism, but conveying a strong sense of the asymmetrical relationship between body and soul, and between identity and alienation, he writes: "Separating the body from the soul pertains only to the One who united them, but [separating] the soul from the body also pertains to those who strive for virtue. For our Fathers call *anachōrēsis* the practice of death and the flight from the body."

And, as if to emphasize that cherishing and cultivating the human spirit's transcendence has nothing to do with contempt of the body, he quotes "that great ascetic" (*praktikōtatos*), Macarius the Egyptian, and writes: "Monks must so keep themselves ready as if they were to die the next day, yet so use their bodies as if they would live with them many years"[38]—an instruction which John Cassian, who sat at Macarius' feet, was to bring with him to the West.[39]

[b] At the root of this intentional anticipation and acceptance of death, in other words, lie neither a morbid preoccupation with death and physical decay (of the kind the late fourteenth and the fifteenth centuries were to display), nor a lack of *joie de vivre*, nor a sick desire to attenuate the enjoyment of present life, but a faithful, hopeful anticipation of life beyond life. Such an anticipation is both content to be in the world and fueled by a native desire for the full revelation of God. Those who so believe are "mindful of the nobility they have from on high";[40] they desire to do justice to their souls, as to the mirror of God. Hence their ultimate serenity in the face of the dynamics of decay, destruction, and even sin inherent in the cosmos and humanity; hence, too, their cultivation, by a disciplined, "mortified" life, of the human spirit, at some expense to the body. After all, in the last resort it is the spirit that must coordinate and govern both the body and the human engagement with the whole world of otherness—conditioned by them of course, but not lost in them.

[c] All of this also explains why Ignatius of Loyola can recommend that, faced with important decisions, we should imagine ourselves at the point of death. What I would like to have decided in the face of death is liable to be the very thing I can profitably decide to do now.[41] For the whole point of the *ars moriendi* is a life inspired by what Ignatius calls "indifference":[42] the inner detachment from self-interest that lends depth and freedom to a life lived right in the thick of things, yet in the expectation of an eternal destiny.

[14] Countless serious contemporary people who believe in God are deeply suspicious of the Christian idioms involving suffering, mortification, and death (no matter how good their New Testament credentials: cf., *e.g.*, 2 Cor 4, 10–12). For example, they find the display of crucifixes (especially realistic ones) downright repugnant. Still, many of them share with Christians a fundamental belief in immortality as well as in the moral imperatives implied in this belief. This drives

home the fact that when Christians anticipate, accept, and even embrace death, they do not do so just for *fundamental* theological reasons —that is, for reasons of the kind explored in the present section.

In fact, the Christian attitude toward death is also (and indeed chiefly) based on positively *doctrinal, christological* grounds. Christians understand Baptism as the voluntary sharing of the death of Christ, (Rom 6, 4); they insist on turning the shame of the Cross and of suffering for the sake of the Gospel into a boast (Gal 6, 14; Rom 5, 3); most of all, they claim that now that Christ is risen, death has lost its "sting" (1 Cor 15, 56)—its power to drive home the dominance of sin and hence, to inflict irreparable harm. These themes will have to occupy us in the fourth and last part of this second volume.

For now, therefore, let us merely note that, if the Christian liturgy refers to the dead as those "who have gone before us marked by the sign of faith,"[43] it is speaking the language, not only of explicit Christian doctrine, but also of fundamental-theological faith-abandon. For in the eyes of all those who, whether thematically or unthematically, seek God, in faith and with increasingly undivided hearts, failure, sin, suffering, dying, and death are a beginning, not the end:

> I do not die,
> I enter into life.[44]

But in that case, the death-dealing dynamics of the cosmos and humanity are not the last word either; only the transcendent, living God, creator of cosmos and humanity, is. Not surprisingly, therefore, one of the finest, most reverential thanksgiving songs of the Psalter can bless God by entrusting to the divine care both sin and mortality:

> For as high as the heavens are over the earth,
> so firm stands his love over those who revere him;
> as far as the East is from the West,
> so far has he removed from himself our transgressions.
> As fathers befriend their children,
> YHWH befriends those who revere him.
> For *He* knows how we are fashioned,
> mindful that clay is all we are.
> People, while they last, are like grass,
> like wild flowers they bloom;
> but let a storm come down upon them, and they are gone;
> not even the place where they lived remembers.
> But YHWH's love stands from everlasting to everlasting
> over those who revere him.
>
> (Ps 103, 11–17)

[15] This abandon to God's merciful acceptance in the face of death is the mature outgrowth of the indelible sense of transcendence at the core of our being, deepened and toughened by the life of active engagement inspired by it. For in the last resort, engaging the world and humanity is a matter of our accepting them at the hands of God, as a trust (cf. §98, 5–6); in the last analysis, it is in *faith* that we engage humanity and the world and take responsibility for them. We are to do so in two ways.

Firstly, we are to respond to the world and humanity *constructively:* as well as we can, we are to discover them and appreciate them and shape them and refine them in the light of our intelligent discoveries and our moral purposes.

But secondly, and at an even deeper level, we are to respond to them *receptively:* we are to balance and heal and restore humanity and the world as they come to us, precarious and conflicted and self-abused. Quite often, too, they will even come to us ill-treated and ravished by immoral human activity, begging for compassion. We are to be responsive to them even though we know that, in the end, the decombination, failure, and sin that mark humanity and the cosmos as we know them will prove too much for us and will defeat our biophysical being. That is, we will find our true selves to the extent that we agree to have our engagement (and hence, ourselves) *tested* by humanity and the world *as they are.*

In this way, human transcendence vis-à-vis the cosmos and humanity as a whole takes the shape of a confident embrace offered to humanity and the world—an embrace sustained and enabled by the sense of native transcendence. And this native transcendence is brought to completion to the extent that we succeed in abandoning ourselves, along with our entire engagement to humanity and the world, to the God who entrusted humanity and the world to us in the first place.

Genuine abandon to God in the face of death, therefore, is the opposite of the resignation of the immature, the lazy, the apathetic, the religiously withdrawn, and those stuck in resentment. All of these will merely resign themselves to the inevitable and beg off when the rigors of life in the real world call for the shouldering of real responsibility. Whether wearily or with childish petulance, they will insist on blaming the powers that be (and ultimately God) for their own troubles as well as for all the world's ills. Genuine abandon, by contrast, coincides with the pride of the servant who has made good use of the talents entrusted to him (Mt 25, 14–30 par. Lk 19, 12–27), and who, even in the defeat of death, meets the Lord in the respectful, yet confident posture of a responsible and reliable partner, not a slave—"as a creditor and not all the time as a debtor" [oo].

[16] This allusion to the parable of the talents calls for a moment of realism. It reminds us that humanity's present situation, like the servants' in the parable while the Lord is away, is one of testing—even crisis; if we work out our salvation, we do so not in uninterrupted, serene obedience to the inner call of our immortal selves, but "in fear and trembling" (Phil 2, 12). The sections just completed have bravely (as well as rightly) commended habitual, mature faith-abandon as the precondition not only of the good life, but also of meaningful living heartened by the anticipation of meaningful dying. But this must not cause us to forget that mature faith in God and abandon to God is only one possible attitude we may adopt as, in our engagement with otherness, we meet with limits, fatigue, failure, boredom, incomprehension, opposition, decomposition, sin, and death. There is another possibility. In the world we live in, it looms large.

THE POWER OF SIN

[§125] "ENSLAVED FOR LIFE, BY FEAR OF DEATH" (HEB 2, 15)

[1] We naturally exist in alienation. It is characteristic of this situation that natural evil is always occurring and the threat of it always impending. Both, it was explained before, are capable of triggering in us the trepidation that is the effect of the "unstable ontological constitution" which is ours by nature (cf. §112, 5; §113, 1). Existence in alienation renders our transcendence over cosmic process, and hence, our spiritual identity, precarious; not even the most mature among us enjoy a wholly unshakable awareness of their deeper dignity. For that awareness is and remains available to us mostly indirectly, unthematically, in action and only slightly more thematically in reflection, in the

---

[oo] Cf. Emmanuel Lévinas: "[For God] to veil his countenance in order to demand—in a superhuman way—everything of Man, to have created Man capable of responding, of turning to his God as a creditor and not all the time as a debtor: *that* is truly divine grandeur! After all, a creditor is one who has faith *par excellence*, but he is not going to resign himself to the subterfuges of the debtor. ... How vigorous the dialectic by which the equality between God and Man is established right at the heart of their incommensurability!" ("Aimer la Thora plus que Dieu" [*Difficile liberté*, pp. 189–93], quotation pp. 192–93). Cf. F. J. van Beeck, *Loving the Torah More than God?*, p. 40; cf. also §99; §117, 3, a–b.

form of the sense of a given that we cannot undo—a transcendental that becomes positively our own only to the extent that we succeed in accepting it (§112).

[a] Here we have to be precise. Only because, at the *anthropological* level, we are natively predisposed to have the *capacity* for trepidation within us triggered, can (and do) *cosmological* factors *de facto* trigger it. If the cosmos tests and tempts us (and it does), this is because *we* are inherently susceptible to inner decay, and even prone to it. Natural concupiscence keeps us off-balance; loss of integrity, authenticity, and identity is forever around the corner. *Capacity* for unbelief and sin is always with us, *naturally*.

[2] But there is more. *Actual* unbelief and sin are with us (§114, 1). As a result, both cosmic evil (§115) and natural human concupiscence (cf. §113, 3, b) are now associated with actual moral evil; they have lost their native innocence, at least indirectly. In this predicament, those who desire to live the good life find themselves habitually thrown off-course, forced into symbiosis with moral evil, whether of the incidental, the casual, the intentional, or the firmly established kind. In this situation, moral duty has ceased to be manifestly rewarding. We find ourselves wearied (and perhaps even made callous) by the unavoidable impact of moral evil on us, as well as by our own inevitable participation in it.

The drudgery of all of this raises the serious question if it is not saner to opt for accommodation and compromise, or at least to settle for a little complicity with evildoers (cf., once again, Ps 73). Even worse, death and the suffering that leads up to it have become inseparable from a pervasive, contagious sense of moral impotence, lack of inner freedom, and pointlessness (cf. DH 227, 239, 378, 622; CF 1903, 1920); this suggests, annoyingly, that life as such is contaminated and infected—that life itself has become a sickness unto death. As a result, far from being an encouragement to live a life enhanced by discipline, asceticism, and probity, the thought of the good life is liable to give way to the thought that we are caught in a bind. It sometimes looks as if the only realistic way to live is to live with the forces of evil and to go along with them pretty much as needed, especially since it does not take long to discover that trying to beat them usually means that you have to join them outright.

In this situation of captivity, consistent desire for the higher goods and responsible anticipation of death are apt to function not as incentives to a fuller life, but as kill-joys and depressing invitations to self-diminishment. Real courage, it is now likely to appear, is possessed by those who think that the only time to die is the hour of death and not a moment sooner; that to be truly alive means to *live*, and not to let the mind turn the indubitable fact of suffering and the bitter anticipation of death into arguments for a life "diminished" by discipline. Those among us who feel like this will say (sometimes in unintentional confirmation of Paul's description of them in Rom 1, 22–32) that making something of life means seizing the opportunity while it lasts while expecting as little as possible from the future.[45] Why not overcome habits of suppressing instinct, and instead start suppressing guilt-feelings and habits of deference to standards set by others? Why not assert our determination to enjoy physical and mental health and happiness, give full play to the life of the senses in all its variety, and thus defy death, courageously—even heroically? And why not publicly recognize this option as a sound, and indeed preferable, alternative to the "repressed" life [*pp*]?

Theologically speaking, what lends plausibility to such hedonistic and vitalist philosophies is sin—both in its actuality and in its effects. "Bondage to sin" (cf. Rom 6, 6. 16–17. 20) has obscured humanity's native sense of God and its consciousness of its relatedness to God; this consciousness is now habitually (if not always actually) unavailable to us [*qq*]. Accordingly, the human sense of identity and hence, the human ability to love and do justice to both things and other persons, have become habitually (if not always actually) scrambled and incapacitated.[46] The fleeting moments when we do feel the stir of deep self-awareness and of the presence of God ("unforseentimes . . . as skies betweenpie mountains"[47]) now serve only to confirm rather than contradict the habitual weakness of our sense of God and of our own identity. Anxiety, loneliness, and self-consciousness (and hence, the sense that in order to *live*, we somehow have no choice but to take care of ourselves and to be self-serving) habitually force us to pursue a variety of self-identifications and postures vis-à-vis the world. Finally, and not at all surprisingly, with humanity feeling both so awkward and so

---

[*pp*] Readers of Norman O. Brown's *Life Against Death* (1959) will have noticed echoes of that provocative book in this paragraph. By the same token, readers of Ernest Becker's *The Denial of Death* (1973) will have heard echoes of this equally provocative but far more profound rejoinder. Becker shows that the posture championed by Brown is in many ways typical of modern North American culture; he also shows that it is far better understood as a form, not of courage or zest for life, but of fear of death.

[*qq*] This has also made all religious knowledge implausible, if not always impossible: DH 2756, 2853, 3875.

heavily responsible for itself and the world, life itself has become encumbered by the awareness of failure and sin.

This awareness is virtually inseparable from a vague sense of guilt, of the kind that is inherent in existence as such, and thus, seemingly unforgivable; only by dint of some kind of resolve, it would often seem, can we succeed in living with it.[48] Thus, too, human life can habitually (if not always actually) feel like a life sentence at hard and thankless labor (cf. Gen 3, 16–19).

In this situation, death might look like a liberation, if its mercilessness did not prevent us from taking such a benign view. For death as we know it is of one piece with our lives: lives that struggle, falter, go astray, and miscarry under the burden of failure, suffering, self-absorption, and downright wickedness. Is it so far-fetched, then, to interpret death, as the Jewish-Christian tradition has done (cf. §116, 5), as punishment for sin—*fit* punishment, since it intrinsically matches sin and certifies its horror?

[a] Small wonder the Christian tradition echoes a theme usually implied (though often quite forcefully stated) by the Hebrew Scriptures as well as by later Jewish wisdom traditions: punishment for sin is not really a sentence extrinsically ("forensically": cf. §124, 12, c) decreed and imposed or inflicted by God, but rather a fitting and just retribution which sinners pull down on themselves in the very act of sinning, along with its dread consequences.[49] These same traditions will also insist that if calamities like cosmic disasters and the ravages of war are to be regarded as divine punishment at all, such punishments are to be interpreted not as acts of divine revenge, but as salutary discipline: they are harsh reminders of our condition and calls to renewal of life, not retributive punishments meant to kill us. For God, the sovereign Judge, delights in life (Wisd 1, 13) and positively wills it, even the sinner's (Ez 18, 32; 33, 11).

Yet for a humanity that insists on arrogating to itself the divine prerogative of sovereignly judging good and evil there is divine punishment indeed. That punishment consists in the denial of humanity's access to the fruit of immortality (Gen 3, 22). In this way, to live in sin is to live in estrangement from, and under the threat of punishment by, the Source of Life and Holiness (cf. Wisd 1, 16–2, 24; 11, 16; 12, 24–27; 15, 18–16, 1);[50] such a life is clinched by a death that lacks any assurance of life. "Death entered the world through sin," Paul can write; accordingly, "the payoff of sin is death"; and conversely, "sin is what gives death its power to hurt [Gk. *kentron*, sting]."

(Rom 5, 21; 6, 23; 1 Cor 15, 56; cf. Rom 8, 2; Jas 1, 15; cf. DH 371, 1512; CF 504, 509).

The great Tradition has not been reluctant to endorse a close mutual link between human sin and death. It has done so by refusing to regard death *as we know it* either as a neutral cosmic occurrence, or as an acceptable passage of human persons to life beyond life. Instead, it has understood human death as a forced, painful passage into an apparent darkness that is natively unfit for human beings— one which, therefore, we have every reason to dread to the point of despair [*rr*].

[3] On the one hand, therefore, living with sin and in sin is now inescapable, and the certainty of death makes sin appear inescapable as well as unforgivable. Yet on the other hand, the fundamental human attunement to God and the deep human sense of responsibility have remained; sinful humanity remains inalienably dedicated to the search for God. And thus, between these two, the worst has come about: the hidden countenance of the transcendent God who inspires desire and prompts awe and intimacy (cf. Is 45, 14–15) has been turned into the faceless mask of a remote deity that reproves concupiscence and sin, and accordingly, inspires fear and revulsion. Even worse, this experience furnishes sinners with the perfect rationalization for their self-

---

[*rr*] Cf. the condemnation of articles adopted at the Synod of Pistoia in 1786, endorsed by Pius VI in 1794. The Pope writes: "death ... *in the present state* is inflicted by way of just punishment for sin, through the deserved removal of immortality" (italics added). In stating this, the pope intends to deny the Jansenist contention that Adam's immortality was, not a divine gift, but humanity's *natural* condition (DH 2617). Vatican II, too, teaches that humanity would have been "exempted" [*subtractus*] from physical death if it had not sinned (GS 18; DH 4318)—an expression implying that immortality is a gift, not humanity's natural destiny. All this is consistent with the age-old catholic teaching on humanity's ("Adam's") state of original justice. Original justice included *natural* integrity, sinlessness, and free will (DH 389, 396, 621; cf. 239; CF 1921; cf. 503) as well as the freely given, *supernatural* gift of friendship with God, and hence, holiness (DH 1511, 2616; cf. 1923, 1926; CF 508, 1984/23, 514/26). Moreover, it involved immortality (DH 222, 1511; CF 508) as a *preternatural* gift—a "gratuitous benefit" (DH 1978, 2617; CF 1984/78; cf. P. Schoonenberg, *Man and Sin*, pp. 182–85). What we have here is another instance of the catholic tradition's conviction that human nature is fully revealed only in the act of being divinely exceeded—that is, in the light of the supernatural, for which human nature has a natural aptitude (cf. §82, 4; cf. §88, 1). In this case, humanity's natural mortality according to the flesh hides a native aspiration to the gift of immortality, which, however, only the encounter with a gracious God can bestow in actuality. The reverse of this proposition is, of course, equally relevant: original justice being removed, mortality has become the painful destiny of a humanity reduced (not to some bland state of natural happiness, but) to a condition contrary to its natural aspiration to life eternal and below its natural dignity (cf. §109, 9, c; §113, 3, f, [*n*]; cf. also §95, 5, [*pp*]).

absorption. Incapable of forgetting God, they lose the ability to love and worship God. They can no longer believe that God's holiness manifests itself, not by the creation of a distance that judges and alienates, but by the offer of leniency and love, which invites awe and intimacy. Living in sin, therefore, perverts the human experience of God's holiness; worship gives way to fear and a sense of estrangement.

In the end, this has repercussions as miserable as they are universal. The dazzling majesty of the cosmos and its complex harmony now frequently look ominous and conspiratorial; its glory, turned suspicious, now often appears to convey veiled threats—a notion the incidence of natural evil only serves to confirm. And human beings, their divine image and likeness paled and their sense of affinity with God dulled, are now predisposed to feel (against their residual better judgment) that, in the last resort, all they can do is to maintain themselves, to fight to stay alive, to devise structures of truth and goodness and religiosity by such lights as they still have at its disposal [ss], and to defend them against rivalry and attack with a vengeance. And most miserably of all, Israel's God, hidden yet present, to whom all that is remains inexorably attracted, is no longer revealed as the God of faithful love. Instead, God has come to look like the very essence of cold justice—a remote Intensity that is unseen yet sees, stays aloof yet judges; an invisible Wrath that remains unaccountable yet punishes, and while giving life, appears to force humanity back into the abyss:

> The frown of his face
> Before me, the hurtle of hell
> Behind, where, where was a, where was a place?[51]

Thus, as the kindly Light turns into a ball of Fire, Heaven's charm turns into the threat of Hell, and (as Martin Luther became so desperately aware) all human attempts at faith and justice tend to become futile and self-defeating—in fact, downright arrogant. The same, or worse, applies to the observance even of the Torah itself. The resolve to live by God's Holy Word is now liable to become doubly sinful, for on the one hand, transgressions of it are unavoidable, and on the other hand, the claim to self-made religiosity and righteousness implied in the claimed observance of it is the height of presumption (cf. Rom 2). In this way, self-serving human endeavor in matters religious will bring about the eclipse of God as much as sin does.

[ss] Cf. Martin Buber's explorations on this subject in *Gottesfinsternis* (ET *Eclipse of God*).

In this terrible predicament, atheism of any kind may look like a relief. But in order to cancel the very thought of God, humanity would first have to become wholly oblivious of itself. But, human nature being what it is, humanity can never succeed in forgetting God altogether; to do that, in Karl Rahner's drastic phrase, it would have to "breed itself back to the level of the clever animal."[52] God, therefore, is liable to be not so much denied as *eclipsed*—overshadowed by counterfeits. For, when the living God becomes too much to live with, what human beings crave for is not denials but easement. Thus, in a world marked by sin, a host of petty tyrants and oppressors of every kind—celestial, semi-celestial, and atmospheric—are ready to pacify the deep sense of pointlessness. Idols, ideals, and ideologies (cf. §114, 4) will oblige; they will offer their services as stand-ins for the living God; they will rush in to fill the theological void. Usually, the passions, fantasies, and self-justifications that lend them credibility will invest them with considerable power. Wearing the masks of demons, they will frighten the soul by threats of destruction. But if unsuccessful, they will try a different tactic; as God's friends have known at least since Anthony in the Egyptian desert, they will transform themselves into angels of light. That is, they will comfort the soul by false assurances—weakening it to the point where it is content to live at levels below its native dignity.[53]

[4] This last realization decisively involves the Jewish-Christian understanding of the invisible powers, angelic as well as demonic. Specifically, in the fallen world in which we live, this understanding involves the recognition that Satan and a host of demonic powers have become the invisible backbone of a worldwide establishment of sin. This issue requires careful explanation and analysis.

[5] Earlier on (§98, 1, a), it was explained that the Jewish and Christian traditions of worship of, obedience to, and faith in the One God succeeded in modifying, in a monotheistic direction, the theological understanding of the invisible powers whose authority is so forcefully suggested by the grandeur of the universe. It continued both to recognize the reality of the powers that be and to respect them as significant and relevant to humanity's relationship with God. Thus, on the analogy of court ceremonial, the community of faith came to imagine the angelic powers as worshiping, obeying, and acknowledging God "with their whole beings"[54] (1 Kings 22, 19; Dan 7, 9–10; Heb 12, 22; Rev 5, 11). Accordingly, it also came to imagine them as occupying a mediating position in the Great Chain of Being: through them, the worship, the obedience, and the faith of all every element in the universe

was carried before God's transcendent Presence (cf. Tob 12, 12; Rev 5, 8; 8, 3; Dan 3, 57–90 LXX). Conversely, the unseen powers also came to be portrayed as God's representatives in caring for human persons (Mt 18, 10!), as bearers of divine messages, and as mediators at the service of those who believe. Accordingly, in the world picture of those whose faith in God is shaped by the monotheistic traditions of the West, the invisible powers are for the most part benevolent: they are models of pure worship, guardians on the paths of goodness and love, and guides to faith [tt].

Still, even in this world picture, natural evil, in the form of both cosmic and involuntary human mishap, remains a force to be reckoned with. It reminds even believers (or, rather, especially them) that there is, in Paul Ricoeur's expression, "a side to our world that confronts us as chaos and is symbolized by the chthonic animal"—the Serpent.[55] There are forces in the universe that not only offer resistance to the cosmic order and humanity's natural and moral fulfillment in it, but positively tend to thwart both of them.[56] Such forces test and imperil, not only humanity insofar as it is as a cosmic, transient phenomenon, but also humanity as it has the distinctive vocation to live responsibly and deliberately, by its native attunement to a transcendent God, and hence, ultimately, to trust and believe in God and glorify God in the perspective of eternity (cf. §117, 3). Once again, therefore, we are reminded that both natural human failure and human sin are connected with the fact that it is humanity's vocation to attain self-actualization under the conditions of alienation. The fact that we are part of a cosmos that tests and tempts us is simply the outside of our inherent ontological instability. This in turn implies that failure and sinfulness as we know them are not just the result of humanity's *interior* experience of instability and temptability, and of wrong choices made in the

---

[tt] It is to be noted that both the liturgical and the ascetical and mystical traditions have associated angels first and foremost with *worship*. Worship offered to God by heavenly beings, so obvious in the Apocalypse and so powerfully evoked by the liturgies of the oriental churches, has not been lost in the Latin Church, witness the "Holy, Holy, Holy" (cf. Is 6, 3) in the eucharistic prayer and the mention of "your holy Angel" in the *Supplices* prayer in the Roman canon. Evagrius Ponticus, too, reflecting the angelology of this liturgical Tradition, associates contemplative worship with angels; he writes: "As good as an angel [*isangelos*]: that is what a monk becomes through true worship [*proseuchēs*], yearning to see the face of the Father in heaven" (cf. Lk 20, 36). He also integrates the idea of *service* into angelic worship by writing: "It is right [*dikaion*] to pray [*proseuchesthai*] not only for one's own purification, but also for every fellow human being's, so as to imitate the manner of the angels." Cf. *De Oratione*, chaps. 113–14, 39 (*PG* 79, 1192D, 1176B; ET *Praktikos* and *Chapters on Prayer*, pp. 74, 61).

secret of our wavering hearts; we also fail and sin by succumbing to forces that attack us from the *outside* in which we are essentially situated (cf. §122, 3, [*i*]).[57] Ricoeur, therefore, is entirely right in observing that there is a "quasi-exteriority" to evil. Humanity's faith in God and in God's plan for its fulfillment is imperiled not only by the innate precariousness of human freedom operating under the conditions of alienation and natural concupiscence (§113, 3, b); it is also put in jeopardy by unseen external powers and authorities bent on promoting natural evil. Accordingly, the Jewish and Christian traditions have thought of these powers as "set loose" by God, and in that sense as "sent" by God to test humanity and even to "defeat" the faithful (Rev 13, 7), while ultimately remaining subject to God's encompassing dominion [*uu*].

Thus is it not surprising to hear Augustine, while explaining to his congregation the pilgrim's prayer known to us as Psalm 61, declare that in the common experience of Christians, testing and temptation and the anxiety caused by them come from outside forces that cause distress. Little wonder, he explains, that in the words of this psalm, the entire Church is crying out to God, in and with the person of Christ.

What is the cry? I just said it: *Hear, God, my supplication, listen to my prayer; from the ends of the earth I have cried out to you.* This means: these were my words when I cried out, and [I cried out] "from the ends of the earth," meaning from everywhere. But why did I cry out in this manner? *As long as my heart was distressed.* The speaker shows he is living, among all the nations everywhere on earth, not in great glory, but in great testing and temptation. And as a matter of fact, our life, while we are on this pilgrimage, cannot be without testing and temptation. For our progress occurs as we are tested and tempted, nor does anyone come to self-knowledge except by being tested and tempted, nor can anyone win the crown except by first being victorious, nor can anyone be victorious except by first doing battle, nor can anyone do battle without first having enemies and tests and temptations. So this person, crying out from the ends of the earth, is distressed. Nevertheless, he is not left alone. For [Christ] wanted to foreshadow our very selves (that is, his body) in his own body—the one in which he has died, and risen again, and ascended into heaven. So the members may be confident that they will fol-

---

[*uu*] On the entire subject of angelology and demonology, both biblical and ancient, cf. *ABDict*, *s.v.* "Angel," "Devil," "Michael," "Satan," as well as monographs like Heinrich Schlier's classic *Mächte und Gewalten im Neuen Testament* (ET *Principalities and Powers in the New Testament*), and Claus Westermann's elegant *Gottes Engel brauchen keine Flügel* (ET *God's Angels Need No Wings*). Cf. also Jean Daniélou, *Les anges et leur mission* (ET *The Angels and Their Mission*) and art. "Devil" in *SacMundi* 2, pp. 70–75 (bibliogr.).

low where the head has gone before. So this is what he was doing when he
let himself be tested and tempted by Satan [Mt 4, 1]: he was transforming us,
in his own person.[58]

[a] In the Bible, the Book of Job is a classic exploration of the human struggle with adverse outside forces. To make its point, it
introduces a differentiation in the heavenly court: God's council,
consisting of the heavenly powers that mediate divine blessings to
the world, includes "the adversary" (or "the accuser"; Heb. *hassatan;*
cf. 1 Chron 21, 1; Rev 12, 10). He is the same malicious spirit whose
indictment of the people's sins, in the prophet Zechariah's vision,
must be silenced by God before temple worship can be restored to
its former glory (Zech 3, 1–5). At God's sufferance, this adversary
may test Job's faith in God, but he must stop short of killing him
(Job 2, 6)—Job's innocence excludes that option as unjust. But he
may use natural evil to get him to disavow God as unjust; once persuaded to commit blasphemy, Job will have to suffer the consequences. Here Job's wife becomes the tempter's mouthpiece: "Curse God
and die" (Job 1, 6–12; 2, 1–10). At the end of the drama, Job has
indeed been brought to the edge of blasphemy and unbelief, yet he
has remained innocent. As a result, he now recognizes, painfully but
happily that God's justice, which he has tried to challenge, is beyond
human grasp; God's mystery is inscrutable; human innocence and
faith are not entitlements to fulfillment in this world. In the end, an
effusion of temporal blessings turns Job's tragic struggle (not wholly
convincingly, perhaps[59]) into a devout comedy: he is more than restored to his former health and happiness, lives to see his children's
children, and dies "old and sated with days" (Job 42, 17). Without
a doubt, however, his turn of fortune does not serve to make the
reader understand that innocent Job, having stood the test of suffering, unconditionally deserves to be rewarded. Rather, it means to
drive home the notion that only those who have learned to acknowledge God's majesty in the midst of undeserved distress can be trust-
ed to enjoy earthly blessings, not as a right but as a gift: "only the
person who recognized the veiled God can demand his revelation."[60]
    No wonder "Satan" (as the Christian community was to call him,
turning a regular Hebrew noun into an ominous proper name)
plays only a marginal part in the Book of Job. Job is a just man from
start to finish. Much as he can be tempted, he is not drawn into sin;
Satan's plan, no matter how menacing, is defeated. Not that Job
had nothing to learn. Only in the end does he know that it is God

and not humanity that governs and judges the world. But this new wisdom springs, not from repentance for any sins he has committed, but from his sustained struggle with God about natural evil and its meaning. Consequently, by virtue of Job's sustained righteousness, Satan has not succeeded in becoming an established power in Job's life; Job has not given him an opportunity to show his true face— which may explain why the Book of Job allows the Tempter to be a member in good standing of God's heavenly council.

[b] Job may be a hero of faith and integrity in the book that bears his name. Still, his wife and especially his friends and antagonists very much inhabit, and speak the language of, a world with which humanity at large is rather more familiar: the world in which Satan is an established influence for evil, having first introduced, by dint of suasion, sin, and consequently, death (cf. Wisd 2, 24; cf. DH 291, 800; CF 609, 19). That is, in the world as we know it, these four are inextricably intertwined: Satan and the unseen powers that be, natural evil, human sin, and death.

This is also the world in which Israel and post-exilic Judaism live: a world marked by the activity not only of good angels, but of a host of demons as well. The Jewish Scriptures bear eloquent witness to this. God can punish sin by withdrawing his dominion from Edom, to deliver it up to unclean animals and to Lilith, the demon of the hurricane (Is 34, 8–17). Unlike the city and the cultivated land, the desert is dominated by fiends like Azazel, the demon of the wasteland where death (and hence, ritual impurity) prevails; accordingly, Azazel is an apt recipient of the scapegoat, condemned to carry the burden of the people's sins out of the encampment (Lev 16, 10). No wonder any observances to contact or invoke either the spirits of the dead or other spirits are banned in Israel (Deut 18, 9–13; Lev 19, 31; 20, 6. 27; 1 Sam 28, 13).

Later Judaism, deeply changed by the transcultural experience of the Exile, was to pick up the age-old association of unseen spirits with the whole array of foreign gods (cf. Beelzebul in 2 Kings 1, 2) and unseen cosmic powers (cf. §98, 1–2); by calling them "demons" (*daimonia*), the Septuagint implicitly unmasks these powers as evil spirits, like the Persian demon Asmodeus (Tob 3, 8). Eventually, mythological accounts of the fall of the rebellious demons, such as the one employed by Second Isaiah to denounce the pride of Babylon's king (Is 14, 4–20, esp. 12–14), come to be used to suggest that the devil is not alone: evil spirits are angels fallen away from the presence of God, an invisible militia under the command of Satan (or Mastêmâ, as the *Book of Jubilees*, so popular at Qumran, calls the chief demon) [*vv*].[61]

In their invisible world, these fallen angels are opposed by the legions of good angels headed by "prince" Michael, the patron angel of the faithful Jews (Dan 10, 13–14. 21; cf. 1QM 17), who will, in the New Testament Apocalypse, figure as the final victor over Satan and his armies (Rev 12, 7–9).

[c] The New Testament continues these Jewish traditions. In fact, Jesus is fully part of it. Much as he can say he had a vision of Satan falling from heaven (Lk 10, 18), and much as the people recognize his power over unclean spirits (Mk 1, 27), when he is accused of being possessed by Beelzebul, or perhaps even of being Beelzebul in person (Mk 3, 22; Mt 10, 25), he acknowledges that Satan does preside over a kingdom (Mk 3, 24 parr.). Its power is manifest in physical and mental illness, possession, and lack of faith, and the principal effective sign of the advent of God's kingdom is the overcoming and healing of these ills by Jesus and his authoritative disabling of the demons that provoke them (Mt 11, 4–5 par. Lk 7, 22)—a mission Jesus calls on his disciples to undertake in their turn (Mk 6, 7. 14–15; Lk 10, 17. 19; cf. Mk 16, 17; Acts 8, 6–7).

[d] The Christian community will be very much aware that the exaltation of Christ has definitively robbed all the powers, whether benign or malignant, of the power to separate those who believe in Christ risen from the love of God (cf. Rom 8, 38–39). Yet in the wake of Jesus' victory over Satan, it does not completely count them out; they remain forces to be reckoned with. In fact, Christian believers are called on to join the battle with the invisible world (Eph 2, 2; 6, 12; Col 1, 13). And not surprisingly, like Judaism, the Christian Churches can have no truck with attempts to get the inside track to the Transcendent by obedience to, or cultivation of, spirits of any kind (Acts 13, 6ff.; 16, 16–18; 19, 11–20; Gal 4, 8–10; 1 Cor 10, 19–21; Col 2, 8. 20–21; cf. DH 205; 283; 459–60; 1859; 2823–25; 3642; CF 402/9).[62] Rather, they live by dint of endurance, test-

---

[*vv*] Note that the Jewish-Christian tradition never represents the diabolical powers, in dualistic fashion, as a counterpart of God—equal but negative (cf. §98, 3–4; §115, 3, [*b*]; §113, 3, e, [*j*]). The evil powers are *created*. This, however, implies that they are natively good, and that their enmity with God must be rooted in *deliberate* aversion: they must have once turned away from God. But being wholly spiritual, they must have done so with their whole being; consequently, they can be thought of only as confirmed in evil (cf. DH 286, 325, 457, 800, 874, 1078; CF 402/7, 19).

ed and tempted at God's sufferance (Rev 13, 5–8), in the expectation of Jesus Christ's final victory over Satan, his demons, and his followers (Rev 20, 1–3. 7–14).

[e] In a world in which Satan's goal—human sin and death (cf. Wisd 2, 23–24)—has been visibly and palpably achieved, Satan has become the invisible commander of an establishment of unholiness and negativity. As such, he enlists as allies not only the forces of cosmic decombination and human inadvertence, but also positive human failure and sin of every kind, as well as prevailing structures of human failure and sin, along with the powers that support and embody them: crude *idols* symbolizing humanity's *degradation*, phony *ideals* representing humanity's *estrangement*, and fraudulent *ideologies* embodying humanity's *self-deification* (cf. §114, 4). In fact, while Satan can be imagined as merely availing himself of blind cosmic forces, he is to be thought of as positively counting on deliberate human failure and sin and their multifarious consequence. After all, if there were no actual sin, Satan and the adverse powers of the universe might still be *tempting* humanity to evil, but they would not have achieved a worldly *establishment*; they would have remained, so to speak, as marginal to humanity and the world as Satan is to Job. But in yielding to temptation humanity has assisted Satan and his retinue in coming to actual power in the world. By sinful human effort and ingenuity, humanity has invested the powers of negativity with substantial credibility and authority. Satan, invisible and always fugitive, is now enthroned on a visible and palpable realm of sin and death which he has helped inspire.

No wonder the New Testament follows Jesus in speaking of sin and confronting it as an established power. Sinners are doomed to death, without possibility of self-redemption; they are living in "slavery" or "captivity" (cf. Gal 4, 8; Rom 8, 21; Heb 2, 15). And the greater tragedy is that they often do so fairly happily—like prisoners managing to avoid despair by making their peace with a life of confinement. Sinful humanity, that is, quietly tends to settle for a lesser life; we will respect gods of our own making; the credible, culturally acceptable human masks they wear make it almost irreverent to unmask them as idols. Prophets with the insight and the courage to denounce systemic evil do occasionally afford us a glimpse, both of our native freedom and of a better world. But it is a measure of our slavery to sin, not only that we tend to eliminate prophets, but also that when we embrace their vision, we characteristically do so with a vengeance: we tend to welcome prophets and follow them in such a way as to overlook the fact that they are *inspired by God*. That is, often we appropriate their message in such a forceful manner as to suggest that we regard the righting of systemic wrongs denounced by them as entirely within our grasp—a matter of purely human responsibility and effort. No wonder we so often end up replacing one systemic sin by another.

[f] In the face of this, the Jewish-Christian tradition has maintained that there is more to the dominion of sin than meets the eye. Not only does the power of sinful habits and of structures of evil suggest that fallen humanity *intrinsically* suffers from a deep-seated moral impotence and from estrangement from God; it also hints at unseen *superior* forces "objectively" doing everything to hold humanity captive and obstructing the kingship of God—a theme which Gerard Lukken has competently shown to be as integral to the Roman liturgy as it is to patristic theology generally.[63]

This "objectivity" does not imply, of course, that it is possible to tell these forces clean apart from the sinful habits and structures they inspire, for it is characteristic of Satan that he hides behind the evil empire he has instigated and the worldly agents he retains [ww]. In fact, having "sinned from the beginning" (1 Jn 3, 8) and being "a liar and the father of lies" (Jn 8, 44), he will even transform himself into an angel of light (cf. 2 Cor 11, 14–15)—a crucial piece of wisdom in the tradition of the discernment of spirits.

[g] Some time ago, it was argued that the ambiguities of cosmic process make it hard to tell *natural* good and natural evil apart (§115, 5; 10, b). Still, it was added that it is possible to identify, by

---

[ww] This is the grain of truth in the oft-heard remark that Satan's biggest success to date is that he has convinced us, modern people, of his non-existence. However, the remark must be called fanciful inasmuch as it claims access to specific knowledge about the unseen powers and their intentions. Theologically speaking, it is as misguided as any claim to information about details of the invisible world; cf. §98, 1, a, [w]. At the other end of this spectrum, however, there are some theological essays suggesting that belief in the "objective existence" of demons is not essential to Christian faith, and that evil is adequately accounted for by recourse to human agency alone. Instances of this are H. A. Kelly's *Towards the Death of Satan* and Herbert Haag's *Abschied vom Teufel.* The careful style of inquiry of these authors merits respect, and charges of heresy are unconvincing (cf. §98, 1, a, [w]); still, their robust anthropological bias, typical of the 1960s and 1970s raises doubts. Tradition (along with experience) suggests that there are powerful supra-human dimensions to human failure and sin; some saints have even claimed to have been forced to engage the devil in direct combat. Is it wise to deny the existence of invisible agents of evil for the same reason that they are not identifiable as *separate* entities in everyday experience?

patient discernment, true instances of natural evil. There are cosmic occurrences that are genuinely harmful to humanity and out of harmony with humanity's legitimate purposes, and hence, capable of awakening the inherent human potential for inauthenticity and estrangement from God (§115, 11; §117, 1–3).

We must now add that the Christian tradition of asceticism and mysticism, ever sensitive to the intricate relationships between the dynamics of the flesh and the life of the human spirit, has insisted that ambiguities even deeper attach to the distinction between *deliberate* (that is, moral) good and evil, and to the "distinguishing between different spiritual influences" that move us in the direction of either (cf. §79, 2, a; §113, 3, d) [*xx*].

No wonder many New Testament traditions contain expressions of high regard for discernment. Those who seek God live in a mixed world; in that world, peace, harmony, and inner assurance can only be the fruit of *God-given* charisms of wisdom and discernment, which enable them to test and tell apart, not only "spirits" (1 Cor 12, 10; 1 Tim 4, 1; 1 Jn 4, 1–2), but also good and evil (Rom 16, 19; Heb 5, 14), true and false prophets and teachers (1 Cor 14, 29; Mt 24, 24; 1 Tim 4, 1; 1 Jn 4, 1), those who truly profess Jesus Christ and "anti-christs" (1 Jn 2, 18; 4, 3), and indeed "everything" (1 Thess 5, 2– 22). Augustine was clearly struggling with an issue both labyrinthine and perennial during the long years when, in writing *The City of God,* he was trying to identify the distinctive differences between the Christian commonwealth and the pagan world (cf. §121, 3).

[*xx*] "Spiritual influences" is the translation of the word *spiritus* in the phrase *discretio spirituum* ("discernment of spirits") in Thomas Corbishley's version of the *Spiritual Exercises* of St. Ignatius of Loyola (*Spir. Ex.* 313). Corbishley must not be lightly accused of capitulating to modern unbelief in the existence of angels; he simply implies, along with the ascetical and mystical traditions, that they cannot be adequately told apart from influences for good, including thoughts, any more than the devil can be adequately told apart from influences for evil. Evagrius Ponticus' belief in the existence of angels and demons is beyond question; yet he, too, uses Gk. *pneuma* ("spirit") as synonymous with both *daimōn* ("demon") and *logismos* ("[tempting] thought"). Cf. A. Guillaumont, "Étude historique et doctrinale," p. 65. Even more interestingly, Denis the Carthusian (1402/3–1471 A.D., known as *doctor ecstaticus* and often called "the last scholastic"), appeals to the prodigious Henry of Hessia (Heinrich Heinbuche von Langenstein, 1325–1397 A. D., known as *doctor conscientiosus*), and offers the following list of "spirits" that require discernment: the happenstance of temperament and physiological states; habits that have become second nature; *fomes* (body heat? excess of sperm?); the fascination of things that are either very good or very evil; vehement passion; the impressions things make on the five senses; the attraction of useful things; the Holy Spirit; the soul; the [guardian?] angel; and the evil spirit. Cf. Dionysius Cartusianus, *De discretione et examinatione spirituum*, article II, *in fine.*

[6] But if it takes God-given discernment to sort out humanity and the world and to read them right, this implies that we realize that they are intrinsically fractured, due to sin. This decisively affects their mutual relatedness: humanity's continuity with the cosmos (§9, 1, [*i*]) is now habitually bedeviled by moral maladjustment. This realization in turn implies another one: humanity must now reckon with elements of *perverse* incoherence and unintelligibility, both in itself and in the world.

    [a] It is important to understand that *this* is not "natural." What *is* natural is that by virtue of ontological constitution, humanity and the world are *finite*—created. This implies that nothing in the world and nothing about humanity is entirely of one piece; finite realities are only imperfectly one and imperfectly distinct from each other (cf. §115, 5, c, [*e*]). Accordingly, alienation naturally blurs boundaries and definitions. Being involved in cosmic process and subject to its hazards, everything cosmic or human is only inadequately identified, and hence, easily thrown off-course. Nothing in the world is ever fully coherent and comprehensible. It takes interpretation (in Newman's terminology, "illative sense") to put the elements together and understand. Still, all these elements of natural concupiscence (§113, 3, b) do not wholly prevent humanity from discovering, by dint of careful interpretation, such coherence and intelligibility as there is in the world, from taking advantage of it, and from turning it to higher purpose. By interpretation we can even come to understand things cosmic and human as depending on, participating in, and oriented to, God, and to act on that understanding. Thus the interpreting mind can discern and develop, at least intermittently, but sometimes even fairly regularly, patterns of deep unity of being and purpose in the world. Accordingly, things human and cosmic are capable of being experienced as at least fundamentally coherent as well as often deeply touching and illuminating, despite their "natural" lack of unity and distinctiveness.

[7] But *this* humanity, and hence, *this* world, are infected by sin. Miserably, the real (if finite) unity, distinctiveness, coherence, and intelligibility of the cosmos and humanity are neither natural nor "innocent" any longer; they are habitually compounded by conditions of negativity *deliberately* (that is, *perversely*) induced, maintained, even promoted. And thus, now that the human ability to do justice to other persons and other things is habitually obscured and incapacitated

(§125, 2), the cosmic knack for natural harmony and its capacity for higher purpose is habitually endangered. This raises the question, How has this come about, how does this keep on coming about?

Thus the historic actuality of human sin raises the issue of *sin's genesis*. The accumulated wisdom of the Jewish-Christian tradition has dealt with this by stating that the power of death and sin over humanity and the world is manifested in free human moves of progressive incoherence. These moves we know from daily experience: we tend to act on anxiety and prejudice, as we try to ensure our survival in the face of both cosmic pressure and human self-assertion. However, the quintessence of these moves lies deeper, in the refusal to acknowledge God by total self-abandon. That is, they tend in the direction of an unintelligibility both fundamental and insuperable.

[8] In affirming this, the Tradition has implicitly claimed to understand these sinful moves to the core. This claim is a paradoxical one, for how can we understand the fundamentally unintelligible? The claim is meaningless indeed, until its true *theological* nature is realized. For, although the human spirit can intuit that the sinful predicament in which it finds itself is an insult to its own attunement to God as well as a distortion of creation (cf. §113, 3, f; §114, 1), it cannot, *from inside the predicament*, understand either the predicament or itself. Sin is an exercise in self-contradiction, and all human beings are caught in this vicious circle; only the living God transcends it, and hence, is capable of taking it on. Consequently, only in the light of God's self-revelation can human sin, its dynamics, and its establishment become intelligible, *in* their very incoherence and perversity (cf. §113, 3, g–j; 5, b, [s]).

Sin, in other words, can be understood only *theologically*. The next part of the second volume of *God Encountered* must develop that understanding, under the subtitle, *The Genealogy of Depravity*.

Notes

Chapter 12

1. "... nur eine kleine Insel in einem unendlichen Ozean des Undurchfahrenen ist, eine schwimmende Insel, die uns vertrauter sein mag als dieser Ozean, aber im letzten getragen und nur so tragend ist": Karl Rahner, *Grundkurs des Glaubens*, p. 33 (cf. ET *Foundations of Christian Faith*, p. 22).
2. Letter VI, 29–30 (*De brieven van Hadewijch*, p. 46; cf. ET *The Complete Works*, p. 57).
3. *Le mystère du surnaturel*, p. 149 (cf. ET *The Mystery of the Supernatural*, pp. 147–48): "De là, chez cette créature à part, cette «constitution ontologique instable» qui la fait à la fois plus grande et plus petite qu'elle-même. De là cette sorte de déhanchement, cette mystérieuse claudication, qui n'est pas seulement celle du péché, mais d'abord et plus radicalement celle d'une créature faite de rien, qui, étrangement, touche à Dieu. *Deo mente consimilis*. À la fois, indissolublement, «néant» et «image»; radicalement néant, et néanmoins substantiellement image." De Lubac's text contains quotations from, and references to, writings by Paul Ricoeur, Maurice Blondel, Boethius (*Deo mente consimilis*: humanity is "similar to God by reason of mind"), and M. D. Chenu.
4. For an insightful, if controversial, psychiatric account, cf. R. D. Laing, *The Divided Self.*
5. *Einai de, mallon ē dokein, Theōi philon* (*Carmina*, II, i, 11, *De vita sua*, 323; *PG* 37, 1029–1166; quotation 1051A). Aelred Squire adopted the phrase as the epigraph of his elegant and wise study of the nature and history of Christian spirituality, *Asking the Fathers.*
6. A. Gesché, *La christologie du «Commentaire sur les Psaumes» découvert à Toura*, p. 185: [Jesus experienced in his soul] "ces émois passagers et furtifs, non délibérés, non peccamineux, ni passionnels, qui l'atteignent sans l'envahir"; "cet état critique, moralement indifférencié puisque inévitable, mais qui, *de soi*, peut précéder une défaillance morale." Origen uses *propatheia* to describe a state of irritation that does not develop into full-blown anger (*Sel. in Ps.* 4, 5; *PG* 12, 1141C); Cyril of Alexandria explains that *propatheia*, understood as an emotional state, can pave the way to temptation and sin (*In Ps. 118*, 67; *PG* 69, 1272B). Aquinas found the Latin equivalent *propassio* attributed to Jerome in the *Glossa ordinaria* (*ad* Mt 26, 37; cf. *PL* 114, 169D), and went on to define it as a passionate experience which, while causing the soul to falter, remains incomplete; it does not lead reason to deviate from right action. Cf. among other instances, *S. Th.*, III, 46, 7, 3 and *ad* 3.
7. *Manere autem in baptizatis concupiscentiam vel fomitem, haec sancta Synodus fatetur et sentit* ("But this holy Synod professes as a matter of both faith and experience that concupiscence, also known as the fuel [of sin], persists in the baptized").

8. Dorotheus of Gaza, quoting Basil, explains that concupiscence, in the sense of disordered affection (*pathē*: "passionateness"), is degenerative, like darkness. It postures as a substantive entity, yet it is mere lack of light; similarly, passionateness is the mere lack of the virtuousness that suits us naturally, by God's design (*Instructions*, XII, §134; *SC* 92, pp. 396–97).
9. *Conf.* X, 29; 31; 37 (*CSEL* 33, pp. 256, 261, 272). The same theme also in *Solil.* I, I, 5–6 (*PL* 32, col. 872); *De pecc. mer.* II, V, 5 (*CSEL* 60, pp. 75–76); *De spir. et lit.* XIII, 22 (*CSEL* 60, pp. 175–76).
10. Quoted by Joan M. Nuth, *Wisdom's Daughter*, p. 57.
11. Gerard Manley Hopkins, *The Wreck of the Deutschland*, stanza 10.
12. On this theme, cf. Irénée Hausherr's profound little monograph *Penthos.*
13. Cf. Peter Brown, *Augustine of Hippo*, p. 388.
14. *CCC* 312.
15. *Ibid.*
16. On the latter theme, cf. esp. Norbert Lohfink, *Der niemals gekündigte Bund* (ET *The Covenant Never Revoked*).
17. Cf. *Wisdom's Daughter*, pp. 27–33 (esp. 28), 56–65; quotation p. 60.
18. Madame de Staël, to whom this widely quoted proverb is attributed, actually wrote *Tout comprendre rend très indulgent.*
19. "Of course [God] will forgive me; it is his trade." Quotation found in Bergen Evans' *Dictionary of Quotations*, p. 158, and identified as Heinrich Heine's reply to a priest who had told him that God would forgive him his sins. On the subject, cf. F. J. van Beeck, *Loving the Torah More than God?*, pp. 51, 91 n. 23.
20. *Apologia Pro Vita Sua*, chapter 5 (ed. Svaglic, pp. 217–18).
21. David Jenkins, *Guide to the Debate About God*, p. 30 (cf. §35, 3).

Chapter 13

1. "Those who know how to distinguish know how to understand."
2. Dr. Rieux to Père Paneloux: "Et je refuserai jusqu'à la mort d'aimer cette création où des enfants sont torturés" (*La Peste*, IV; *Théâtre, Récits, Nouvelles*, p. 1395; cf. ET, pp. 196–97).
3. Gerard Manley Hopkins, "That Nature is a Heraclitean Fire and of the Comfort of the Resurrection." "Sheer off, disseveral": utterly individual, unlike any other.
4. Cf. *Theodizee* (ET *Theodicy*), I, 20–21; cf. III, 241–50; II, 119.
5. For some of the theological consequences of this understanding, cf. A. Hulsbosch, *De schepping Gods: Schepping, zonde en verlossing in het evolutionistische wereldbeeld* (ET *God in Creation and Evolution*), and P.J.A.M. Schoonenberg, *Gods wordende wereld* (ET *God's World in the Making*).
6. Cf. James Gleick, *Chaos.*
7. "... in der Erfahrung des sich im Gleichgewicht befindenden, durch den Ausgleich der Kräfte bestimmten Seins": *Das Erbe Europas*, p. 95.
8. On these themes, cf. H.-G. Gadamer, *Über die Verborgenheit der Gesundheit*, pp. 189–200.
9. On the latter, cf. works like Stephen M. Hawking, *A Brief History of Time: From the Big Bang to Black Holes.*
10. Cf. Christopher F. Mooney, "The Anthropic Principle in Cosmology and Theology."
11. Cf. Pierre Teilhard de Chardin, *Le phénomène humain*, pp. 180ff. (ET pp. 164ff.).
12. On teleology, cf. also Edward T. Oakes' illuminating essay "Final Causality."
13. *CCC* 310.
14. Aquinas explains that this genuine, if limited, asymmetry is a matter of the "incomplete return to self" characteristic of sentient life forms (*non completur eius* [= *sensus*] *reditio*): *Q. D. de veritate*, 1, 9, *in c.*; on this matter, cf. §115, 9, a.
15. "... daß kein Lebewesen seine eigene Umwelt so zur Kulturwelt umarbeitet wie

der Mensch": H.-G. Gadamer, *Über die Verborgenheit der Gesundheit*, p. 25.
16. Cf. *De hom. opif.*, VII–XI, a passage that ends with the inference that the human spirit "bears an accurate resemblance to what is superior to it, since, by the fact that it is unknowable in its own regard, it shows forth the incomprehensible nature [of God]" (*akribē pros to hyperkeimenon echei tēn homoiotēta, tōi kath 'heauton agnōstōi charakterizōn tēn akatalēpton physin*: PG 44, 140D–156B; ET *The Making of Man*, NPNCF, Second series, vol. 5, pp. 392–97).
17. "Das noch nicht festgestellte Tier": *Jenseits von Gut und Böse*, 92. Quoted by H.-G. Gadamer, *Über die Verborgenheit der Gesundheit*, p. 26.
18. *S. Th.* I, 76, 5, *ad 4*: "anima intellectiva, quia est universalium comprehensiva, habet virtutem ad infinita: et ideo non potuerunt sibi determinari a natura vel determinatæ existimationes naturales, vel etiam determinata auxilia vel defensionum, vel tegumentorum, sicut aliis animalibus, quorum animæ habent apprehensionem et virtutem ad aliqua particularia determinata." *S. Th.* I, 91, 3, *ad 2*: "cornua et ungulæ, quæ sunt quorumdam animalium arma, et spissitudo corii, et multitudo pilorum ac plumarum, quæ sunt tegumenta animalium, attestantur abundantiæ terrestris elementi, quæ repugnat æqualitati et teneritudini complexionis humanæ; et ideo homini non competebant. Sed loco horum habet rationem et manus quibus potest parare sibi arma, et tegumenta, et alia vitæ necessaria, infinitis modis; unde et manus dicitur *organum organorum*. Et hoc etiam magis competebat rationali naturæ, quæ est infinitarum conceptionum, ut haberet facultatem infinita instrumenta sibi præparandi." For comparable passages, cf. *S. Th.* I–II, 5, 5, *ad 1*; 95, 1, *in c..*
19. " . . . illa quae sunt perfectissima in entibus, ut substantiae intellectuales, redeunt ad essentiam suam reditione completa: in hoc enim quod cognoscunt aliquid extra se positum, quodammodo extra se procedunt; secundum vero quod cognoscunt se cognoscere, iam ad se redire incipiunt . . . Sed reditus iste completur secundum quod cognoscunt essentias proprias": *Q. D. de veritate*, 1, 9, *in c*.
20. Cf. Louis Dupré, *Passage to Modernity*, pp. 39–41.
21. "We triumph over nature by obeying it": cf. Hans-Georg Gadamer, *Über die Verborgenheit der Gesundheit*, p. 76.
22. Robert Murray, *The Cosmic Covenant*, p. 175.
23. In teaching this bioethical ground rule, the *magisterium* of the Catholic Church has adhered to a strict construction of it, at least thus far. That is to say, it has excluded as immoral any termination of harmless human life, not only when the termination is intended *as an end*, but also when it is intended *merely as a means to achieve the end of saving another human life*. It is well known that this issue is under serious discussion today, especially in the context of the debate about the morality of surgical procedures to terminate, say, ectopic pregnancies to save the mother's life, or to separate conjoined twins that have vital organs in common. On the fundamental aspects of this discussion, cf. *Moral Norms and Catholic Tradition*, edited by Charles E. Curran and Richard A. McCormick.
24. Cf. *Evangelium Vitae*, 75.
25. *Ibid.*
26. The problem here discussed is found in *Veritatis Splendor*, 76. In that passage, the fundamental moral "precepts" are not only called exceptionless, but also "particular" or "specific." This language is apt to confuse fundamental rules of the game with specific directives to players.
27. *Evangelium Vitae*, 75.
28. *Ibid.*, 62, 65.
29. "The Incredible Christian Capacity For Missing the Christian Point," p. 400 (italics added).
30. *S. Th.* I–II, 94, 2, *in c*.
31. Cf., for instance, *S. Th.* II–II, 179, 1, 1 and *ad 1*, quoting Aristotle's *De anima* II,

415^{b}13: *to de zēn tois zōsi to einai estin* ("for living beings, to be alive is to be")—a *locus classicus* (cf. *AristBWks*, p. 561).

32. *S. Th.* II–II, 64, 6, *in c.*, supplemented with details from articles 2, *in c.* and *ad 2*; 3, *in c.*
33. *Evangelium Vitae*, 56.
34. *Ibid.*
35. *Ibid.*, 58.
36. Cf. J. Cheryl Exum, *Tragedy and Biblical Narrative*, p. 13.
37. Cf. H.-G. Gadamer, *Über die Verborgenheit der Gesundheit*, pp. 133–39.
38. Cf. J. Cheryl Exum, *Tragedy and Biblical Narrative*, p. 13.
39. Cf. Emmanuel Lévinas, "To Love the Torah More than God," in F. J. van Beeck, *Loving the Torah More than God?*, p. 37; cf. also pp. 45–47.
40. *Le phénomène humain*, p. 346–48 (cf. ET pp. 311–13): "Jusque dans ses zones ré-fléchies, nous l'avons vu, le Monde procède à coup de chances, par tâtonne-ment. Or de ce seul chef, jusque dans le domaine humain (celui cependant où le hasard est le plus contrôlé), que de ratés pour une réussite, — que de misères pour un bonheur, — que de péchés pour un seul saint . . . Simple in-arrange-ment ou dérangement physiques d'abord, au niveau de la Matière; mais souf-france bientôt, incrustée dans la Chair sensible; et, plus haut encore, méchan-ceté ou torture de l'Esprit qui s'analyse et choisit: statistiquement, à tous les de-grés de l'Évolution, toujours et partout, c'est le Mal qui se forme et se réforme, implacablement, en nous et autour de nous! . . . Ainsi l'exige, sans recours possible, le jeu des grands nombres au sein d'une Multitude en voie d'organisation. . . . D'une manière ou de l'autre, il reste que, même au regard du simple biologiste, rien ne ressemble autant que l'épopée humaine à un che-min de la Croix."
41. Cf., *e.g.*, Plato, *Timaeus*, 29^{d}7–31^{b}3 (*PlatoCDia*, pp. 1162–63); Marcus Aurelius, *Meditations*, X, 1 (ed. Farquharson, vol. I, pp. 190–93).
42. *De Oratione*, XXXIII (formerly attributed to the Abbot St. Nilus of Sinai) (*PG* 79, 1173CD; cf. Evagrius Ponticus, *The Praktikos* and *Chapters on Prayer*, p. 60; cf. *Philok* I, p. 60). Interestingly, it is clear, from the phrasing of the Greek text, that Evagrius does not have in mind Mk 10, 18 ("No one is good except God a-lone"). Instead, he is probably using a Stoic idiom.
43. On this theme, cf. also Charles Curran's "Providence and Responsibility."
44. On this theme, cf. Charles H. Talbert's lucid and informative little book *Learning Through Suffering: The Educational Value of Suffering in the New Testament and in Its Milieu.*
45. *limos, loimos, abrochia, nosoi, polemoi*: Dorotheus of Gaza, *Instructions* XIV, §155 (*SC* 92, pp. 436–37).
46. W. H. Auden, "As I walked out one Evening," in *Collected Shorter Poems 1927–1957*, pp. 85–86.
47. One of the principal theses of Robert Markus' attractive book *The End of Ancient Christianity.*
48. Cf. H.E.W. Turner's fine summary *The Patristic Doctrine of Redemption*, which illustrates the point made in the text without, however, emphasizing its impor-tance.
49. *Theodizee* (ET *Theodicy*), I, 8–10; cf. III, 416.
50. "Faith in progress."
51. *Das Erbe Europas*, p. 18: "Im Zeichen der modernen Wissenschaft gibt es, um es so zu nennen, den pfeilgeraden Willen."
52. On *phronēsis*, cf. John Henry Newman, *Grammar of Assent*, pp. 276–81.
53. For this basic (and pervasive) concept in Sullivan's work, cf. esp. *The Interpersonal Theory of Psychiatry*, pp. 28–29; *Conceptions of Modern Psychiatry*, p. 92, and the es-say by Patrick Mullahy appended to this work: "A Theory of Interpersonal Re-lations and the Evolution of Personality," pp. 239–94; and *The Fusion of Psychiatry*

     and Social Science, pp. 22–31, published, respectively, in volumes I and II of *The Collected Works of Harry Stack Sullivan.*

54. Cf. *Leven in Meervoud*, pp. 247–62 (ET *Divided Existence and Complex Society*, pp. 215–28).

55. H.-G. Gadamer, *Über die Verborgenheit der Gesundheit*, p. 102.

56. H.-G. Gadamer, *Das Erbe Europas*, p. 21: "eine mühsame Arbeit der Einschränkung und Steuerung jenes pfeilgeraden Willens."

57. Cf. again William B. Frazier, "The Incredible Christian Capacity For Missing the Christian Point."

58. *Collected Works*, p. 828 (italics added). The reference is to Pierre Teilhard de Chardin's treatment of the divinization of the dynamics of disintegration, in *Le milieu divin*, pp. 80–102 (ET *The Divine Milieu*, pp. 80–94).

59. *Collected Works*, pp. 830–31 (italics added). For Camus, cf. also §115, 2, note 10.

60. Cf. *Über die Verborgenheit der Gesundheit*, esp. pp. 36ff., 55ff., 60ff., 98ff., 116ff., 128ff., 138ff., 145ff., 166ff.

61. "Was ist dem Geist, der zu sich selbst gekommen ist, thematisch oder unthematisch vertrauter and selbstverständlicher als das schweigende Fragen über alles schon Eroberte und Beherrschte hinaus, als das demütig liebende Überfragtsein, das allein weise macht? Nichts weiß der Mensch in der letzten Tiefe genauer als daß sein Wissen, d.h. das, was man im Alltag so nennt, nur eine kleine Insel in einem unendlichen Ozean des Undurchfahrenen ist, eine schwimmende Insel, die uns vertrauter sein mag als dieser Ozean, aber im letzten getragen und nur so tragend ist, so daß die existentielle Frage an den Erkennenden die ist, ob er die kleine Insel seines sogenannten Wissens oder das Meer des unendlichen Geheimnisses mehr liebe; ob ihm das kleine Licht, mit dem er diese Insel ableuchtet—man nennt es Wissenschaft—, ein ewiges Licht sein soll, das ihm (das wäre die Hölle) ewig leuchtet": Karl Rahner, *Grundkurs des Glaubens*, p. 33 (cf. ET *Foundations of Christian Faith*, p. 22). – Incidentally, a passage like this shows that Hans Urs von Balthasar was overlooking Rahner's considerable literary talent when he declared (in an otherwise fascinating interview) that, though Karl Rahner was the greater speculative theologian by far, his weakness lay in his fundamental devotion to transcendental reflection cultivated as a system. This was due, he added (not without a trace of self-congratulation), to a fundamental difference of perspective between himself and Rahner: Rahner had opted for Kant, while he had opted for Goethe. Cf. "Geist und Feuer: Ein Gespräch mit Hans Urs von Balthasar."

62. *Ita fit ut neque illa bona quae a peccantibus adpetuntur ullo modo mala sint neque ipsa uoluntas libera, quam in bonis quibusdam mediis numerandam esse comperimus, sed malum sit auersio eius ab incommutabili bono, et conuersio ad mutabilia bona; quae tamen auersio atque conuersio quoniam non cogitur, sed est uoluntaria, digna et iusta eam miseriae poena subsequitur: De Libero Arbitrio* II, XIX, 53 (*CC* 29, p. 272; cf. *PL* 32, 1269).

63. *Est autem peccatum hominis inordinatio atque peruersitas, id est a praestantiore auersio et ad condita inferiora conuersio: De div. quœst. ad Simplicianum* I, II, 18 (*CC* 44, p. 45; cf. *PL* 40, 122).

64. Cf. Peter Brown, *Augustine of Hippo*, pp. 299–329.

65. "*Fecerunt itaque ciuitates duas amores duo, terrenam scilicet amor sui usque ad contemptum Dei, caelestem vero amor Dei usque ad contemptum sui. Denique illa in se ipsa, haec in Domino gloriatur. Illa enim quaerit ab hominibus gloriam; huic autem Deus conscientiae testis maxima est gloria. Illa in gloria sua exaltat caput suum; haec dicit Deo suo: Gloria mea et exaltans caput meum* (Ps 3, 4). *Illi in principibus eius uel in eis quas subiugat nationibus dominandi libido dominatur; in hac seruiunt inuicem in caritate et praepositi consulendo et subditi obtemperando. Illa in suis potentibus diligit uirtutem suam; haec dicit Deo suo: Diligam te, Domine, uirtus mea*" (*De Civitate Dei*, XIV, 28; *CC* 48, p. 451).

66. "... rationalis creatura ... ita facta est, ut sibi ipsi bonum, quo beata fiat, esse non possit, sed mutabilitas eius, si conuertatur ad incommutabile bonum, fiat beata; unde si auertatur, misera est": *Ep.* 140 (*Liber de gratia Novi Testamenti ad Honoratum*) XXIII, 56 (*CSEL* 44, p. 202; *PL* 33, 561).
67. Both the reference to Ambrose (*Ep.* 77, 10, 14) and the quotation from Augustine's *Enarr. in Ps.* 5, 10 [392] are found in Brian E. Daley, *The Hope of the Early Church*, pp. 98, 140.

Chapter 14

1. *Ep. Barn.* 4, 10.
2. Cf. art. "alienation" in *EncPhil* I, pp. 76–81 (bibl.)
3. Cf. Louis Dupré, *Marx's Social Critique of Culture*, p. 19.
4. *Das Erbe Europas*, p. 29: "Gibt es überhaupt Anderes, das nicht das Andere unserer Selbst ist? Jedenfalls keinen, der ein anderer, der auch ein Mensch ist."
5. For a good example, cf. Elizabeth A. Johnson, *She Who Is*, pp. 67–69.
6. On God's "vrochtbaerre natuere," cf. *Van .vii. trappen in den graed der gheesteliker minnen*, VII, E; *RW* III, pp. 269–72.
7. Cf. *Die geestelike brulocht*, pp. 584–91 (*The Spiritual Espousals and Other Works*, pp. 148–49.
8. Cf. the observations, both sensible and philosophically sound, made by J. A. Appleyard, in his *Becoming a Reader*, p. 97.
9. On responsive identity, cf. also F. J. van Beeck, *Christ Proclaimed*, esp. pp. 243–51, 406–38.
10. "Hier liegt am Ende die letzte Wurzel der Freiheit, die den Menschen zum Menschen macht: die Wahl. Er hat zu wählen, und er weiß—und er weiß zu *sagen*—, was er damit zu tun beansprucht: das Bessere auszulesen und als der Bessere das Gute, das Rechte und Gerechte zu wählen. Ein ungeheurer Anspruch—und am Ende ein übermenschlicher. Der Mensch muß ihn aber erheben, weil er wählen muß": Hans-Georg Gadamer, *Das Erbe Europas*, pp. 132–33.
11. *Eth. Nic.* II, 6 (*AristBWks*, pp. 957–59).
12. *Letters*, IV (*Vanden blinkenden steen*, etc., pp. 592–93).
13. *Chapters on Theology, Gnosis, and Practice*, I, 7–8 (*SC* 51ᵇⁱˢ, pp. 44–45).
14. *Antigone*, 360–62 (ed. Pearson).
15. Hilaire Belloc, Sonnet XI (*Sonnets and Verse*, p. 17).
16. An eloquent account of this in Joseph P. Whelan, "How I Pray Now."
17. Cf. Plato, *Socrates' Defense (Apology)*, 29·9 (oide men gar oudeis ton thanaton, oud'ei tygchanei tōi anthrōpōi pantōn megiston on tōn agathōn). Cf. *PlatoCDia*, p. 15.
18. Hilary of Poitiers, *De Trinitate* I, 2 (*CC* 62, p. 2; cf. ET *FC* 25, p. 4): "... et idcirco ad aliquas se patientiae et continentiae et placabilitatis uirtutes et doctrina et opere transtulisse, quod bene agere adque intelligere id demum bene uiuere esse opinabantur; uitam autem non ad mortem tantum ab inmortali Deo tribui existimandam, cum boni largitoris non esse intelligeretur, uiuendi iucundissimum sensum ad tristissimum metum tribuisse moriendi."
19. "Un poème n'est jamais achevé — c'est toujours un accident qui le termine, c'est-à-dire qui le donne au public": *Oeuvres*, II, p. 553 (ET *Analects*, p. 104). Note that Valéry continues: "never does the actual state of the work (unless the author is a fool) demonstrate that it could not be carried further, changed, and treated as a first rough draft or the starting point of some new venture."
20. Cf. Karl Rahner, *Grundkurs des Glaubens*, p. 265 (ET *Foundations of Faith*, p. 270). Cf. also, Robert Ochs' moving *The Death in Every Now*.
21. Cf. F. J. van Beeck, *Loving the Torah More than God?*, pp. 60–65; however, cf. also pp. 47–53 for some important caveats.
22. On these themes, cf. Karl Rahner's brilliant article, "Immanente und transzendente Vollendung der Welt" (ET "Immanent and Transcendent Consummation

of the World").
23. Brian E. Daley, *The Hope of the Early Church*, p. 29, 5152.
24. Cf. *S. Th.* I, 93, 7, *ad 4*.
25. On this notion, cf. Brian E. Daley's appeal to Ambrose: *The Hope of the Early Church*, p. 98.
26. For examples, cf. Brian E. Daley, *The Hope of the Early Church*, pp. 21 (Justin), 36–37 (Tertullian), 39–40 (Hippolytus), 51 (Origen), 95 (Hilary), 98–99 (Ambrose), 111 (Cyril of Alexandria), 118 (ps.-Macarian homilies), and esp. 160 (Paulinus of Nola). Most Fathers interpret the "first resurrection" either as Baptism (the sounder approach, it would seem) or as the first installment of the eschaton, to be followed by the "second resurrection," which then introduces the definitive state of the world to come. Cf. the index in Daley's *The Hope of the Early Church*.
27. Cf. Brian E. Daley, *The Hope of the Early Church*, pp. 137–41.
28. *Ibid.*, p. 49–50, quotation from Origen; cf. *ibid.*, p. 109, for a similar idea in Chrysostom.
29. Cf. F. J. van Beeck, *Christ Proclaimed*, pp. 331–34.
30. Roman Missal, Fourth Eucharistic Prayer.
31. Cf. Brian E. Daley, *The Hope of the Early Church*, pp. 27, 46, 57, 88–89, 91, 98, 138–41.
32. Cf. Erich Fleischhack, *Fegfeuer*.
33. On "sacrificial system," cf. esp. David Power, *The Sacrifice We Offer*.
34. *Hōs kath' hēmeran apothnēskontas zēn*: *Life of Anthony*, 89 (p. 95; *PG* 26, 968AB); Anthony's own explanation, which also contains the quotation from Paul, is at 19 (872A); cf. also 91 (969C).
35. *Apophthegmata*, 1 (*PG* 34, 233A). Cf. the *Imitation of Christ*, Bk. I, chap. 23 (*De meditatione mortis*), 2: *Beatus, qui horam mortis suae semper ante oculos habet et ad moriendum quotidie se disponit* ("Blessed are those who always have the hour of their death before their eyes and ready themselves to die every day").
36. *Ou «meletēn thanatou» ton bion poioumetha?*: *Oration* XXVII (= *Or. theol.* I), 7, 15 (*SC* 250, p. 86–87; *PG* 36, 20C [49]), quoting Plato, *Phaedo* 81a (*PlatoCDia*, p. 64).
37. On Clement of Alexandria's appeal to Plato, cf. Brian E. Daley, *The Hope of the Early Church*, p. 44.
38. *Praktikos*, 52; 29 (*SC* 171, pp. 618–21; 566–71). These pages also contain A. Guillaumont's excellent notes, and his references to, among others, Clement of Alexandria, *Strom.* V, 11, 67, 1 (*GCS* 15, p. 370), and Gregory Nazianzen, *Letters* 31 (*PG* 37, 68C). Guillaumont quotes Plato's *Phaedo*, 67 c–e, Plotinus' *Enneads*, I, 9, and Porphyry's *Aphormai pros ta noēta*, 8–9 as Clement's and Gregory's sources. Cf. also Evagrius' *De Oratione*, 61: "by reason of your great desire for God, your mind takes off, little by little, and takes its distance from the flesh [*hypanachōrei tēs sarkos*] ..." (*PG* 79, 1179C).
39. Cf. *Institutiones coenobiticae*, V, 41 (*SC* 109, p. 256): "Ita inquit debere monachum ieiuniis operam dare ut centum annis in corpore commoraturum, ita motus animi refrenare et iniuriarum oblivisci tristitiasque respuere, dolores quoque ac detrimenta contemnere tamquam cotidie moriturum."
40. "*memnēmenoi tēs anōthen eugeneias*": Gregory Nazianzen, *Oration* XXVII (= *Or. theol.* I), 7, 16–17 (*SC* 250, p. 88–89; *PG* 36, 20C [49–50]).
41. *Spir. Ex.*, [186], [340].
42. *Ibid.*, [23].
43. "... *qui nos præcesserunt cum signo fidei*": from the commemoration of the dead in the Roman canon—now the first eucharistic prayer.
44. "Je ne meurs pas, j'entre dans la vie": St. Thérèse of Lisieux, letter of June 9, 1897 (*Une course de géant*, p. 426; cf. ET *General Correspondence*, II, p. 1128).
45. Horace, *Odes*, III, xi, 8: *carpe diem, quam minimum credula postero*.
46. On the inability to love, cf. P. Schoonenberg, *Man and Sin*, pp. 70–79.

47. Gerard Manley Hopkins, "My own heart let me have more pity on."
48. Cf. Martin Heidegger, *Sein und Zeit* (ET *Being and Time*), §§58, 62.
49. For examples, cf. Brian E. Daley, *The Hope of the Early Church*, pp. 232, n. 12 (Irenaeus), p. 56 (Origen), and esp. p. 140 (Augustine).
50. Cf. P. Schoonenberg, *Man and Sin*, pp. 57–59.
51. Gerard Manley Hopkins, "The Wreck of the Deutschland," st. 3.
52. Cf. K. Rahner, *Grundkurs des Glaubens*, pp. 57–60; quotation p. 58: "Er hätte sich zurückgekreuzt zum findigen Tier" (ET *Foundations of Christian Faith*, pp. 47–51).
53. Cf. Athanasius' *Life of Anthony, passim*, but esp. 5–6, 51–53 (*PG* 26, 845C–852A, 917A–920A).
54. *CCC* 329.
55. "... il y a ainsi un côté de notre monde qui nous affronte comme chaos et que l'animal chthonique symbolise": P. Ricoeur, *La symbolique du mal*, p. 242 (ET *The Symbolism of Evil*, p. 258.
56. For an ambitious attempt to create order in the great variety of images and conceptions of "the Devil," cf. Neil Forsyth, *The Old Enemy*.
57. Cf. *La symbolique du mal*, pp. 239–43 (ET *The Symbolism of Evil*, pp. 256–59).
58. *Enarr. in Ps. 60*, 2–3 (*PL* 36, 724; text emended as *per* footnote): "Quid autem clamat? Quod supra dixi, *Exaudi, Deus, deprecationem meam, intende orationi meæ; a finibus terræ ad te clamavi.* Id est, hoc ad te clamavi: *a finibus terræ:* id est, undique. Sed quare clamavi hoc? *Dum angeretur cor meum.* Ostendit se esse per omnes gentes toto orbe terrarum [non] in magna gloria, sed in magna tentatione. Namque vita nostra in hac peregrinatione non potest esse sine tentatione: quia provectus noster per tentationem nostram fit, nec sibi quisque innotescit nisi tentatus, nec potest coronari nisi vicerit, nec potest vincere nisi certaverit, nec potest certare nisi inimicum et tentationes habuerit. Angitur ergo iste a finibus terræ clamans, sed tamen non relinquitur. Quoniam nos ipsos, quod est corpus suum, voluit præfigurare et in illo corpore suo, in quo jam et mortuus est, et resurrexit, et in cœlum ascendit; ut quo caput præcessit, illuc secutura membra confidant. Ergo nos transfiguravit in se, quando voluit tentari a satana."
59. On this subject, cf. J. Cheryl Exum, *Tragedy and Biblical Narrative*, pp. 11–15.
60. Emmanuel Lévinas, "Aimer la Thora plus que Dieu" (*Difficile liberté*, pp. 189–193), p. 193; cf. F. J. van Beeck, *Loving the Torah More than God?*, p. 40.
61. Cf. Jub 10, 3ff., esp. 8. 11 (ed. R. H. Charles, p. 28).
62. It is notable that J. Neuner and J. Dupuis have adopted only one of the texts in DH in *The Christian Faith* (a canon from the sixth-century local council in Braga, Portugal), leaving it to the reader to speculate whether their decision is based on the judgment that the matter itself is marginal (which is doubtful) or on the judgment that it is irrelevant to modern Catholics (one wonders).
63. Cf. his *Original Sin in the Roman Liturgy*, esp. pp. 157–265.

Bibliography

Allen, William. *A Defense and Declaration of the Catholike Churchies Doctrine touching Purgatory, and Prayers of the Souls Departed.* Menston: Scolar Press, 1970.

Appleyard, J. A. *Becoming a Reader: The Experience of Fiction from Childhood to Adulthood.* Cambridge, MA: Cambridge University Press, 1990.

Athanasius, Saint. *The Life of Anthony and the Letter to Marcellinus.* Translated by Robert C. Gregg. *The Classics of Western Spirituality.* New York, Ramsey, and Toronto: Paulist Press, 1980.

Auden, W. H. *Collected Shorter Poems 1927–1957.* London, Faber and Faber, 1966.

Augustine, Saint. *Confessions.* Translated with an Introduction and Notes by Henry Chadwick. Oxford: Oxford University Press, 1991.

———. *S. Aurelii Augustini De Libero Arbitrio Voluntatis: St. Augustine on Free Will.* Translated by Carroll Mason Sparrow. *University of Virginia Studies,* 4. Charlottesville, VA: The University of Virginia, 1947.

Baillie, Donald M. *God Was in Christ: An Essay on Incarnation and Atonement.* New York: Scribner's, 1948.

Balthasar, Hans Urs von. "Geist und Feuer: Ein Gespräch mit Hans Urs von Balthasar." *Herder-Korrespondenz* 30(1976): 72–82.

Becker, Ernest. *The Denial of Death.* New York: The Free Press; London: Collier Macmillan, 1973.

Beeck, Frans Jozef van. *Christ Proclaimed: Christology as Rhetoric.* New York, Ramsey, NJ, and Toronto: Paulist Press, 1979.

———. *Loving the Torah More than God? Towards a Catholic Appreciation of Judaism.* Chicago: Loyola University Press, 1989.

Belloc, Hilaire. *Sonnets and Verse.* New edition. London: Duckworth, 1938.

Berg, J. H. van den. *Leven in meervoud: Een metabletisch onderzoek.* Nijkerk: G. F. Callenbach, 1963 (ET *Divided Existence and Complex Society: An Historical Approach.* Pittsburgh: Duquesne University Press, 1974).

Bernardin, Joseph Cardinal, and others. *Consistent Ethic of Life.* Edited by Thomas G. Fuechtmann. Kansas City, MO: Sheed & Ward, 1988.

Birnbaum, David. *God and Evil: A Unified Theodicy/Theology/Philosophy.* Hoboken, NJ: Ktav Publishing House, 1989.

Bonhoeffer, Dietrich. *Ethik.* Edited by Eberhard Bethge. München: Chr. Kaiser Verlag, 1975 (ET *Ethics.* New York: Macmillan, 1965).

Bonica, John J. *The Management of Pain.* Second edition. 2 vols. Philadelphia and London: Lea and Febiger, 1990.

Bremer, Jan Maarten. "Death and Immortality in Some Greek Poems." In *Hidden Futures: Death and Immortality in Ancient Egypt, Anatolia, the Classical, Biblical and Arabic-Islamic World*. Edited by J.M. Bremer, Th. P.J. van den Hout, and R. Peters. Amsterdam: Amsterdam University Press, 1994, pp. 109–24.

Brown, Norman O. *Life Against Death: The Psychoanalytical Meaning of History*. New York: Viking Books, 1959.

Brown, Peter. *Augustine of Hippo: A Biography*. Berkeley, Los Angeles, and London: University of California Press, 1969.

Buber, Martin. *Gottesfinsternis: Betrachtungen zur Beziehung zwischen Religion und Philosophie*. In *Werke*, vol. 1, *Schriften zur Philosophie*. München: Kösel; Heidelberg: Lambert Schneider, 1962, pp. 503–603 (ET *Eclipse of God: Studies in the Relation Between Religion and Philosophy*. New York: Harper & Row, 1957).

Buytendijk, F. J. J. *Over de pijn*. Third edition. Utrecht: Het Spectrum, 1957 (ET *Pain*. London: Hutchinson & Co., 1961).

Camus, Albert. *La Peste*. In *Théâtre, Récits, Nouvelles*. Edited by Roger Quilliot. *Bibliothèque de la Pléiade*, 61. [Paris]: Gallimard, 1962, pp. 1211–1472 (ET *The Plague*. New York: Alfred A. Knopf, 1971).

Canévet, M. "L'humanité de l'embryon selon Grégoire de Nysse." *Nouvelle revue théologique* 114(1992): 678–95.

Catherine of Genova, Saint. *Purgation and Purgatory: The Spiritual Dialogue*. New York and Ramsey, NJ: Paulist Press, 1979.

Caussade, Jean Pierre de. *L'abandon à la providence divine*. Edited by Michel Olphe-Gailliard. *Collection Christus*, 22. Paris: Desclée de Brouwer, 1966 (ET *Abandonment to Divine Providence*. Image Books. Garden City, NY: Doubleday, 1975; *The Sacrament of the Present Moment*. San Francisco: Harper & Row, 1989).

———. *Instructions spirituelles en forme de dialogues sur les divers états d'oraison suivant la doctrine de M. Bossuet*. Edited by Henri Bremond. Paris: Bloud et Gay, 1931 (ET *Spiritual Instructions on the Various States of Prayer According to the Doctrine of Bossuet, Bishop of Meaux*. Translated by Algar Thorold. Introduced by John Chapman. New York, Benzinger, 1931).

Comstock, Craig. See Sanford, Nevitt.

Congregation for the Doctrine of the Faith. *Letter on Certain Questions Concerning Eschatology*. *Origins* 9 [1979]: 131–33 (original: "Recentiores episcoporum synodi." *Acta Apostolicae Sedis* 71[1979]: 940–42).

Connor, James L. "Original Sin: Contemporary Approaches." *Theological Studies* 29(1968): 215–40.

Curran, Charles E. See *Moral Norms and Catholic Tradition*.

———. "Providence and Responsibility: The Divine and the Human in History from the Perspective of Moral Theology." In *The Catholic*

Theological Society of America: Proceedings of the Forty-Fourth Annual Convention 44(1989): 43–64.

Daley, Brian E. *The Hope of the Early Church: A Handbook of Patristic Eschatology.* Cambridge: Cambridge University Press, 1991.

Daniélou, Jean. *Les anges et leur mission.* Chevetogne: Éditions de Chevetogne, 1953 (ET *The Angels and Their Mission.* Westminster, MD: Newman Press, 1957).

Denis the Carthusian. *De discretione et examinatione spirituum.* In *Doctoris ecstatici Dionysii Cartusiani opera minora.* Vol. VIII (= *Opera Omnia.* Vol. 40). Tournai: Cartusia S. M. de Pratis, 1911, pp. 261–319.

Dorotheus of Gaza, Saint. (Dorothée de Gaza). *Oeuvres spirituelles. Sources chrétiennes,* 92. Paris: Éditions du Cerf, 1963 (ET *Discourses and Sayings. Cistercian Studies Series,* 33. Kalamazoo, MI: Cistercian Publications, 1977).

Dostoyevsky, Fyodor. *The Brothers Karamazov.* Translated by David Magarshack. Harmondsworth, Middlesex: Penguin Books, 1958.

Dulles, Avery. "Henri de Lubac: In Appreciation." *America* 165(1991): 180–82.

Dupré, Louis K. *Marx's Social Critique of Culture.* New Haven and London: Yale University Press, 1983.

———. *Passage to Modernity: An Essay in the Hermeneutics of Nature and Culture.* New Haven and London: Yale University Press, 1993.

Eadie, Betty J. With Curtis Taylor. *Embraced by the Light.* Placer, CA: Gold Leaf Press, 1992.

Eliade, Mircea. *The Myth of the Eternal Return: or, Cosmos and History. Bollingen Series,* XLVI. Princeton, NJ: Princeton University Press, 1971.

———. *Patterns in Comparative Religion.* New York: The New American Library, 1974.

Epictetus. *The Discourses as Reported by Arrian, the Manual, and Fragments.* Edited by W. A. Oldfather. 2 vols. Cambridge, MA: Harvard University Press; London: William Heinemann, 1951.

Evagrius Ponticus. See Guillaumont, Antoine.

———. *The Praktikos* and *Chapters on Prayer.* Edited by John Eudes Bamberger. Spencer, MA: Cistercian Publications, 1970.

Exum, J. Cheryl. *Tragedy and Biblical Narrative: Arrows of the Almighty.* Cambridge: Cambridge University Press, 1992.

Farley, Edward. *Good and Evil: Interpreting a Human Condition.* Minneapolis: Fortress Press, 1990.

Fleischhack, Erich. *Fegfeuer: Die Vorstellung vom Geschickder Verstorbenen geschichtlich dargestellt.* Tübingen: Katzmann, 1969.

Forsyth, Neil. *The Old Enemy: Satan and the Combat Myth.* Princeton, NJ: Princeton University Press, 1987.

Fowler, James W. *Stages of Faith: The Psychology of Human Development and the Quest for Meaning.* San Francisco: Harper & Row, 1981.

Francis of Sales, Saint. (Saint François de Sales). *Introduction à la vie dévote.* Paris: Nelson, [1951] (ET *Introduction to the Devout Life.* Westminster, MD: The Newman Press, 1948).

Frazier, William B. "The Incredible Christian Capacity For Missing the Christian Point." *America* 167(1992): 398–400.

Gadamer, Hans-Georg. *Das Erbe Europas: Beiträge.* Bibliothek Suhrkamp, 1004. Frankfurt am Main: Suhrkamp, 1989.

———. *Über die Verborgenheit der Gesundheit: Aufsätze und Vorträge.* Bibliothek Suhrkamp, 1135. Frankfurt am Main: Suhrkamp, 1993.

Gesché, Adolphe. *La christologie du «Commentaire sur les Psaumes» découvert à Toura.* Gembloux: J. Duculot, 1962.

Gibson, H. B. *Pain and its Conquest.* London and Boston: Peter Owen, 1982.

Gleick, James. *Chaos: Making a New Science.* New York: Penguin Books, 1987.

Greene, Graham. *A Burnt-out Case.* London: Heinemann, 1961.

———. *The Power and the Glory.* New York: The Viking Press, 1946.

Gregory of Nyssa, [Saint]. *The Catechetical Oration.* Edited by James Herbert Srawley. Cambridge: The University Press, 1956 (ET "An Address on Religious Instruction." In *Christology of the Later Fathers.* Edited by Edward Rochie Hardy, with Cyril C. Richardson. *The Library of Christian Classics.* Philadelphia: Westminster, 1954, pp. 268–325).

Guardini, Romano. *Die Annahme seiner selbst: Den Menschen erkennt nur, wer von Gott weiß.* Topos-Taschenbücher, 171. Mainz: Matthias Grünewald-Verlag, 1987.

———. *Vom Sinn der Schwermut.* Topos-Taschenbücher, 130. Mainz: Matthias-Grünewald-Verlag, 1983.

Guillaumont, Antoine. "Étude historique et doctrinale." In *Évagre le Pontique. Traité pratique ou Le moine.* Vol. 1. *SC* 170, pp. 21–125.

Haag, Herbert. *Abschied vom Teufel.* Einsiedeln, Zürich, and Köln: Benziger, 1969 (FrT *Liquidation du diable.* Paris: Desclée De Brouwer, 1971).

Hadewijch. *The Complete Works.* Translated and introduced by Mother Columba Hart. The Classics of Western Spirituality. New York: Paulist Press, 1980.

———. See Mommaers, Paul.

Happel, Stephen, & James J. Walter. *Conversion and Discipleship: A Christian Foundation for Ethics and Doctrine.* Philadelphia: Fortress Press, 1986.

Häring, Bernard. *Sin in the Secular Age.* Garden City, NY: Doubleday, 1974.

Hausherr, Irénée. *Penthos: The Doctrine of Compunction in the Christian East.* Cistercian Studies Series, 53. Kalamazoo, MI: Cistercian Publications, 1982.

Hawking, Stephen M. *A Brief History of Time: From the Big Bang to Black Holes.* Toronto, New York, London, Sidney, and Auckland: Bantam Books, 1988.

Heidegger, Martin. *Sein und Zeit.* Fifteenth edition. Tübingen: Max Niermeyer Verlag, 1979 (ET [seventh German edition] *Being and Time.* Translated by John Macquarrie and Edward Robinson. New York, Hagerstown, San Francisco, and London: Harper & Row, 1962).

———. *Was ist Metaphysik?* Seventh edition. Frankfurt a. M.: Klostermann, 1955.

Hevenesi, Gabriel. *Scintillae Ignatianae.* New York and Cincinnati: Pustet, 1919.

Hopkins, Gerard Manley. [*Works.*] Edited by Catherine Phillips. *The Oxford Authors.* Oxford and New York: Oxford University Press, 1986.

Hulsbosch, A. *De schepping Gods: Schepping, zonde en verlossing in het evolutionistische wereldbeeld.* Third edition. Roermond: J.J. Romen en Zoon, 1964 (ET God in Creation and Evolution. New York: Sheed and Ward, 1965).

Ignatius of Loyola, Saint. *The Spiritual Exercises of Saint Ignatius.* Translated by Thomas Corbishley. London: Burns and Oates, 1963.

Jenkins, David. *Guide to the Debate About God.* London: Lutterworth Press, 1966.

John Paul II, Pope [Karol Wojtyla]. Encyclical *Evangelium Vitae.* Washington, DC: United States Catholic Conference, 1995.

———. Encyclical *Veritatis Splendor.* ET in *Origins* 23(1993): 297. 298–334.

Johnson, Elizabeth A. *She Who Is: The Mystery of God in Feminist Theological Discourse.* New York: Crossroad, 1992.

Journet, Charles. *Le mal: Essai théologique.* Bruges: Desclée De Brouwer, 1960 (ET *The Meaning of Evil.* New York: P. J. Kenedy, 1963).

Kelly, Henry Ansgar. *Towards the Death of Satan: The Growth and Decline of Christian Demonology.* London, Dublin, and Melbourne: Geoffrey Chapman, 1968.

Laing, R. D. *The Divided Self.* New York: Pantheon Books, 1969.

Le Goff, Jacques. *La naissance du Purgatoire.* Paris: Gallimard, 1981 (ET *The Birth of Purgatory.* Chicago: University of Chicago Press, 1983).

Leibniz, Gottfried Wilhelm. *Die Theodizee. Philosophische Bibliothek,* 71. Second Edition. Hamburg: Verlag Felix Meiner, 1968 (ET *Theodicy: Essays on the Goodness of God, the Freedom of Man, and the Origin of Evil.* Translated by E. M. Huggard. London: Routledge & Kegan Paul, 1951 [=1952]).

Le Roy Ladurie, Emmanuel. *Montaillou, village occitan de 1294 à 1324.* Paris: Gallimard, 1975. Revised edition 1982 (ET *Montaillou: The Promised Land of Error.* New York: G. Braziller, 1978).

Lévinas, Emmanuel. *Difficile liberté: Essais sur le judaïsme.* Second edition. Paris: Albin Michel, 1976.

Lewis, C. S. *The Allegory of Love: A Study in Medieval Tradition.* London: Oxford University Press, Geoffrey Cumberlege, 1936.

Linnæus, Carolus. *Systema Naturæ.* Facsimile of the First Edition of 1735. Stockholm: Bokförlaget Rediviva, 1977.

Lohfink, Norbert. *Der niemals gekündigte Bund: Exegetische Gedanken zum christlich-jüdischen Dialog.* Freiburg, Basel, and Wien: Herder, 1989 (ET *The Covenant Never Revoked: Biblical Reflections on Christian-Jewish Dialogue.* New York: Paulist Press, 1991).

Lorimer, David. *Whole in One: The Near-Death Experience and the Ethic of Interconnectedness.* London: Penguin, 1990.

Lubac, Henri de. See Dulles, Avery.

——. *Le mystère du surnaturel. Theologie,* 64. [Paris]: Aubier, Éditions Montaigne, 1965 (ET *The Mystery of the Supernatural.* New York: Herder and Herder, 1967).

Lukken, G. A. *Original Sin in the Roman Liturgy: Research into the Theology of Original Sin in the Roman Sacramentaria and the Early Baptismal Liturgy.* Leiden: E. J. Brill, 1973.

MacIntyre, Alasdair. *After Virtue: A Study in Moral Theory.* Notre Dame, IN: University of Notre Dame Press, 1981.

Marcus Aurelius. *Markou Antōninou Autokratoros Ta Eis Heauton: The Meditations of the Emperor Marcus Antoninus.* Edited by A.S.L. Farquharson. 2 vols. Oxford: Clarendon Press, 1944.

Markus, Robert A. *The End of Ancient Christianity.* Cambridge: Cambridge University Press, 1990.

Martelet, Gustave. *The Risen Christ and the Eucharistic World.* New York: Seabury Press, 1976.

McCabe, Herbert. "Manuals and rule books." *The Tablet* 247(1994): 1649–50 (Also in *Considering* Veritatis Splendor. Edited by John Wilkins. Cleveland, OH: The Pilgrim Press, 1994, pp. 61–68).

McCormick, Richard A. See *Moral Norms and Catholic Tradition.*

Meier, John P. *A Marginal Jew: Rethinking the Historical Jesus.* Volume 2: *Mentor, Message, and Miracle. The Anchor Bible Reference Library.* New York: Doubleday, 1994.

Mommaers, Paul. *De brieven van Hadewijch.* Averbode: Altiora, 1990.

——. *Hadewijch: Schrijfster–Begijn–Mystica.* Averbode: Altiora, 1989.

Moody, Raymond A. *Life After Life: The Investigation of a Phenomenon–Survival of Bodily Death.* Toronto and New York: Bantam Books, 1975.

——. *Reflections on Life After Life.* Toronto and New York: Bantam Books, 1977.

Mooney, Christopher F. "The Anthropic Principle in Cosmology and Theology." *Horizons* 21 (1994): 105–29.

Moral Norms and Catholic Tradition. Edited by Charles E. Curran and Richard A. McCormick. *Readings in Moral Theology*, 1. New York: Paulist, 1979.

More, Saint Thomas. *The Supplication of Souls.* Westminster, MD: Newman Press, 1950.

Morse, Melvin. *Closer to the Light: Learning from Children's Near-Death Experiences.* With Paul Perry. New York: Villard Books, 1990.

Müller-Eckhard, Hans. *Die Krankheit nicht krank sein zu können.* Second edition. Stuttgart: Ernst Klett Verlag, 1955.

Murdoch, Iris. *The Sovereignty of Good.* London and Henley: Routledge and Kegan Paul, 1970.

Murray, Robert. *The Cosmic Covenant: Biblical Themes of Justice, Peace, and the Integrity of Creation. Heythrop Monographs*, 7. London: Sheed & Ward, 1992.

Newman, John Henry. *Apologia Pro Vita Sua, Being a History of His Religious Opinions.* Edited by Martin J. Svaglic. Oxford: Clarendon Press, 1967.

———. *An Essay in Aid of a Grammar of Assent.* Edited by Nicholas Lash. Notre Dame and London: University of Notre Dame Press, 1979.

Niebuhr, H. Richard. *The Responsible Self: An Essay in Christian Moral Philosophy.* New York, Evanston, and London: Harper & Row, 1963.

Noonan, John T., Jr. "Development in Moral Doctrine." *Theological Studies* 54(1993): 662–77.

Nuth, Joan M. *Wisdom's Daughter: The Theology of Julian of Norwich.* New York: Crossroad, 1991.

Oakes, Edward T. "Final Causality: A Response." *Theological Studies* 53 (1992): 534–44.

Ochs, Robert. *The Death in Every Now.* New York: Sheed and Ward, 1969.

O'Connor, Flannery. *Collected Works.* Edited by Sally Fitzgerald. *The Library of America*, 39. New York: Literary Classics of the United States, Inc., 1988.

Pascal, Blaise. *Oeuvres complètes.* Preface by Henri Gouhier. Introduced and annotated by Louis Lafuma. Paris: Éditions du Seuil, 1963.

Pope, Stephen J. *The Evolution of Altruism and the Ordering of Love.* Washington, DC: Georgetown University Press, 1994.

Power, David. *The Sacrifice We Offer: The Tridentine Dogma and Its Reinterpretation.* Edinburgh: T. & T. Clark, 1987.

Rabik, Bernard J. Freedom in Fundamental Option: Delineation of Freedom in Fundamental Option as Found in Recent Theological Writings. Rome: Faculty of Theology of the Pontifical University of St. Thomas, 1972.

Rahner, Karl. *Geist in Welt: Zur Metaphysik der endlichen Erkenntnis bei Thomas von Aquin.* Second edition, revised and augmented by Johannes

Baptist Metz. München: Kösel-Verlag, 1957 (ET *Spirit in the World.* Translated by William Dych. New York: Herder and Herder, 1968).

———. *Grundkurs des Glaubens: Einführung in den Begriff des Christentums.* Third edition. Freiburg, Basel, and Wien: Herder, 1976 (ET *Foundations of Christian Faith: An Introduction to the Idea of Christianity.* Translated by William V. Dych. New York: Seabury, 1978).

———. "Immanente und transzendente Vollendung der Welt." In *SchrzTh,* 8, pp. 593–609 (ET "Immanent and Transcendent Consummation of the World." In *TheoInv,* 10, pp. 273–89).

———. "Zum theologischen Begriff der Konkupiszenz." In *SchrzTh,* 1, pp. 377–414 (ET "The Theological Concept of Concupiscentia." In *TheoInv,* 1, pp. 347–82).

———. *Zur Theologie des Todes, mit einem Exkurs über das Martyrium.* Quaestiones disputatae, 2. Freiburg: Herder, 1958 (ET *On the Theology of Death.* Second edition. New York: Herder and Herder; London: Burns and Oates, 1965).

Richter, Horst Eberhard. *Wer nicht leiden will, muß hassen: Zur Epidemie der Gewalt.* Hamburg: Verlag Hoffmann und Campe, 1993.

Ricoeur, Paul. *Finitude et culpabilité.* Vol. II. *La symbolique du mal.* Paris: Aubier, Éditions Montaigne, 1960 (ET *The Symbolism of Evil.* Boston: Beacon Press, 1969).

Riesman, David. *The Lonely Crowd: A Study of the Changing American Character.* New Haven and London: Yale University Press and Oxford University Press, 1970.

Robinson, John A. T. *The Body: A Study in Pauline Theology.* London: SCM Press, 1952.

———. *The Human Face of God.* Philadelphia: Westminster Press, 1973.

Rogers, Carl R. *On Becoming a Person: A Therapist's View of Psychotherapy.* Boston: Houghton Mifflin, 1961.

Ruusbroec, Blessed Jan van. *Die geestelike brulocht.* [*The Spiritual Espousals;* Ioannis Rvsbrochii *De ornatv spiritualivm nvptiarvm*]. *Corpus Christianorum, Continuatio Mediaevalis,* 103. Tielt: Lannoo; Turnhout: Brepols, 1988.

———. *The Spiritual Espousals and Other Works.* Introduced and translated by James A. Wiseman. The Classics of Western Spirituality. New York, Mahwah, and Toronto: Paulist Press, 1985.

———. *Vanden blinkenden steen. Vanden vier becoringen. Vanden kerstene ghelove. Brieven.* [*The Sparkling Stone. The Four Temptations. The Christian Faith. Letters.*] Ioannis Rvsbrochii *De calcvlo sev perfectione filiorvm Dei. De qvattvor svbtilibvs tentationibvs. De fide et ivdicio. Epistolae.*] *Corpus Christianorum, Continuatio Mediaevalis,* 110. Tielt: Lannoo; Turnhout: Brepols, 1991.

Sanctions for Evil. See Sanford, Nevitt.

Sanford, Nevitt, Craig Comstock, and others. *Sanctions for Evil: Sources of Social Destructiveness*. San Francisco: Jossey-Bass, 1971.

Scheler, Max. *Der Formalismus in der Ethik und die materiale Wertethik: Neuer Versuch der Grundlegung eines ethischen Personalismus. Gesammelte Werke*, 2. Bern and München: Francke Verlag, 1954 (ET *Formalism in Ethics and Non-Formal Ethics of Values: A New Attempt Toward the Foundation of an Ethical Personalism*. Evanston: Northwestern University Press, 1973).

――――. *Die Stellung des Menschen im Kosmos*. In *Späte Schriften. Gesammelte Werke*, 9. Bern and München: Francke Verlag, 1976, PP. 7–71 (ET *Man's Place in Nature*. New York: The Noonday Press, 1971).

――――. *Wesen und Formen der Sympathie*. In *Wesen und Formen der Sympathie. Die deutsche Philosophie der Gegenwart. Gesammelte Werke*, 7. Bern and München: Francke Verlag, 1973, pp. 3–258 (ET *The Nature of Sympathy*. New Haven: Yale University Press, 1954).

Schlier, Heinrich. *Mächte und Gewalten im Neuen Testament. Quaestiones Disputatae*, 3. Freiburg: Herder, 1958 (ET *Principalities and Powers in the New Testament. Quaestiones Disputatae*, 3. New York: Herder and Herder, 1961).

Schoonenberg, P.J.A.M. *Gods wordende wereld: Vijf theologische essais. Woord en beleving*, 13. Tielt: Lannoo, 1962 (ET *God's World in the Making. Duquesne Studies: Theological Series*, 2. Pittsburgh, PA: Duquesne University Press; Louvain: Editions E. Nauwelaerts, 1964).

――――. *Man and Sin: A Theological View*. [Notre Dame, IN]: University of Notre Dame Press, 1965.

Sertillanges, A.G. *Le problème du mal*. 2 vols. Paris: Aubier, Éditions Montaigne, 1948–1951.

Sophocles. *Fabvlae*. Edited by A.C. Pearson. Reprint. Oxford: Clarendon Press, 1967.

Squire, Aelred. *Asking the Fathers: The Art of Meditation and Prayer*. Second edition. Wilton, CT: Morehouse-Barlow; New York and Ramsey, NJ: Paulist Press, 1976.

Sullivan, Harry Stack. *The Collected Works of Harry Stack Sullivan, M. D.* Edited by Helen Swick Perry and others. Two vols. New York, W. W. Norton and Co., [no yr.].

Talbert, Charles H. *Learning Through Suffering: The Educational Value of Suffering in the New Testament and in Its Milieu*. Collegeville, MN: The Liturgical Press, 1991.

Teilhard de Chardin, Pierre. *Le milieu divin: Essai de vie intérieure. Oeuvres de Pierre Teilhard de Chardin*, 4. Paris: Éditions du Seuil, 1957 (ET *The Divine Milieu*. New York: Harper & Row, 1965).

―――. *Le phénomène humain. Oeuvres de Pierre Teilhard de Chardin*, 1. Paris: Éditions du Seuil, 1955 (ET *The Phenomenon of Man*. Harper Torchbooks. New York: Harper & Row, 1961).

―――. *Science et Christ. Oeuvres de Pierre Teilhard de Chardin*, 9. Paris: Éditions du Seuil, 1965 (ET *Science and Christ*. New York and Evanston: Harper & Row, 1968).

Thérèse de l'Enfant-Jésus et de la Sainte-Face, Sainte. *Une course de géant: Lettres*. Édition intégrale. Paris: Éditions du Cerf et Desclée De Brouwer, 1977 (ET St. Thérèse of Lisieux. *General Correspondence*. 2 vols. Translated by John Clarke. Washington, DC: ICS Publications, 1982, 1988.

―――. *J'entre dans la vie: Derniers Entretiens*. Paris: Éditions du Cerf et Desclée De Brouwer, 1973 (ET St. Thérèse of Lisieux. *Her Last Conversations*. Translated by John Clarke. Washington, DC: ICS Publications, 1977).

Tillich, Paul. *Systematic Theology*. Three volumes in one. Chicago: University of Chicago Press, 1967.

Troisfontaines, Roger. *«Je ne meurs pas . . . »* Paris: Éditions universitaires, 1960 (ET *I Do Not Die*. New York: Desclee Company, 1963).

Turner, Henry Ernest William. *The Patristic Doctrine of Redemption: A Study of the Development of Doctrine During the First Five Centuries*. London: Mowbray, 1952.

Valéry, Paul. *Oeuvres*. Edited by Jean Hytier. *Bibliothèque de la Pléiade*, 147–48. Paris: Gallimard, 1960.

Walter, James J. See Happel, Stephen.

Westermann, Claus. *Gottes Engel brauchen keine Flügel*. Stuttgart: Kreuz Verlag, 1978 (ET *God's Angels Need No Wings*. Philadelphia: Fortress Press, 1979).

Whelan, Joseph P. "How I Pray Now: A Conversation." *America* (November 20, 1993), 17–20.

Woolf, Virginia. *The Waves*. Reprint of the 1931 edition. A Harvest/HBJ Book. New York and London: Harcourt Brace Jovanovich, 1978.

Subject Index

Name Index

Virgil, *20*

Walter, James J., *131*
Weiszäcker, Viktor von, 99

Westermann, Claus, 168
Whelan, Joseph P., *182*
Woolf, Virginia, 141

Scripture Index

Frans Jozef van Beeck, S.J., is the author of eleven books and about fifty essays and articles. In the area of theology, examples are "Towards an Ecumenical Understanding of the Sacraments" (1966); "Sacraments, Church Order, and Secular Responsibility" (1969); *Christ Proclaimed: Christology as Rhetoric* (1979); *Fifty Psalms: An Attempt at a New Translation* (with Huub Oosterhuis and others; 1969); *Grounded in Love: Sacramental Theology in an Ecumenical Perspective* (1981); "Professing the Uniqueness of Christ" (1985); *Catholic Identity after Vatican II: Three Types of Faith in the One Church* (1985); "The Worship of Christians in Pliny's Letter" (1988); *Loving the Torah More than God? Toward a Catholic Appreciation of Judaism* (1989); "Tradition and Interpretation" (1990); "Divine Revelation: Intervention or Self-Communication?" (1991); "Professing Christianity Among the World's Religions" (1991); "Two Kind Jewish Men: A Sermon in Commemoration of the Shoa" (1992); "The Quest of the Historical Jesus: Origins, Achievements, and the Specter of Diminishing Returns" (1994) "Christian Faith and Theology in Encounter with Non-Christians: Profession? Protestation? Self-maintenance? Abandon?" (1994); "Fantasy, the Capital Sins, the Enneagram, and Self-Acceptance: An Essay in Ascetical Theology" (1994); "My Encounter with Yossel Rakover" (1995). In the area of literature, there are pieces like *The Poems and Translations of Sir Edward Sherburne (1616-1702)* (1961); "Hopkins: *Cor ad Cor*" (1975); "A Note on *Ther* in Curses and Blessings in Chaucer" (1985); "The Choices of Two Anthologists: Understanding Hopkins' Catholic Idiom" (1989). The following parts of *God Encountered: A Contemporary Catholic Systematic Theology* appeared previously: Volume One, *Understanding the Christian Faith* (1989), Volume Two/1, *The Revelation of the Glory: Introduction and Fundamental Theology* (1993), and Volume Two/2, *The Revelation of the Glory: One God, Creator of All That Is* (1994). Volume Two/4 is in process. Father van Beeck's personal predilections include liturgy, preaching, teaching, spiritual direction, good conversation, and music (he used to be a decent violinist), as well as some bird watching.

230.2
B414
1993
v.2
pt.3

98386

LINCOLN CHRISTIAN COLLEGE AND SEMINARY

3 4711 00151 7111